The Next Los Angeles

The publisher gratefully acknowledges the generous contribution to this book provided by the General Endowment Fund of the University of California Press Associates.

The Next Los Angeles

The Struggle for a Livable City

Updated with a New Preface

ROBERT GOTTLIEB,
MARK VALLIANATOS,
REGINA M. FREER,
AND PETER DREIER

University of California Press

BERKELEY   LOS ANGELES   LONDON

University of California Press, one of the most distinguished
university presses in the United States, enriches lives around
the world by advancing scholarship in the humanities, social sciences,
and natural sciences. Its activities are supported by the UC Press
Foundation and by philanthropic contributions from individuals
and institutions. For more information, visit www.ucpress.edu.

University of California Press
Berkeley and Los Angeles, California

University of California Press, Ltd.
London, England

Library of Congress Cataloging-in-Publication Data

The next Los Angeles : the struggle for a liveable city :
updated with a new preface /
  Robert Gottlieb . . . [et al.].
      p.   cm.
  Includes bibliographical references and index.
  ISBN-13: 978-0-520-25009-3 (pbk. : alk. paper)
  ISBN-10: 0-520-25009-5 (pbk. : alk. paper)
  1. Los Angeles (Calif.)—Social conditions—
  20th century. 2. Los Angeles (Calif.)—
  Social conditions—21st century. 3. Los Angeles
  (Calif.)—Politics and government—20th century.
  I. Gottlieb, Robert.

HN80.L7N49 2006
306.09794'940904—dc22   2006044496

15   14   13   12   11   10   09   08   07   06
10   9   8   7   6   5   4   3   2   1

This book is printed on New Leaf EcoBook 50, a 100% recycled
fiber of which 50% is de-inked post-consumer waste, processed
chlorine-free. EcoBook 50 is acid-free and meets the minimum
requirements of ANSI/ASTM D5634-01 (Permanence of Paper).

For our families and loved ones:

Marge Pearson and Casey and Andie Pearson-Gottlieb

Johanna Smith and Evaggelos, Crista, and Corinna Vallianatos

Phillips B. Freer, Rudell S. Freer, and Wendell P. Freer

Terry Meng and the twins (Amelia and Sarah Dreier)

Contents

Illustrations

TABLE

Preface to the 2006 Edition

Has the Next Los Angeles—a more socially just, democratic, and livable city—finally arrived? This book seeks to answer that question and to examine the continuing debates about the city's history and its future. The book was conceived following the defeat of a candidate and a political campaign that had reflected many of the visions and causes of the social movements that had inspired the idea of a Next Los Angeles. Four years later, that candidate—Antonio Villaraigosa—won a landslide victory (59 percent to 41 percent) over incumbent mayor James Hahn, a moderate Democrat. An instant national celebrity, Villaraigosa could be found everywhere in the media in the days and months that followed his election.

For Los Angeles' progressive activists, the Villaraigosa victory raised hopes about moving the city in a new direction. We chronicled the work of these progressives as a political force in our book *The Next Los Angeles*, which was published in the beginning of 2005.

As described in the book, the city's progressive movement—a force we call Progressive L.A., embodied in the work of community groups, unions, environmentalists, housing activists, feminists, and others—had worked on Villaraigosa's inspiring but ultimately unsuccessful campaign against Hahn in 2001. Now, with Villaraigosa's victory in 2005, progressives have become excited about the possibilities of turning their vision into a reality.

At the same time, Villaraigosa's victory has raised many questions. What does it mean to be a progressive at the municipal level when so many powerful forces—a city whose financial needs far exceed its revenue-raising capacity; a president and governor hostile to the plight of cities and the poor; a business and development community that has been resistant to taxes, living wages, and regulations; and the ever-present threat of capital mobility—are arrayed against reform? His election enhanced, but in no way guaranteed, Los Angeles' chances of becoming the most progressive city in the country. "I'm an unabashed progressive," Villaraigosa told an enthusiastic standing-room-only crowd at the Take Back America conference in Washington, D.C. a week after his victory, "but I'm not a knee-jerk."

This new preface to the second edition describes what has happened to Los Angeles since the book was first published. It contrasts the 2001 and 2005 mayoral elections and analyzes the early direction of the Villaraigosa administration. We explore the excitement and dilemmas created by Villaraigosa's victory and the ways that members of the political force we call Progressive L.A. have attempted to maneuver as both insiders and outsiders in the new mayor's governing coalition.

We consider our effort a "scholarship of engagement." The four of us have been writing about and have been participants in this aspiring progressive political force that has taken shape in Los Angeles since the civil unrest in April 1992. That turbulent event catalyzed a renewed commitment on the part of the city's networks of organizers and activists. Our book sought to describe—in a decade-by-decade portrait—Los Angeles' complex and often hidden progressive history. It explored the massive demographic and economic changes, and vibrant social and cultural undercurrents, that transformed Los Angeles into the most exciting and tumultuous city and region in the country. We also analyzed whether the city's progressive forces could gain sufficient political influence to significantly shape its future. We argued that, despite Villaraigosa's defeat in 2001, there were still opportunities for turning Los Angeles in a more progressive direction. At the same time, we recognized that those opportunities could be eclipsed by the continuing and intense racial and ethnic conflicts, widening disparities in income, and protracted social, environmental, and economic problems that plagued Los Angeles—and every other major metropolitan region in the country. Now, with the political shift represented by the 2005 election, the possibilities for a progressive transformation appear even closer, and increasingly capable of turning this decade into the most exciting period in Los Angeles' history.

THE 2001 MAYORAL RACE AND AFTER

During the 2001 election, Villaraigosa became a symbol and a magnet for Progressive L.A. due to his campaign's vision and policy agenda as well as his personal background as a student activist, union organizer, civil liberties advocate, and progressive elected official. As a member of the California State Assembly, where he had also served as Speaker, Villaraigosa earned a reputation as a champion of environmental and economic justice. During his 2001 mayoral run, Villaraigosa's campaign platform paralleled the values and policy ideas of the Progressive L.A. groups. His campaign themes of inclusion, diversity, and justice in 2001 inspired activists.

Hahn, the longtime city attorney, beat Villaraigosa by a 54 to 46 percent margin. Hahn's electoral coalition included strong support among White homeowners (especially in the San Fernando Valley) and among African Americans, a legacy of the popularity, among black voters, of his father, Kenneth Hahn (who represented South L.A. on the City Council and County Board of Supervisors). Some African American support for Hahn in 2001 was linked to fears about the political ascendancy of Latinos—a trend that could lessen the power of African American voters and elected officials. At the same time, Hahn resorted to classic dirty and racist campaign tactics to undermine Villaraigosa's credibility and to exploit racial fears, linking Villaraigosa, among other charges, to drug dealers.

Despite Villaraigosa's loss in 2001, the broad progressive coalition that came together during the campaign helped accelerate the city's reform agenda. One example of this development was the relationship that the L.A. County Federation of Labor and its leader Miguel Contreras established with Mayor Hahn. In 2001, the County Fed and most of its constituent unions had passionately endorsed Villaraigosa and mobilized thousands of union members and staffers in his campaign. After Hahn won, Contreras and his union colleagues pushed the new mayor to support prolabor policies. Hahn dutifully complied, although—as was the case for most of his commitments—without much enthusiasm. He supported labor's successful effort to get an ordinance through the City Council to restrict the ability of big-box stores like antiunion Wal-Mart to build stores in Los Angeles. He endorsed the labor movement's campaign to unionize security guards in the office buildings across the city. He walked the picket lines when grocery workers were engaged in a bitter four-month strike with three national supermarket chains. He supported (albeit reluctantly) an unprecedented city-funded $100 million annual housing trust fund proposed by Housing L.A., a coalition of union, church, and community activists. Following a grassroots campaign led by the community group ACORN, the Los Angeles City Council passed and Mayor Hahn signed a strong law against banks' predatory lending practices that charge high interest rates to unsuspecting—predominantly elderly and working-class—home buyers. The labor movement also joined Hahn in opposing a 2002 ballot initiative to allow the San Fernando Valley to secede from Los Angeles and form a separate city. Hahn's opposition to secession won points with the unions, particularly the public employee unions who feared that a breakaway conservative Valley could reduce union representation and its overall clout.

After the 2001 campaign, L.A. progressives consolidated their gains in various ways. In 2003, Martin Ludlow, who had also served as the County Fed's political director and had been a key aide to Villaraigosa in the state legislature, was elected to the L.A. City Council. That same year, Villaraigosa also won a City Council seat, defeating an incumbent from the heavily Latino 14th district. The Villaraigosa-Ludlow team on the City Council symbolized the potential for a Latino–African American coalition and, along with Eric Garcetti and Ed Reyes, strengthened the progressive bloc within the City Council. Fabian Nunez, who had also served as the County Fed's political director and was a veteran activist for immigrant rights, was elected to the state Assembly in 2002 and catapulted to the powerful position of Speaker two years later. In November 2004, Karen Bass, an African American and a longtime community organizer, was elected to the state Assembly to represent the 47th Assembly district, a polyglot area with significant black, Latino, and Jewish populations. Indeed, the Los Angeles area delegations in both the state legislature and the U.S. Congress were, by 2005, probably the most progressive of any city in the country.

VILLARAIGOSA'S 2005 VICTORY

Shortly after *The Next Los Angeles* was published, the 2005 mayoral campaign moved into high gear. As in 2001, many of the progressive social movements and constituent groups that were part of Progressive L.A. coalesced around Villaraigosa's candidacy. This time it was the incumbent Hahn with a lackluster record—including ongoing "pay-to-play corruption" scandals—who turned out to be most vulnerable.

In the March 2005 mayoral preliminary election, Villaraigosa garnered the most votes among the five major candidates, a margin that was spread across all key demographic, racial, ethnic, economic, and geographic groups. He won 33 percent of the total vote compared with Hahn's 24 percent. But Villaraigosa had topped the ballot four years earlier, and he knew that the crucial question was which candidate—he or Hahn—would gain the support in the runoff of voters who had cast their ballots for the three defeated candidates.

When the runoff votes had been counted, Villaraigosa's wide victory margin was spread across all key demographic groups. He won majorities among all income groups, from 54 percent among those earning over

$100,000 to 67 percent among voters below $20,000. He carried 77 percent of voters between 18 and 29 years old and 70 percent of those between 30 and 44.

Compared with 2001, Villaraigosa strengthened his base of support among Latinos (he won 84 percent of their vote), union members (60 percent), and Jews (55 percent). While in 2001 Villaraigosa won only 20 percent of the African American vote, one poll indicated that in 2005 he received as much as 58 percent of the African American vote, a huge swing.[1] Among Whites, his share of the vote grew from 41 percent to 50 percent. Among White voters in the suburban middle-class San Fernando Valley, he garnered 48 percent of the vote, compared with 34 percent four years earlier.

The collapse of Hahn's support among San Fernando Valley Whites and among South Los Angeles African Americans was particularly decisive. In their first battle, White voters in the Valley (which represents one-third of the city's residents) feared what they perceived to be Villaraigosa's radicalism. Four years later, Hahn's Valley support had dramatically eroded, due in part to the growing Latino migration to the East Valley as well as unhappiness among White voters in the West Valley with Hahn's strong opposition to the unsuccessful secession initiative in 2002.

The shift among African American voters was particularly important to Villaraigosa's victory and the opportunity to build a progressive multiracial coalition. After four years in office, Hahn could no longer rely upon his late father's popularity among African Africans to translate into votes. Young African Americans, in particular, turned out for Villaraigosa. More significantly, Hahn lost considerable African American support when he fired police chief Bernard Parks, an African American with his own political ambitions. Villaraigosa would pick up the support of many Black elected officials like Congresswoman Maxine Waters, business leaders like former basketball star Magic Johnson, and key church figures who played a critical role in influencing community opinion. (Parks himself ran successfully for City Council in 2003 and placed fourth in the 2005 primary election for mayor, subsequently throwing his support to Villaraigosa in the runoff.)

The 2005 runoff election also differed significantly from 2001 in how the two candidates were perceived and how the media focused on the election. In their second rematch, Hahn's uninspiring performance as mayor allowed Villaraigosa to take the offensive. The most visible themes of Villaraigosa's campaign—crime, transportation gridlock, the environment, and the state of public schools in Los Angeles—helped shift the focus to Hahn's limited appeal. Hahn tried again to link Villaraigosa to drug dealers and radical politics (including his involvement in Latino student politics at UCLA many years earlier). But these tactics didn't resonate with the media or with voters. By 2005, having run once for mayor and then having served on the City Council, Villaraigosa was much better known among Los Angeles voters. The second time around, Hahn could no longer define Villaraigosa.[2]

Progressive L.A. activists viewed the 2005 election as a pivotal victory for their movement. Though their participation was not as visible as it had been in the mobilizations four years earlier, thousands of activists had volunteered for Villaraigosa. His campaign put long-term organizer Anthony Thigpenn—an African American activist with two decades of experience in the peace and community organizing movements—in charge of its field operation. The campaign paid particular attention to mobilizing such constituencies as younger African Americans, the growing Latino community, and liberal White middle-class voters, especially Westside Jews.

This time around, L.A.'s labor movement, having successfully engaged the incumbent mayor, confronted a dilemma about whom to endorse. Contreras hoped to orchestrate a dual endorsement of both candidates, but most L.A. union leaders believed that rewarding incumbents for good behavior was a cardinal principle ("reward your friends, punish your enemies"), and on those grounds Hahn got the County Federation of Labor's support. Villaraigosa gained the endorsement of several unions, including United Teachers of Los Angeles, but Hahn got the lion's share of labor's money and mobilization. Even so, most observers noted that labor's effort on Hahn's behalf was less enthusiastic than its work for Villaraigosa four years earlier. Fewer rank-and-file union members, and even staffers, participated in the County Fed's voter registration and turnout campaign for Hahn.

The County Fed's endorsement of Hahn dismayed many progressive L.A. activists who saw Villaraigosa as the very symbol of the kind of Latino/labor/liberal alliance that Contreras and many unions had championed. Nevertheless, Villaraigosa received 35 percent of the votes of union members in the five-candidate primary race compared with Hahn's 27 percent.

Then, suddenly, just weeks before the runoff, the fifty-two-year old Contreras died unexpectedly of a heart attack. At the funeral, Villaraigosa, with his long history and close friendship with both Contreras and Contreras's widow, Maria Elena Durazo, the head of the Hotel Employees and Restaurant Employees Union in Los Angeles, was one of the pallbearers. Less than a week later, 60 percent of union members voted for Villaraigosa in the runoff, despite the County Fed's endorsement.

Villaraigosa ran two parallel campaigns. One was a media-oriented, sound bite campaign that put Hahn on the defensive. The other was a spirited, volunteer-heavy, grassroots mobilization that included an energetic and peripatetic candidate reaching out to different constituencies across the city. The two campaigns came together in an astounding landslide victory for Villaraigosa.

Instantly, the face of Los Angeles' new mayor was everywhere: on the cover of newsmagazines, on the network news stations, profiled on National Public Radio and in nearly every major newspaper in the country. The new mayor was called "bold" and "charismatic." The stories focused on his prominence as a Latino mayor in the country's second largest city—a city with the largest Latino population in the nation.

The stories also highlighted Villaraigosa's early years—the son of an abusive father, a rebellious teenager, a reformed substance abuser—and described his growth as a progressive activist, an elected official, and now a public figure with a major bully pulpit. It was an updated version of the American dream. "Blending the idealism of the 1960s, when all things seemed possible, with the realism of the 21st century, when it's clearer what is possible," wrote *U.S. News and World Report*, "Villaraigosa puts his life story on the line as proof of what can be accomplished no matter how hard it seems."[3]

VILLARAIGOSA TAKES OFFICE

As Villaraigosa assembled his transition team, he requested, as a kind of cautionary exercise, that each person on the team see *Crash*, a new film that depicted the intense, day-to-day ethnic and racial clashes in Los Angeles and the almost inexorable spiral toward violence. Then, literally almost as soon as the inaugural party had dispersed, tension and violence flared at a local high school that pitted Latino against African American students. Villaraigosa immediately arrived on the scene and in this and several other instances continued to be vocal around his theme of racial and ethnic inclusion.

Despite the euphoria, it was clear that the challenges facing the new mayor—and his Progressive L.A. supporters—were deep and very visible. Racial and ethnic conflict was only one of a wide range of issues and potential sources of discord that Los Angeles, the new mayor, and the Progressive L.A. forces had to address. Villaraigosa's major campaign themes—declining public schools (and the need for mayoral intervention), transportation gridlock (and the need for transit alternatives), and neighborhood crime and violence (and the need for more police and community responses)—were enormously complex and not easily resolvable. Other controversial issues—for example, the rapid expansion of the L.A. port and the truck and rail traffic moving goods inland, which generated enormous negative environmental and community impacts for nearby neighborhoods—rose to the surface as well. How would the new mayor address those issues as well as continue to use his bully pulpit? How would the Progressive L.A. forces position themselves—as insiders, outsiders, or both? These became the postelection challenges and opportunities for the Next Los Angeles.

For the mayor, two approaches stood out in his first six months: creating a vision for the city he loved and continuing to promote his language of inclusion. His vision drew on some of the themes of Progressive L.A.: making L.A. the "greenest and cleanest big city in America" (planting a million trees, for example); creating a transit future (with a strong focus on expanded rail); building a denser and taller planned city (through transit-oriented development and other strategies favored by the new urbanists); implementing clean and sustainable economic development (attracting new technologies such as digital media); and continuing to emphasize Los Angeles as a "world city" (transforming L.A. into "the Venice of the 21st century," as Villaraigosa often put it).

There were also differences with Progressive L.A. that the new mayor and his allies had to work out. During the campaign, for example, Villaraigosa had pledged his support for inclusionary zoning, a policy that would require all new residential developments to include at least 15 percent affordable housing units. The Housing L.A. coalition—which had successfully pushed for a municipal housing trust fund four years earlier—had been lobbying for two years to get the City Council to adopt inclusionary zoning, triggering strong opposition from the business-sponsored Central City Association. Once Villaraigosa took office, however, the housing activists backed off, wanting to give the new mayor breathing room and an opportunity to forge a broader coalition for housing reform. Villaraigosa told housing activists that he would push for inclusionary zoning as part of a comprehensive housing agenda but that he first needed to get some traction on less controversial issues.

The controversy over the city's port and the transport of goods tested the new mayor's ability to forge a progressive governing coalition that included unions, environmentalists, neighborhood groups, and business, including economic interests such as the shippers who were in sharp disagreement with some of the Progressive L.A. forces. On the one hand, Villaraigosa appointed strong community and environmental advocates to the Harbor Commission, which oversaw port-related activities. He vowed to address the impacts on neighborhoods, including some low-income communities that had been marginalized in prior discussions of port expansion during the Hahn administration. On the other hand, Villaraigosa accepted the business community's core argument that the movement of goods from the port to trucks that traveled along major road corridors was key to the region's economy and should be encouraged to expand. To environmentalists, this argument failed to address the consequences of the likely increases from the most serious and protracted sources of pollution in the region, as air quality officials continued to point out. To residents of nearby communities, these views ignored the impacts of traffic, noise, and pollution on their well-being. Even the unions representing the dockworkers, truckers, and rail yard workers expressed concern for workers' health.

Villaraigosa's appointments indicated a partial embrace of the Progressive L.A. agenda and its key figures. A number of appointments to bodies like the Planning Commission, the Department of Water and Power Board, the Board of Public Works, the Harbor Commission, and the Police Commission included a wide array of environmental, social justice, and civil rights figures. Several appointments were in important, though less visible, positions, such as local (area-wide) planning commissions.

Many of Villaraigosa's appointees had never served on municipal boards. They viewed their appointments as a way to influence, even transform, the priorities of municipal government. But Villaraigosa also drew on a handful of traditional insiders for some appointments, including people who had served with Hahn and even his predecessor, Republican Richard Riordan. It remains to be seen whether and how Villaraigosa will confront underlying differences and tensions among this diverse array of appointees.

Villaraigosa's progressive allies understood that to be an effective mayor he needed to build a diverse governing coalition. The new mayor wanted to reassure the business community that his progressive views did not conflict with a strong belief in strengthening the city's economic prosperity. But Villaraigosa wanted to redefine a "healthy business climate" to mean a prosperity that would be widely shared by working people, one that would lift the working poor into the middle class, provide good schools and affordable housing, and protect the environment. He wanted to promote a more enlightened view of business's responsibility to the broader community. He picked his core staff and appointed board members who could help him accomplish that difficult balancing act.

On several occasions during his first six months in office, Villaraigosa also demonstrated his willingness to oppose the position of the business community. For example, over the objections of the Chamber of Commerce, the new mayor supported (and the City Council passed) an ordinance that made it harder for a company that buys a grocery store to fire employees for at least three months. The law, drafted by the United Food and Commercial Workers union, was designed to thwart the possibility that the Idaho-based Albertsons grocery chain (which has about twenty stores in Los Angeles and whose workers are covered by a union contract) would be sold to a nonunion company. Also, despite the opposition of the Central City Association, Villaraigosa named to the Homeless Services Authority three leaders of the American Civil Liberties Union (which had won an injunction and a legal settlement from the city over the Police Department's treatment of the homeless).

For Progressive L.A., the biggest challenge was how to reconcile the potentially conflicting roles of insider policy makers and outsider advocates. Villaraigosa named Larry Frank, a longtime labor and community organizer, as a deputy mayor. Frank, who had been an important field organizer in both Villaraigosa mayoral campaigns, spoke frankly of the challenge. "I've never been an insider," Frank said at a talk at Occidental College, six months after the election. He told the *Los Angeles Times* that the central dilemma was "competing demands": "How do you move an agenda forward, and how do you hold a coalition together?" But, he warned, "If all you're concerned about is holding your coalition together, you can't push on issues."[4]

While Villaraigosa was assembling his team and formulating his agenda, various parts of the Progressive L.A. world came together to identify new issues and policies that they hoped would coincide with the mayor's plans. One group of planners drafted a document called "Planning for a Livable City" that they hoped would guide Villaraigosa's planning and transportation agenda.[5] A second (somewhat overlapping) group, consisting of environmental, environmental justice, and "livable city" advocates, which called itself the Los Angeles Working Group on the Environment, included both "outsiders" and "insiders" who sought to ease the transition from being part of an electoral coalition to being part of a governing coalition. They hoped to shape the work of key departments like Water and Power, City Planning, Transportation, and the Port.

Those who had studied L.A. history recognized the moment's similarities to the situation in 1938, when a progressive coalition had helped oust the incumbent mayor, Frank Shaw, in a recall election and elect a "good government" reformer, a pro–New Deal Republican named Fletcher Bowron. Bowron helped enact some important changes in the city during his fifteen-year run as mayor. While the business elites of the city, led by the *Los Angeles Times*, characterized him as a "son of a bitch, but our son of a bitch," they eventually lost patience with him when he refused to abandon his support for public housing. The same business elites ousted him as mayor in 1953—the height of the McCarthy era—by orchestrating a charged red-baiting campaign on behalf of their handpicked successor, Congressman Norris Poulson.[6]

Progressives also saw parallels between Villaraigosa's victory and the excitement generated by Tom Bradley's victory in 1973. Bradley, too, had forged an interracial coalition and built on the momentum of the civil rights movements and other progressive forces. As we describe in *The Next Los Angeles*, Bradley brought key activists into his administration and initially made some significant changes. But he soon accommodated himself to the downtown business community's agenda and lost his reformer's zeal, especially when the federal government slashed funds to help cities.

The leaders of L.A.'s progressive movement understood that Villaraigosa's election could be a key turning point in the city's history. They wanted to seize the opportunity to push for significant reform, but they also recognized that others in Villaraigosa's electoral and governing coalitions would surely push back, leading to conflict and thus threatening his ability to successfully govern. Realizing that reform is a long-term project, they wanted to find policy initiatives that could serve as stepping-stones to significant change. At the same time, they did not want L.A.'s progressive movement to become so dependent on Villaraigosa's administration that they neglected to "build the base"—recruit new activists, strengthen their organizing and forge new coalitions, and improve their capacity to mobilize for elections, grassroots campaigns, and protests.

PROGRESSIVES AND THE URBAN FUTURE

Unlike Bowron and Bradley, Antonio Villaraigosa came out of "movement" politics. He emerged in high school as an activist committed to grassroots organizing, a progressive vision, and a passion for public service. Few people in Los Angeles—either his allies or skeptics—doubt the new mayor's dedication to those values. In his first six months in office, he reminded anyone who would listen that he wanted to be judged by those standards. "What's the point of having power," he often said, "if we can't use it to improve people's lives?"

But if Villaraigosa's Los Angeles were unique—an island of progressivism in a much larger sea of conservativism—it would hardly be more than an interesting experiment with little relevance for people elsewhere. Fortunately, around the country, progressives have become more sophisticated at municipal policy as well as politics in the past decade. A growing number of progressive activists have been catapulted to municipal office. This is a tribute to the alliances between unions, community organizations, environmentalists, faith-based groups, and others that have emerged in the past decade. As their numbers expand, they are beginning to make connections and learn from each other's successes and mistakes.[7]

There is growing momentum for progressive municipal reform—to improve housing conditions, unionize low-wage workers in the service and light manufacturing sectors, enact living-wage laws, resist bank redlining and predatory lending, improve public schools, fight against environmental hazards, and expand public transit. But many problems simply cannot be solved at the local level alone. Indeed, in some ways, this is a terrible time to be mayor of a major American city. The Bush administration and the GOP-controlled Congress have turned their backs on cities and inner-ring suburbs. Federal funds for affordable housing, schools, public transit, public safety, and health care are woefully inadequate. Many city officials, reeling from the loss of federal and state aid, have had no choice but to cut essential services, including public safety, libraries, road repair, and public schools. Bush's priorities—cutting taxes for the rich; spending huge amounts on the war in Iraq; weakening regulations on business that protect consumers, workers, and the environment; and reducing spending for domestic social programs—come at the expense of cities and inner-ring suburbs. Bush has imposed many new mandates on cities—such as increased homeland security and No Child Left Behind requirements for schools—without providing the funds necessary for the cities to comply. It could be called fend-for-yourself federalism.

The result is that most big-city mayors are trapped in a fiscal straitjacket, and Congress, now dominated by suburban districts because of both changing demographics and gerrymandering, routinely overlooks this situation. We cannot significantly solve our nation's urban problems without federal reforms. As a result, progressives have increasingly recognized that an effective urban progressive movement must start in cities and move outward to working-class suburbs and some liberal middle-class suburbs to create the political momentum for a renewed federal commitment to urban America.

That is part of Villaraigosa's challenge. As the mayor of America's second largest city, Villaraigosa is playing on a much larger stage than his progressive counterparts in other cities. He recognizes, as he said soon after taking office, that "the world will be watching—and judging—the grand social experiment before them."[8] If he can't make a progressive agenda happen in L.A., it will be a significant setback for progressives elsewhere. But if Mayor Villaraigosa and his allies in Progressive L.A. can demonstrate that cities can be well managed as well as become laboratories of progressive policy reform, they will help lay the political groundwork not only for the Next Los Angeles but for the revival of a new progressive politics—and progressive agenda—throughout the country.

Robert Gottlieb, Mark Vallianatos, Regina Freer, and Peter Dreier
Los Angeles, February 2006

1. The 58 percent support among African American voters was identified in an exit poll conducted by the Center for the Study of Los Angeles at Loyola Marymount University. It differed from the results of a *Los Angeles Times* exit poll that situated Villaraigosa's support among African American voters at 48 percent, a still substantial swing though not as dramatic as indicated by the Loyola poll. The Loyola Center argued that their poll was specifically designed to better measure "the opinions of L.A.'s diverse electorate than other methodologies currently in use." See African American Voter Registration, Education, and Participation Project, "African American Voters Turn Out in Support of Antonio Villaraigosa," *AAVREP Newsletter*, May/June 2005, aavrep.org/pubarchives.html (accessed 16 February 2006). The *L.A. Times* analysis is discussed in an article by Raphael J. Sonenshein and *L.A. Times* pollster Susan Pincus, "Latino Incorporation Reaches the Urban Summit: How Antonio Villaraigosa Won the 2005 Los Angeles Mayor's Race," *PSOnline*, October 2005, 713–21, www.apsanet.org (accessed 16 February 2006).

2. The change in focus from 2001 to 2005 was similar to Tom Bradley's defeat of incumbent mayor Sam Yorty in a rather low-key election in 1973, four years after Yorty's successful slash-and-burn tactics against Bradley in 1969, when those two candidates first faced off. Both the 1969 and 2001 elections were intense, ideological, pivotal political moments in the history of the city, with major participation by progressive social movements. In contrast, the 1973 and 2005 elections shifted the focus to the performance of the incumbent mayor at a time when the two challengers, Bradley and Villaraigosa, had become less controversial and better known to the public. In the process, both Bradley and Villaraigosa ran more traditional campaigns in 1973 and 2005, and the more incendiary charges of the previous elections fizzled during the rematches.

3. "Leading with His Life," *U.S. News and World Report*, 31 October 2005, 34.

4. Presentation by Larry Frank, "Inside-Outside Politics: A Deputy Mayor and Long Time Organizer's Perspective," Occidental College, Los Angeles, 16 November 2005; Abel Salas, "Grass-Roots Government: An Old Block Organizer Heads Back to the Neighborhood," *Los Angeles Times Magazine*, August 16, 2005, 6.

5. See Urban and Environmental Policy Institute, "Planning for a Livable City," 2005, http://departments.oxy.edu/uepi/planning_director/index.htm (accessed 16 February 2006).

6. Robert Gottlieb and Irene Wolt, *Thinking Big: The Story of the Los Angeles Times, Its Publishers, and Their Influence on Southern California* (New York: Putnam, 1977), 259–61. One of the casualties of that episode was Frank Wilkinson, one of Bowron's top housing aides, who was forced out of his job with the Housing Authority because of his radical views. Wilkinson, who was an inspiring figure for several generations of progressive activists and went on to become a leading civil liberties activist, died in January 2006.

7. See David B. Reynolds, ed., *Partnering for Change: Unions and Community Groups Build Coalitions for Economic Justice* (Armonk, NY: M. E. Sharpe, 2005); John Nichols, "Urban Archipelago: Progressive Cities in a Conservative Sea," *Nation*, 20 June 2005; Joel Rogers, "Cities: The Vital Core," *Nation*, 20 June 2005; Peter Dreier, "Can a City Be Progressive?" *Nation*, 15 June 2005.

8. Richard Fausset, "Mayor Shares Vision for L.A.," *Los Angeles Times*, 9 December 2005.

Introduction

A Land of Extremes

Los Angeles: our country's worst nightmare, or a model for a changing nation?

The nightmare seems easy enough to identify. The first horrific smog attack occurred in Los Angeles, on Black Monday in June 1943. By the 1940s, L.A. had become a segregated "northern" city, the setting for two major outbursts of civil unrest and racial turmoil. It gave birth to Sam Yorty, Ronald Reagan, and a string of police chiefs who took special pride in keeping the city safe from Okies, Mexicans, Blacks, and Reds. Los Angeles was also one of the first cities to embrace a systematic anti-union policy known as the "Open Shop," and was the site of some of the worst abuses of labor during the twentieth century. Huge economic disparities can be found in L.A., including concentrated pockets of wealth and poverty less than a mile apart. It is the land of extremes: mild climates and turbulent floods, asphalt and concrete-encased rivers, endless landscapes of subdivisions, freeways, and malls. For many, Los Angeles is the ultimate urban, social, and environmental disaster.

But look again. Los Angeles has also become the home of a new kind of labor movement, of a community-oriented environmentalism, and of a multiethnic coalition politics. It has been and continues to be a place where reformers, radicals, and visionaries help shape the future. For Los Angeles, as Carey McWilliams wrote more than fifty years ago, is not merely a testing ground, but also "a forcing ground, a place where ideas, practice, and customs must prove their worth or be discarded." It is "a land of magical improvisation," a place that "creates its own past."[1] Los Angeles, in fact, has continually reinvented itself and tested out new ideas. It is also the place that may help identify a new progressive politics in regions around the country and help set the standard for political and social change in the years to come.

UNDERSTANDING LOS ANGELES

To understand the future of America, one needs to understand Los Angeles. Nearly every trend that is currently transforming the United States— immigration, economic polarization, metropolitan sprawl, the decline of traditional political organization, the provisional rebirth of the labor movement, the struggle to remake cities as more livable places—has appeared in some form in Los Angeles. The changes that L.A. witnessed in the second half of the twentieth century—from the city that celebrated its White, Protestant character to one that has become synonymous with diversity; from an antilabor bastion to the headquarters of the new, organizing-oriented unionism—reflect changes that have begun to appear or may come to pass in other major metropolitan areas. Los Angeles has also been profoundly shaped by the forces of globalization. Much of its manufacturing base has been dismantled, with whole new economic sectors created in its stead. Its major corporate headquarters have moved elsewhere, and its middle class has shrunken. And Los Angeles' cultural and political life has been profoundly reshaped by a wave of immigration on a scale seen only in New York a hundred years ago.

In Los Angeles, the separation of the suburbs from the central city; the decline of upper-middle-class support for such public needs as schools, parks, libraries, and sidewalks; and the emergence of the first serious secession movement in American urban history have made it the very symbol of the dysfunctional urban area. But, with its new immigrant population, its newly reenergized labor movement, and its dynamic community and environmental and social movements, Los Angeles is also the place where the next generation of American progressive thought and action is being defined.

Everybody wants to know about Los Angeles. But for all its importance as the point of creation for global pop culture, as the symbol of urban sprawl, or as the cutting edge of multiculturalism, it still remains difficult to get a handle on this city of improvisation. Los Angeles is a complex place. Beyond the traditional historical story line of right-wing elites, real estate speculators, and Hollywood moguls resides a different and largely invisible story. To understand Los Angeles ultimately requires understanding the origins and evolution of its social movements, of its rich traditions of community activism, and of its alternative cultural life, which has often been marginalized or ignored. Los Angeles, for all its celebrated *difference*, is in fact becoming *representative*, providing lessons about the coming challenges and opportunities for a politics of social change in the new century.

THE NEXT LOS ANGELES

In October 1998, hundreds of activists, young and old, gathered at Occidental College to explore the history, present, and future opportunities for progressive social movements and progressive policy in the Los Angeles region. The participants came to commemorate the seventy-fifth anniversary of a notable moment in Los Angeles history: when Socialist writer Upton Sinclair, in support of striking dockworkers, was arrested for reading the Bill of Rights at a section of the harbor area of San Pedro, which became known as Liberty Hill. The conference also highlighted the twentieth anniversary of the social change–oriented Liberty Hill Foundation, which had taken its name from that 1923 episode.

The L.A.-area progressives gathered that day also referenced another historical moment—Sinclair's 1934 gubernatorial campaign, with its legions of Southern California–based organizers and volunteers, which launched a presumably quixotic campaign, End Poverty in California (EPIC)—and nearly revolutionized the politics of California and the country. What was most striking about EPIC was its capacity to pull together different social movements through a unifying vision of change. And while Sinclair did not win the election, the EPIC campaign helped to reconfigure the political landscape in the region and the state, stimulating new movements and important policy changes.

This book explores how a wide array of social movements throughout the twentieth century—what we call Progressive L.A.—has helped to make L.A. a better city. In doing so, we argue that Progressive L.A. movements provided a vision about Los Angeles and its much-maligned river and landscapes, its multiracial and immigrant cultures and communities, and its social, economic, and environmental conditions of daily life. Our text is at once a history, a policy analysis, and an evaluation of the opportunities for change, both in Los Angeles and in other regions of the country. And we write at a political moment that is ripe for either a grassroots progressive policy agenda or a form of protracted political, economic, and cultural balkanization.

The book is divided into three sections. The first section provides a historical discussion of a changing Los Angeles. Chapter 1, "A Mosaic of Movements," offers a decade-by-decade historical snapshot of Los Angeles' progressive social movements. Chapter 2, "Charlotta Bass," extends that historical snapshot by chronicling the life of this key African American newspaper editor and activist, and by exploring her positions on labor, race and discrimination, the "foreign born" and immigration, and women's rights—all of which prefigured contemporary political themes.

The second section provides an in-depth exploration of key economic, social, and environmental trends that shaped Los Angeles at the end of the twentieth and beginning of the twenty-first centuries. It also examines the responses of the Progressive L.A. movements to those trends. Chapter 3, "The Continuing Divide," analyzes L.A.'s changing demographics and economics and their impact on the region. Chapter 4, "Stresses in Eden," explores concerns about the region's livability, including issues such as transportation, land use, housing, the food system, criminal justice, and the changing urban environment.

The third section addresses L.A.'s changing political landscape. Chapter 5, "Shifting Coalitions," analyzes the evolution of L.A.'s social movements and the political shifts from the 1950s to the present day. Chapter 6, "Setting an Agenda," analyzes two recent top-down efforts to address L.A.'s protracted economic and social tensions—the L.A. 2000 Partnership, formed in the late 1980s, and Rebuild L.A., formed in the aftermath of the 1992 civil unrest. The chapter then compares those efforts to a more bottom-up grassroots initiative—the convening of a series of task forces, through the Progressive Los Angeles Network (PLAN), that drew on the themes and campaigns of community activists and social movements in the region. The concluding chapter, "A Vision for the City," describes conflicting interpretations of the Next L.A. and the prospects for a revitalized progressive politics in this country. Will Los Angeles become a balkanized region dominated by the forces of secession, ethnic and geographic conflicts, and economic polarization? Or will there emerge a Los Angeles transformed by social movements, demographic changes, and new political coalitions that seek to make Los Angeles a more democratic, just, and livable region?

The book's appendix, "A Policy Agenda for the Next L.A.," provides a partial template, developed for the 2001 mayoral primary election, of a new progressive, community-based agenda for Los Angeles. While the book's four authors shared in the research and writing of each of the chapters (and Harold Meyerson coauthored chapter 5), the appendix reflects the work of the leading community organizers, activists, and progressive policy analysts who pulled together the different components of the PLAN agenda. This book, in many respects, is a product of that work and the discussions that shaped it.

CONTEMPORARY PROGRESSIVES

In *The Next Los Angeles,* the term *Progressive L.A.* is used to describe an emerging social change movement concerned with issues of social and economic justice, democracy, and livability. The book describes earlier social movements that participated in the struggles to transform L.A. and make it a more just and livable city.

Our use of the word *progressive*, however, does differ in some respects from the way the term has been used to characterize earlier periods and movements, such as the "Progressive Era" of the early twentieth century or the popular front groups of the 1940s and early 1950s. The Progressive Era, from 1900 to 1920, with its much celebrated "gospel of efficiency," has come to be associated with technical and scientific expertise, public-private partnerships, overcoming (and sometimes ignoring) class division, and, among some of the more conservative progressives of that era, hostility to democratic participation. Responding to the excesses of early industrial capitalism, many of these progressives were elite reformers who trusted technological change more than democratic process and who promoted moral reformation rather than social justice. In contrast, other progressives, such as Jane Addams and Florence Kelley, advocated for a more radical and democratic approach to social and environmental reform.

All of the popular front progressives of the 1940s and early 1950s, on the other hand, raised the banner of social and economic justice. Despite this emphasis, popular front progressives were swept up and often trapped by the Cold War dilemma—you had to identify with either the Communist or anti-Communist left, often by declaring support for or opposition to the Soviet Union. This choice undermined and even precluded the development of grassroots cultural, labor, and community politics and made little or no reference to a sense of place and vision about Los Angeles. It was difficult (although not impossible) for social change advocates or radical thinkers such as Carey McWilliams to escape those tensions. Nevertheless, even in the midst of the bleakest days of the Cold War, the desire to remake Los Angeles still motivated much of the community, union, and issue-based activism that survived this period.

After the demise of the popular front—and ultimately of much of the "Old Left"—during the McCarthy era of the 1950s, the term *progressive* fell out of favor with the 1960s generation of activists and organizers. Many of these activists proudly proclaimed themselves "New Left" and "radical," while rejecting connections to earlier social justice movements. The New Left provided a refreshing burst of new political energy, new social movements such as feminism, environmentalism, and gay liberation, and a new consideration of the crucial importance of race, class, and gender in American society. But the New Left, despite its concern with "community," was often divorced from a community politics associated with the everyday lives of people living and working in urban neighborhoods. This disconnectedness, moreover, made the New Left's version of social change advocacy more abstract. A politics of the imagination was created (to paraphrase the slogan used in France in May 1968), but one that was not necessarily rooted in community.

By the 1970s, many of the new social movements had begun to organize in communities and workplaces. During the subsequent two decades, despite political reversals, progressive activism broadened its appeal and deepened its roots. By the new century, Los Angeles' progressive tradition—a century of struggle for social change—had given birth to a new set of voices and a broader, deeper vision of possibility, and the term *progressive* began to reenter the political vocabulary. The new progressives also began to identify with a history that provided insight about contemporary struggles and visions of the future. Today, Progressive L.A. is more than just a disparate set of historical and contemporary movements and ideas. It is, instead, on the leading edge of making the Next Los Angeles a better place to live.

PART I

Progressive Legacies

Social Movements in the Twentieth Century

Introduction

"We have a history," longtime housing and civil liberties activist Frank Wilkinson said of Los Angeles' progressive social movements. "But it's a history that's been neglected and often dismissed." Wilkinson, speaking at the October 1998 conference on progressive movements in Los Angeles, might have been referring to his own battles on behalf of public housing or the actions of his fellow panelists who had built economic and social justice. While Los Angeles is often seen as a bastion of conservative, probusiness, and antilabor perspectives and policies, it has also been able to reinvent itself politically and culturally, welcoming innovative and radical ideas. While L.A.'s progressive movements have often suffered in a hostile political culture, marginalized by an entrenched conservative political and business elite, they have nevertheless helped to shape the region's political, economic, and cultural life in ways little recognized by mainstream historians.

The history of progressive social movements in Los Angeles reflects the same kind of point-counterpoint argument that is made about Los Angeles itself—the land of dreams and possibility versus the "day of the locust" imagery of ecological disaster and reactionary power. The history of Los Angeles—and its progressive movements—includes moments when opportunities for change and "reinvention" seemed great, as well as periods when the prospects for change seemed bleak. The 1930s, for example, was clearly a period of great political and social ferment, in which progressive social movements extended their reach into every arena of political, economic, and social life. But the forces of political and cultural reaction were also powerful. For example, the End Poverty in California electoral movement in 1934 triggered the first dramatic use of the media as part of a concentrated—and ultimately successful—counterattack, staged by hired public relations firms and orchestrated by the business and political elite.

9

Similarly, the 1950s in Los Angeles was a period of blacklists, political reaction, and the dismantling of progressive social policies such as affordable public housing. But progressive social movements also regrouped during that decade, and within a few years they had catalyzed a new wave of civil rights and environmental and community organizing.

This section explores that complex history by providing a portrait of many of the progressive movements, personalities, and issues of twentieth-century Los Angeles. It also examines how many of the themes of the past reverberate today. It documents progressives' efforts to address the changing conditions of the city's culturally, ethnically, and socially diverse constituencies. The first chapter provides a decade-by-decade historical snapshot of Progressive L.A. and its evolution through different political periods. The second chapter profiles journalist and activist Charlotta Bass, an African American woman whose wide-ranging political activity symbolizes the complexity of Progressive L.A. These historical sketches, in turn, reflect a major theme of this book: by recovering the history of Progressive L.A., we can not only learn from that history but help make history as well.

1   A Mosaic of Movements

Progressive L.A. in the Twentieth Century

The history of twentieth-century Los Angeles is a tale of conflicting visions and agendas. The better-known story depicts corporate and political elites promoting unregulated development, civic boosterism, cheap labor, exploited immigrants, and endless sprawl. But Los Angeles also has a vibrant history of reformers and radicals—the activists of Progressive L.A.—who offered an alternative vision of social justice and an agenda of workplace reform, civil rights, gender equity, a healthier environment, and more livable communities. While this vision and agenda are less well known, they have at different times successfully influenced the social, economic, environmental, and political dynamics of the region and helped to improve the daily lives of its residents.

During much of the twentieth century, Progressive L.A. resembled a mosaic of separate struggles around particular problems and issues. While L.A.'s diverse progressive social movements were able to win specific victories and lay the groundwork for reform, they rarely built the momentum necessary to unite sometimes contending constituencies in order to gain the political power needed to change public policy. There were, however, historical moments when greater unity and a compelling vision made possible a broader transformation of the political landscape. At the same time, the forces arrayed against those alternative visions and agendas remained formidable, helping to secure L.A.'s reputation as a bastion of reactionary, anti-labor, antienvironmental, and anti-immigrant politics. L.A.'s mosaic of movements was, at times, marginalized, not only due to the ferocious counterreaction to their actions and goals, but also as a consequence of the divisiveness within movements, of agendas that became divorced from

11

community issues and needs, and of a politics that looked outside Los Angeles' capacity to reinvent itself.

As the twenty-first century approached, momentum began to build for a new, more unified Progressive L.A. The challenges for progressive unity remained enormous, compounded by the September 11, 2001, terrorist attacks and parallel political and economic shocks, including efforts to break Los Angeles apart, which created powerful obstacles for progressive change. By exploring L.A.'s progressive social movements from the past century, we can better understand how progressives today can overcome those obstacles.

THE FIRST DECADE:
WHAT KIND OF CITY WILL LOS ANGELES BECOME?

It was, to be sure, a most unusual election. Coming just a few years after Los Angeles had become one of the first cities to adopt a charter amendment that allowed, among other reforms, the recall of elected officials, the 1906 mayoral election included a Democrat, a Republican, and a candidate of the newly formed Public Ownership Party (POP). This new electoral grouping brought together Socialists, labor, and advocates of the public ownership of utilities. The POP offered a prolabor and "living wage" platform and supported municipal ownership of the new hydroelectric power plant and a proposed electric railway from downtown to the port at San Pedro. The POP's candidate, Stanley Wilson, was not given much of a chance against the organizational resources of the two major parties. Key business and political figures sharply attacked this new force in the city, prefiguring the antilabor, antiradical onslaught that would characterize the reactionary elites during the next three decades. Though Wilson, as expected, lost the election, he injected a new type of progressive politics into the political discourse of the time. The local Democratic Party, for instance, jumped on the municipal ownership bandwagon. Wilson and the POP's efforts helped progressives gain credibility about both social- and economic-justice issues as well as what kind of city Los Angeles would become.[1]

By the new century, Los Angeles, in the wake of boom-and-bust cycles and rampant real estate speculation, was seeking to redefine itself. Conflicts were emerging about whether, where, and how the city would grow, how its politics would be defined, what resources would be available, whether the Los Angeles River would become a community haven or an industrial sewer, and how Los Angeles would be planned in the years to come. Some reformers, like City Beautiful advocate Dana Bartlett, argued that Los

Angeles showed signs of becoming a "city of homes, without slums," where the poor could "live in single cottages with dividing fences and flowers in the front yard, and often times with vegetables in the backyard." This was the image of Los Angeles as Eden, a region blessed with a Mediterranean climate (the "Land of Sunshine"), agricultural abundance, a variety of wildlife and vegetation, an optimistic attitude, and a welcoming spirit toward new residents.[2]

But others argued that Los Angeles was beset with a complex of environmental, political, and social problems, creating challenges for those reformers and radicals seeking to make Los Angeles a more livable, equitable, and democratic place. The city's old guard had already begun to promote visions of an Open Shop city based on cheap, nonunion labor; of expanding the city's geographical boundaries, orchestrated through real estate syndicates and imported water; and of a growth strategy fueled by continuous waves of new residents migrating from the Midwest and elsewhere. At the same time, a persistent anti-immigrant strain characterized much of the old guard's politics. The focus on "foreigners," moreover, was not directed just at Asians and Mexicans, the primary target of anti-immigrant politics. "Why should [Los Angeles] be made a dumping ground for the scum of Europe?" snarled a 1904 editorial in the *Los Angeles Times*.[3]

An important political shift also began to occur in this period, associated with the new progressive reform movements advocating the direct recall, the initiative, and the referendum.[4] More radical forces also began to gather, including a more assertive labor movement and an expanding Socialist Party, focused on social and economic reforms more than on political change. They promoted utopian ideas that had a pragmatic twist—such as worker-owned and cooperative organizations. Los Angeles had active Nationalist Clubs, groups associated with the ideas of Edward Bellamy, author of the utopian novel *Looking Backwards*. In 1902, the newly formed Los Angeles Cooperators opened a cooperative grocery store on South Main Street, based on the Rochdale Plan advocated by several labor groups. The store, which had over two hundred members at its launching, was designed so that its working-class members could share in merchandise discounts and company profits. Unable to attract sufficient capital, the Main Street store folded three years later. Despite this failure, the cooperative concept continued to resonate and reemerged in the 1930s and again in the 1960s and 1970s as an important part of the broader political agenda of Los Angeles progressives.[5]

The 1906 mayoral election also helped to establish a progressive coalition that became one of four key political groupings in the city. At one end of the spectrum were the conservative forces that promoted the Open Shop, pri-

vate control of the utilities and the transportation system, real estate subdivision and speculation, and permanent population growth through migration from within the United States. A second group, a moderate reform faction, promoted good government concepts to make cities run more
efficiently, but essentially accepted the approach of the conservatives on
labor and social reform issues. A third group, the radical wing of the progressive reformers, called for a stronger role for government and sought to
mediate between the contending forces of labor and capital. A fourth group,
including parts of the labor movement and the emerging Socialist Party,
combined a justice agenda based on the rights of labor and the welfare of the
community with support for municipal planning and controls on unregulated growth. While the newspapers, banks, private utilities, railroads, and
real estate syndicates made plans for expansion in anticipation of a new
water supply from Owens Valley, radical reformers questioned these plans.
None of the four factions was entirely able to control the political process.
Whether in relation to the Open Shop, the rights of labor, electoral reforms,
or the use of imported water for real estate speculation, the city was at a critical juncture.

THE 1910S:
SOCIALISTS TO POWER?

Ironmolder and union activist Dan Grayson, fresh from successfully overcoming charges that he had violated a Los Angeles antipicketing ordinance,
ran for governor of California on the Socialist Party ticket—and won. Once
in office, he signed into law a bill that guaranteed jobs and a living wage for
all wage earners.

Sound far-fetched? This election took place in *From Dusk to Dawn*, a
silent film that drew large audiences when it first opened at a Socialist
movie hall on Broadway in downtown Los Angeles. With a cast of over ten
thousand, *From Dusk to Dawn* realistically portrayed life in the era's
poverty-stricken slums, the brutality of dangerous workplaces, the violence
used by companies and local police to destroy union organizing, and the
struggle of ordinary people for better lives and working conditions.[6]

From Dusk to Dawn was not Hollywood escapism. On the contrary, its
nationwide popularity was rooted in its close reflection of the political
times and popular mood. Socialists in Los Angeles were aspiring to power.
In 1911, labor lawyer and Socialist leader Job Harriman, who made a
cameo appearance in *From Dusk to Dawn*, was nearly elected mayor of Los
Angeles.

An important figure in L.A.'s progressive history, Harriman has yet to receive a much-deserved full-length biographical assessment of his critical role in promoting an alternative vision for Los Angeles. In the 1911 primary election for mayor, Harriman electrified local residents and national progressives by coming in first, barely a thousand votes short of a 50 percent majority and outright victory. Harriman had effectively crafted a coalition of Socialists, union members, and the radical wing of the progressive reform and good government movements. Harriman's first-place finish also generated near panic among both moderate progressives and conservative business forces about a Socialist takeover of the municipal government. These groups mobilized to support the reelection of Mayor George Alexander, a relatively weak reformer, who had been scorned in the primary by several of the most powerful and reactionary of the business elites. Harriman's campaign was ultimately undermined by a plea bargain announced just before election day. Harriman was one of the lawyers for the McNamara brothers, accused of the October 1, 1910, bombing of the *Los Angeles Times* building, which resulted in the deaths of twenty people. Though he was part of the defense team for the brothers (one of whom was a top union official), Harriman was unaware of their guilt or of the deal pursued by the lead attorney, Clarence Darrow, to prevent a death sentence. It was clear that the plea bargain was designed to influence the outcome of the election. Tarred by his association with the McNamaras and a vitriolic, anti-Socialist, and anti-union campaign led by the *Times*, Harriman's political support dissipated, and he lost the runoff election.[7]

Despite Harriman's defeat, Socialist candidates for the State Assembly and Los Angeles City Council did well. Several Socialist candidates were elected or came close to winning, in both the 1911 and 1913 elections, on platforms that included an industrial policy based on "closed-shop" union contracts and a "fair day's wage for a fair day's work." The Socialists also promoted a water, energy, and land use policy that included growth boundaries and livable cities, and a "good government" program to fight political corruption and challenge the elite power structure that ruled Los Angeles. The size of the Socialist vote in the 1911 and 1913 elections, upward of 40 percent, even caused prominent progressive reformer John Randolph Haynes to declare that Los Angeles politics had shifted from Democrat versus Republican to Socialist versus Anti-Socialist. "The principles of Socialism will ultimately—in fact, I may say in the not distant future—be incorporated into the systems of government of all civilized nations," Haynes wrote in one widely circulated 1913 essay.[8]

Despite the strong showing of the Socialist candidates, the structure of electoral representation in Los Angeles and nearly all other U.S. cities failed to provide a place for forceful radical voices. In 1912, a People's Charter Commission that included progressive reformers and Socialists proposed a series of Charter amendments, including a system of proportional representation for municipal elections. This provision would have allowed for representation of dissenting voices on the City Council, including those who, like the Socialists, failed to secure outright majorities but nevertheless represented a significant portion of the electorate. Though several of the other proposed amendments passed in a subsequent election, a major business-led attack against the idea of proportional representation led to its defeat.[9]

The upsurge of radical politics in Los Angeles eroded during World War I due to patriotic appeals, attacks on civil liberties, and hostility to antiwar views. Innovative institutions and public strategies were also undercut, such as the city funding for a municipal newspaper *(The Municipal News)*, a new voice that for a short period provided refreshing and often comprehensive accounts of public policy debates. The *Municipal News* demonstrated how an alternative news medium could influence political debates, particularly in contrast to the sensationalist Hearst papers and the reactionary *L.A. Times.*[10] The *Times*, especially, had become a direct, unfettered instrument of local business elites, including Harry Chandler, the son-in-law of the *Times*'s publisher, Harrison Gray Otis. Chandler, who replaced his father-in-law after Otis's death in 1914, was also a major real estate speculator and behind-the-scenes political and business figure. He worked closely with such reactionary, antilabor leaders as Paul Shoup of the Southern Pacific Railroad and Harry Haldeman (grandfather of Watergate figure H. R. Haldeman, a top aide to President Richard Nixon) to place Los Angeles at the forefront of opposition to progressive change.[11]

Reactionary political forces began to consolidate their power at the end of the decade, but Los Angeles maintained its reputation as a place for utopian experiments and innovation. Job Harriman, for one, left the Los Angeles political arena to help to establish a communal living arrangement at Llano del Rio, at the edge of the Mojave Desert. He recruited a local architect, Alice Constance Austin, to create what Harriman called an alternative city, which would, among other goals, "make homes for many a homeless family" and demonstrate how one could "live without war or interest on money or rent on land or profiteering in any manner."[12] Experiments in innovative workers' housing had already been introduced in Southern California, such as Lewis Court in Sierra Madre, which had a ring of small concrete houses that enclosed a large communal garden. Llano del Rio was more ambitious, reflecting communitarian traditions of the nineteenth and early twentieth centuries, but it lasted only three years. Its members relocated to Louisiana, a casualty of economic barriers and the complexities of maintaining a self-contained community separate from the urban core. It became another symbol of Progressive L.A.'s quest for innovation as well as of the difficulties of establishing radical alternatives in a hostile political environment.

THE 1920S:
A FRAGMENTED METROPOLIS

Striking dockworkers, including members of the Industrial Workers of the World (nicknamed the Wobblies), were constantly harassed. In defense of their rights, Upton Sinclair—journalist, novelist, political activist, Socialist candidate for Congress, screenwriter, and film producer—joined a rally in San Pedro in 1923 and started to read from the Bill of Rights. "This is a delightful climate," Sinclair began his talk—and was promptly arrested along with hundreds of others. "We'll have none of that Constitution stuff," the arresting officer declared. Sinclair was subsequently held incommunicado for eighteen hours. The scandal that ensued led to an exposé of police corruption and the arrest of the chief of police. It also led to the founding of the American Civil Liberties Union of Southern California. The site of the protest came to be known as Liberty Hill, which ever since has been associated with the rights of labor and the defense of free speech.[13]

In Los Angeles history, the 1920s has typically been viewed as a period of reaction—overt racism against Asians and Mexicans, the triumph of the big studios in Hollywood, the oil boom and the environmental degradation that went with it, and the consolidation of business's plan to decimate the labor movement and make Los Angeles a bastion of cheap labor. Indeed, by 1929, John Porter, auto-parts dealer and former member of the Ku Klux Klan, had been elected mayor. Porter benefited from the support of Reverend Robert "Fighting Bob" Shuler, whose anti-Catholic, anti-Jewish, anti-Black invectives were also spiced with criticism of the teaching of evolution and hostility to those who opposed the Klan. At the same time, organizations such as the anti-union, anti-immigrant, and misogynist Better America Federation helped to unite the most reactionary forces among political and civil elites.[14]

The 1920s was also a time of economic and demographic change. Los Angeles more than doubled in size, from a population of 577,000 in 1920 to more than 1.2 million at the end of the decade. While L.A. continued to attract an influx of White middle-class and lower-middle-class Midwesterners influenced by images of L.A. as a kind of Eden of the imagination, non-White immigrants also arrived in search of jobs. Many of these immigrants settled along the Los Angeles River corridor in the "Eastside Industrial District" to the south and east of downtown Los Angeles, where some factories were concentrated. This area also came to be known as the "foreign districts," due to the high concentration of immigrant neighborhoods.[15]

Los Angeles developed a more diverse industrial base in this period, although the major industries—motion pictures and oil especially—still dominated much of the region's economic activity. The 1920s also witnessed another boom cycle, in which population expansion, continually promoted as L.A.'s "growth industry" by such groups as the Chamber of Commerce's All Year Club, coincided with the development of new imported water supplies and the rapid geographic expansion of Los Angeles' land base. From 1913 to 1928, the city's size grew fourfold. The city—and the surrounding region—became increasingly dependent on imported water and energy resources and a vast grid-based transportation system of interurban trolley lines.[16]

Much of the expansion in manufacturing and agriculture was related to the area's population growth and development of regional markets. Companies such as Goodyear and Firestone built branch plants in L.A., attracted by the new availability of resources like water and energy, the region's expanding labor pool, and the invidious anti-union activities of groups like the Better America Federation. Hostility to unions characterized the region's business climate and dominated the politics of the era. For example, Los Angeles became the headquarters of the "American Plan," the national campaign to establish open-shop policies in every workplace and every industry, also linking population growth to anti-unionization initiatives. As the *L.A. Times,* the local champion of the American Plan, argued, any step back from the open shop would cause the city's growth to "slow down, stop, or even reverse its direction."[17]

Many people, however, were left out of the boom or were treated as marginal to the dominant culture of growth and expansion. Racism, directed particularly at the growing Latino, Asian, and African American populations, became more prevalent in this period. A revealing study by USC sociology professor Bessie Averne McClenahan documented efforts by middle-class Whites in the Vermont-Jefferson area of South Los Angeles to keep African Americans and Japanese Americans from moving into their neighborhood. Employing such tactics as restrictive housing covenants to ensure "White-only sales," and even trying to keep a local elementary school all White, these residents panicked over the prospect of racial inclusion. "Fear was aroused and resentment stirred," McClenahan wrote, "of what was believed to be the slogan of the Negroes, 'On to Vermont.'"[18]

But progressives regrouped in the 1920s. They successfully challenged some of the more reactionary elected officials and sponsored modest efforts toward cooperative organization, which extended to such industries as bakeries, laundries, auto parts, and banking. One such group was the labor-backed Southern California Cooperative Association, formed in 1921 to assist the unemployed as well as to compete with nonunion businesses. This interest in alternative forms of social and economic organization paralleled cultural experiments of the period. Political radicals and literary bohemians formed circles in places like Pasadena and Venice, along Central Avenue in South L.A., on the Eagle Rock campus of Occidental College, in Boyle Heights, in the back room at Musso and Frank's restaurant in Hollywood, and at Jake Zeitlin's At the Sign of the Grasshopper bookstore in downtown Los Angeles. There and elsewhere, journalists, planners, essayists, novelists, union organizers, and others attempted to craft an alternative vision of Los Angeles as a place of possibility and experimentation, a city that was also "gaudy, flamboyant, richly scented, noisy [and] jazzy," as one newcomer, Carey McWilliams, characterized its emerging reputation.[19]

The first wave of feminism also made an impact. Socialist and progressive women had been active in Los Angeles since the turn of the century, organizing Socialist women's clubs as well as a Los Angeles branch of the Women's Trade Union League. In 1913, a new group called the Women's Wage League linked up with the Socialist Party and the Central Labor Council to push for an ordinance to establish a Women's Living Wage Investigation Board. The ordinance was designed to identify which employers had failed to pay what the California Bureau of Labor Statistics identified as a living wage and then to use that information to organize boycotts against those companies. The issue of women's suffrage also resonated in Southern California. Dora Haynes organized the city's League of Women Voters chapter in 1919, and helped to mobilize support for the state's ratification of the women's suffrage constitutional amendment. Support for women's suffrage in Southern California had been particularly strong prior to the passage of the Nineteenth Amendment in 1920, which gave women the vote and helped to stimulate another wave of interest in women's participation in politics and in advocacy for women's rights in the workplace and the home.[20]

The small but growing African American community also experienced the first stirrings of a new radicalism, particularly among some of the younger members of the Los Angeles branch of the NAACP, which hosted that organization's national convention in 1928. The rapidly growing Mexican American community also began to explore its own complex, binational political and cultural identities during the 1920s. For example, the first commercial recording of a popular Mexican musical genre, the *corrido,* occurred in 1926 in Los Angeles. The *corrido* offered a narrative designed to "interpret, celebrate, and ultimately dignify events already thoroughly familiar to the *corrido* audience," as one analyst put it. The 1926 recording of "El Lavaplatos," for example, describes a Mexican immigrant who comes to Los Angeles to make his fortune but is forced to take a job as a dishwasher. The narrator concludes, "Goodbye dreams of my life, goodbye movie stars. I am going back to my beloved homeland, much poorer than when I came."[21]

The hidden strands of 1920s Progressive L.A. also included a burgeoning grassroots environmentalism, such as when working-class communities were able to restrain "Big Oil" from drilling in—and destroying—their neighborhoods. Oil drilling at beach sites became a highly charged issue during the '20s. Large majorities of Angelenos maintained consistent support for public access to beaches and favored a ban on pier drilling. By the end of the decade, urban planners Frederick Law Olmsted, Jr., and Harlan Bartholomew had authored a major urban greening plan for Los Angeles that included large-scale development of parks, limits on urban sprawl, and restrictions on inappropriate development. The Olmsted-Bartholomew approach contrasted with the push by real estate developers and other commercial interests to "penetrate the wild virgin areas of the region," as the *Los Angeles Times* put it, and make Los Angeles into a permanently expanding—and fragmented—metropolis.[22]

THE 1930S:
EPIC STRUGGLES

In 1933, in the depths of the Depression, Upton Sinclair published *I, Governor of California and How I Ended Poverty: A True Story of the Future.* In this slim volume, Sinclair described how, as governor, he would put the state's unemployed to work in state-aided "production for use" cooperative enterprises as part of the public takeover of bankrupt factories and idle farmland. The book launched what Sinclair regarded as an educational campaign for governor around a simple slogan—"End Poverty in California," or EPIC.

Sinclair's genius was his ability to bring together the broad spectrum of progressives and radicals around a common vision and a concrete reform agenda. In a state where Republicans had long dominated the statehouse, Sinclair shocked the political establishment and won the Democratic Party nomination in 1934, attracting more primary votes than any candidate in the party's history. More than two-thirds of those votes came from Southern California. Fearful that L.A. had become a hotbed of radical thought and action, big business—led by the Hollywood studios, the *Los Angeles Times*, and the big agricultural growers—mobilized an extraordinary media campaign that undermined his chances to win in November.[23]

Despite Sinclair's defeat and the continuous onslaught against radical groups and immigrants (including, for the first-time, U.S.-born "Okies" and "Arkies"), economic decline and political disenfranchisement fueled the drive for a new progressive politics. A greatly expanded Red Squad in the Los Angeles Police Department led the antiradical drive, operating as a near-autonomous instrument of business elites under the direction of Police Captain William "Red" Hynes. Housed in the Chamber of Commerce building and with ties to the Ku Klux Klan, Red Squad members were also hired by employers to help to break labor strikes, guard borders against immigrants, and undercut any manifestation of progressive politics in the city.[24]

But harassment by the Red Squad failed to stop the momentum for progressive politics. Amid the social and economic chaos of the Depression, the political sparks ignited by the 1934 EPIC campaign and parallel political, social, and cultural movements soon spread. EPIC clubs sprang up at a phenomenal rate in Southern California and became just one component of a broad progressive drive that included a flourishing cooperative movement; a revived labor movement led by the new Congress of Industrial Organizations (CIO) and its Labor Non-Partisan League; and a cultural and literary renaissance of writers, artists, photographers, and independent filmmakers exploring a range of social themes. Voters elected several EPIC candidates to the state legislature. Some of them—like Augustus Hawkins of Los Angeles and Jerry Voorhis of Whittier—were later elected to Congress, while EPIC supporter Culbert Olson was elected governor in 1938.[25]

The EPIC campaign became part of the broader political upheaval of the 1930s. Workers in Los Angeles and elsewhere joined unions in unprecedented numbers and engaged in civil disobedience and general strikes. In 1933, Mexican and Japanese berry workers in El Monte went on strike to demand an increase in their nine-cents-an-hour pay. They were soon joined by several thousand workers in Culver City, Venice, and Santa Monica, an uprising that led to a twenty-cents-an-hour settlement. That same year, union organizer Rose Pesotta and a number of Latina organizers in the International Ladies Garment Workers' Union led the predominantly Latina workforce in the garment industry in one of the few industrywide strikes in Los Angeles' history.[26]

The 1933 Dressmakers' Strike was notable for several reasons. The garment industry workers in Los Angeles, half of them Mexican immigrant or Mexican American employees (most of whom were women) as well as Russian, Polish, Italian, and Jewish workers, were an early reflection of the increasingly multiethnic low-wage Los Angeles workforce. The strike, led by Latinas who were part of an emerging radical as well as ethnic-based politics in the region, put pressure on the international union to open up its leadership to the rapidly growing number of Latina workers. As historian George Sanchez argued, the strike was crucial in "redefining the oppositional culture of Mexican organized workers during the 1930s." "Building on histories of Mexican cooperative organization and memories of radicalism on both sides of the border," Sanchez wrote, "these organizers placed this history within the context of current labor struggles and encouraged workers to see themselves living out an important American tradition of radicalism." By the end of the decade, several Latina labor organizers, led by Luisa Moreno of the United Cannery, Agricultural, Packing and Allied Workers, had organized the L.A.-based El Congreso Nacional de Habla Espanola. El Congreso became a leading Latino advocacy group, linking civil rights for all Spanish-speaking people in the United States with labor rights and economic justice issues.[27]

Aside from the labor insurgencies, activism spread to nearly every facet of daily life. Community groups blocked landlords and police from evicting unemployed renters. Mexican American activists in the CIO organized a dance attended by fifteen hundred Mexican gang members that helped to mobilize them to support campaigns around schools, better recreational facilities, and more job opportunities for young people.[28] Seniors mobilized around the Townsend Plan, initiated by the charismatic, eccentric, and at times crackpot doctor Francis E. Townsend in Long Beach in 1933. This movement and similar insurgencies, like the Ham 'n Eggs pension plan advocacy, took an increasingly unpredictable if not near fascistlike turn, approximating the kind of right-wing populism that had emerged in Europe and other parts of the United States. Nevertheless, the revolt of the seniors, born and bred in the hothouse utopian politics of Southern California, combined with a broad array of social movements to push Congress to pass major New Deal reforms, such as the federal Social Security Act. In the midst of this protest, Sinclair's campaign, even in defeat, made radical ideas seem like common sense. In this climate, President Roosevelt sought to contain the rebellion by humanizing capitalism with a reform agenda that included the Wagner Act, Social Security, and a jobs program for the unemployed.[29]

Despite its intent to contain the radical upsurge, the early reforms of the New Deal only seemed to inspire further activism. Within a year after Sinclair's defeat in the governor's race, for example, several of the city's labor, progressive, and radical organizations had formed the United Organization for Progressive Political Action, and three of its candidates had won election to the Los Angeles City Council. That same year, Tokijiro Saisho, a Japanese immigrant and a Socialist, helped to launch a Japanese workers' organization, the California Farm Laborers Association, headquartered in Los Angeles. Workers at the Douglas Aviation plant in Santa Monica organized a sit-down strike in 1937, which led to the greatest mass arraignment in Los Angeles County history. Other efforts to organize workers that same year included an unsuccessful organizing drive at Lockheed and a successful campaign at Northrop. Ultimately, by the war years, the unions had succeeded in organizing nearly the entire aircraft industry, and by doing so raised the next generation of aerospace workers into the middle class.

Among low-wage agricultural workers, including Asian, Mexican, and transplanted Midwestern and southwestern farmers, bitter farm strikes in Los Angeles and the Imperial Valley foreshadowed the rise of farmworker unions in the 1940s and again in the 1960s. To offset these strikes, groups like the Associated Farmers utilized tactics that amounted to "organized terrorism," designed to produce "a system of peonage," as Herbert Klein and Carey McWilliams wrote in the *Nation*.[30] At the same time, LAPD Captain Hynes sent his police army to close the borders against the "immigrant" Okies and Arkies, and politicians continued to use racial fears to divide the voters. Even so, a progressive coalition continued to grow in strength. The Labor Non-Partisan League launched a series of campaigns with progressive candidates, including John Anson Ford's close but unsuccessful race in 1937 against mayoral incumbent Frank Shaw. The Ford campaign, however, anticipated the successes of progressive electoral coalitions, including, one year later, a successful recall of the corrupt Shaw and the consequent election of Fletcher Bowron. Bowron, a conservative Superior Court judge willing to forge alliances with progressives, was attacked by the *Los Angeles Times* as an "honest reformer who has become the unwitting dupe of the CIO, the Communists, and certain crackpot reformers." Despite the continuing attacks of the *Times*, Bowron implemented important reforms in his first year as mayor, including the dismantling of the Red Squad and the firing of Captain Hynes.[31]

By the end of the 1930s, Los Angeles progressives had finally succeeded in overcoming the intensive three-decade effort led by business elites and growth promoters to keep Los Angeles an Open Shop citadel and a conservative political and cultural enclave. As the war in Europe began to reorient the U.S. economy, an era of organizing, new ideas, program experimentation, and robust political coalition building had created important political openings in Los Angeles. Change was in the air, though new battle lines were being drawn.

THE 1940S:
RESTRICTIVE COVENANTS, WHITE RIOTS, AND BLACKLISTS

Three months after the end of World War II, African American defense workers Anna and Henry Laws were found guilty of violating a restrictive covenant in the deed on their small home on East 92nd Street. The covenant stated that the premises should not be "used or occupied by any person not of the Caucasian race." The Lawses and their daughter were fined and imprisoned. Reformers and radicals formed several support organizations, including the Home Protective Association, organized by African American community leader Charlotta Bass, and the Committee for the Defense of Henry Laws, under the chairmanship of Daniel Marshall, leader of the Catholic Inter-Racial Council of Los Angeles.

The Lawses' experience was not unique for African Americans. Ironically, the Lawses had tried to locate another house, placing ads in the African American press, interviewing real estate agents, and spending evenings and weekends looking for a home, to no avail. African Americans accounted for only 7 percent of Los Angeles' postwar population (nearly doubling during the war years), but they made up 46 percent of all the applications filed for the city's tiny inventory of government-subsidized public housing. Growing awareness of racist and anti-Semitic restrictive covenants coincided with a severe postwar housing shortage. The Lawses' case triggered a grassroots crusade for civil rights and better housing. This movement ultimately prevailed in the courts (a 1948 Supreme Court ruling found restrictive covenants in violation of the Fourteenth Amendment, although the practice continued informally for more than another decade) and in the neighborhoods (where a vibrant movement sought to promote centrally located, affordable public housing for African Americans, Latinos, and other working-class residents of the city).[32]

The politics of race emerged during and after the war as a critical issue for

L.A.'s progressives. It helped to define the nature of the city as it evolved into a major urban and industrial center. Restrictive covenants turned out to be just one component of a wide range of racist policies.

During World War II, reactionary forces in California launched racist fear campaigns, directed in particular against Japanese Americans. While conservative civic leaders beat the drums to herd Japanese Americans into internment camps during World War II, a new generation of activists joined with such progressive voices as newspaper publisher Charlotta Bass, writer Carey McWilliams, the American Civil Liberties Union's A. L. Wirin, and State Attorney General Bob Kenny to fight for the civil rights and the civil liberties of Los Angeles' diverse residents. In the fall of 1947, a group of Japanese American activists formed the Nisei Progressives organization to support the 1948 presidential campaign of former vice president Henry Wallace. Wallace was running on the Progressive Party ticket on a platform that challenged the Cold War, the arms buildup, and racial segregation. Though the campaign was plagued by charges of association with the Communist Party, it provided an important forum in Los Angeles for a diverse cross-section of progressive thinking and activity not tied to the Communists.[33]

The intersection of race and politics spilled over into the East L.A. barrios during the war, when another racially oriented campaign, led by the Hearst press, attacked Los Angeles' Mexican American residents as "greasers," "pachucos," and "zoot suiters," using blatant racist stereotypes. The police, using the pretext of the death of a young Mexican American on a ranch near an open reservoir called the Sleepy Lagoon, rounded up hundreds of Mexican Americans. This provided an open season for anyone to bring charges against those rounded up. Twenty-three Mexican American youths were subsequently charged with the Sleepy Lagoon murder. An impressive community-based mobilization to defend them was led by Mexican American activists such as El Congreso executive director Josefina Fierro (with support from African American activists, Hollywood liberals, and organizers such as Carey McWilliams's protégé Alice McGrath). Seventeen of the defendants were found guilty of charges ranging from assault to first-degree murder. Coverage of the trial further inflamed the city's racial climate. Months later, a "White riot" occurred, involving servicemen stationed at Los Angeles' large naval and marine bases. Soldiers randomly attacked the "zoot suiters," transforming Los Angeles' Eastside into a racial war zone. Later, the U.S. District Court of Appeals overturned the Sleepy Lagoon convictions as a miscarriage of justice. All the defendants were acquitted and freed in October 1944. By then, eight of the defendants had spent two years in San Quentin, but the case represented a major organizing victory for the city's Mexican American community.[34]

These racist campaigns were part of a systematic effort to undermine the progressive gains made during the 1930s. These crusades gathered momentum after World War II and became part of the fabric of anti-Communist politics that dominated the political landscape during much of the late 1940s and 1950s. In fact, Los Angeles became a volatile cauldron of reaction and extreme right-wing politics. The mainstream assault on civil liberties— what came to be known as McCarthyism—began in Los Angeles, with Congress's investigation of alleged Communist infiltration in Hollywood. In May 1947, Congressman J. Parnell Thomas held secret hearings at the Biltmore Hotel in downtown Los Angeles to probe "Communist infiltration" of Hollywood, the initial investigation that launched the House Un-American Activities Committee's (HUAC) ubiquitous political onslaught against progressives.[35]

The attack on Communists was part of a broader and sometimes bloody battle in the mid-1940s in Hollywood over union representation (and jurisdictional battles between progressive and reactionary unions), the role of organized crime in unions and the studio system, and the content of the films themselves. The bitter strike and subsequent lockout in 1945 and 1946 of the painters, grips, electricians, and other film technicians associated with the Conference of Studio Unions (CSU) also laid the groundwork for the 1947 HUAC hearings and resulting blacklist.[36]

Months after the crushing of the CSU and the HUAC hearings, the "Hollywood Ten" were among the first victims of the domestic Cold War, even as the Red Scare and the blacklist cast a much wider net, beyond the film industry. It snared trade unionists, academics (such as UCLA history professor John Caughey, who was fired for refusing to sign a loyalty oath), public officials, writers, actors, and filmmakers. The University of California Regents, for example, issued a proclamation demanding "loyalty to American institutions and to the American system of government," amid charges that UCLA had become "a hotbed of foreign-type radicalism."[37] Los Angeles' burgeoning housing movement became one of the key victims of the Cold War hysteria. Plans developed by city housing official Frank Wilkinson to build mixed-income, racially integrated public housing throughout the city were thwarted by real estate industry interests who linked government-sponsored housing to "Socialism."[38]

Against this hostile backdrop, however, activists sought to create some political space for progressive ideas and policies. During the late 1940s, culture, politics, and social issues were linked in a number of ways. While the major Hollywood studios caved in to the Red Scare and fought efforts by employees to unionize, some writers, directors, and producers sought to make films about postwar social problems like racism and anti-Semitism, such as the 1947 films *Crossfire* and *Gentlemen's Agreement*. In May 1948, thirty-one thousand people jammed into Gilmore Stadium to hear a speech by Progressive Party candidate Wallace. As part of this campaign, Los Angeles radical Harry Hay, a union organizer, Communist, screen extra, and stunt rider, developed an ingenious strategy to mobilize gays and lesbians, at that point a nearly invisible constituency. Hay had been a member of the Communist Party, involved in the arts and entertainment arena of radical politics, since 1934. In 1946, he founded Los Angeles People's Songs, which affiliated with Pete Seeger's People's Songs, Inc., to promote folk music as a "barometer of the class struggle," as Hays put it in a course he taught at the Los Angeles People's Educational Center. At the time of the Wallace rally in 1948, Hays proposed establishing "Bachelors Anonymous" to support Wallace while signaling to gays that the Progressive Party campaign provided a political home not available elsewhere. Though this effort never got off the ground, two years later, using the political skills he'd learned within the progressive and union movements, Hay formed the Los Angeles–based Mattachine Society. This was the nation's first modern gay rights organization—the first group to insist that lesbians and gay men be treated as equals, while identifying gays as a cultural and political minority. Despite the Cold War and rampant homophobia at the time, more than five thousand gays participated in the group in its first three years.[39]

During and immediately after the war, the civil rights movement also began to expand its membership and its actions, embracing the increasing diversity of 1940s Los Angeles. The struggle for Black civil rights was the initial cutting edge in this process. In 1941, the NAACP's newly formed Youth Council organized protests against racial discrimination. The next year, hundreds of African American women flooded the downtown U.S. Employment Service office, forcing the end of racial and gender discrimination in the war industries. As described in the next chapter, Charlotta Bass, the editor of the *California Eagle*, the city's longest-running Black paper, was at the center of this campaign as well as a wide range of community-based progressive movements. At the seventieth anniversary party for the *Eagle*, on October 1, 1949, ten thousand people filled L.A.'s Wrigley Field to hear Black actor, singer, and radical activist Paul Robeson speak and perform, and to affirm Robeson's right to perform across the country. (This was soon after the "Peekskill incident" in upstate New York, when Robeson supporters were attacked, after a concert, by a right-wing vigilante mob.) Ultimately, Los Angeles became one of the first cities outside the South where antidiscrimination and civil rights struggles included diverse racial and ethnic groups, a precursor of the "multicultural" politics that emerged four decades later.[40]

There was perhaps no more compelling figure of Progressive L.A. during the 1940s than Carey McWilliams (1905–80). A writer, journalist, author, housing commissioner, and political activist, McWilliams effectively chronicled and captured the moods and contradictions of prewar and postwar Los Angeles. His advocacy work and writing (including the 1939 *Factories in the Field*, about the exploitation of California farmworkers, and the 1946 *Southern California: An Island on the Land*) drew attention to the problems of economic injustice, racism, and anti-Semitism. He was the leading interpreter of the region as an incubator of progressive movements and ideas. He also chronicled efforts by Los Angeles' political and social elites to resist labor and civil rights demands while promoting sprawling development. In contrast, McWilliams, whom agribusiness interests called the "number one pest of California," championed farmworker rights. Perhaps most strikingly, McWilliams helped to articulate the notion of Los Angeles as a center of innovative progressive thought and action. His departure for New York at the end of the decade, to become editor of the *Nation* magazine, never diminished his attachment and connections to Progressive L.A.[41]

THE 1950S:
GOVERNING ELITES AND THE EXPLODING METROPOLIS

During much of the 1950s, *Frontier* magazine, the idiosyncratic, muckraking Los Angeles–based monthly journal (a kind of West Coast soulmate of the *Nation* that continued the McWilliams tradition of critical commentary and investigative journalism), seemed to be a lonely voice within a political wilderness. With commentaries on such issues as L.A.'s housing crisis, the dearth of a civic culture, and the behind-the-scenes activities of powerful conservative figures such as O'Melveny and Myers attorney James "Lin" Beebe and insurance executive Asa Call, *Frontier* explored issues that would have otherwise received little public attention. On the political front, *Frontier* promoted the idea that a progressive revival in Los Angeles and California was possible, even with a business-dominated mayor and a conservative governor. *Frontier* identified and promoted a reemergent progressive political coalition, both inside and outside the Democratic Party. It advocated that progressive government could solve problems and create opportunities for jobs, education, and livable communities.[42]

These ideas seemed less fanciful by the end of the decade, after Republicans had self-destructed in the 1958 gubernatorial and Senate races. Opportunities for progressive political action increased significantly. Even in this most conservative of decades in Los Angeles, a progressive agenda, focusing on the dynamics of a changing region and state, still appeared capable of influencing the political discourse. New public initiatives were developed in such areas as education and infrastructure development.

By the 1950s, Los Angeles had become a major urban-industrial behemoth. Despite its limited rainfall and modest local water resources, the region's expansion-minded water wholesaler, the Metropolitan Water District, put forth the "Laguna Declaration," which proclaimed that water from distant, imported sources could and would be made available for any future urban growth, including conversion of farmland to suburban development.[43] Southern California grew astronomically in this period, from a population of 5 million in 1950 to 7.8 million at the end of the decade. The region also became the second largest manufacturing center in the country. Extending earlier growth patterns, Los Angeles became the very symbol of suburbanization and sprawl as a substitute for planning and good land use policy. One study noted how Los Angeles residents most commonly characterized their region through such terms as *spread out, spacious, formless,* and *without centers.* "It's as if you were going somewhere for a long time," one resident commented to researchers, "and when you get there, you discovered there was nothing there, after all."[44]

Los Angeles shifted to the right during the early and mid-1950s, securing its place as a home of reactionary politics. The counterattack against progressives, which extended to city hall, reached a crescendo during this period. Fletcher Bowron, who had served fifteen years as mayor, was increasingly under attack, partly due to his support of affordable public housing. The L.A. business elite, led by Call (who had helped to orchestrate the anti-EPIC campaign of 1934); Harry Chandler's son Norman Chandler, of the *Los Angeles Times;* and O'Melveny attorney Beebe, enlisted Los Angeles congressman Norris Poulson to run against Bowron for mayor in 1953. Enticing him by promising ample campaign funds, a raise in the mayor's salary, and a chauffeur-driven Cadillac to "strut around in," as they put it in a letter to their prospective candidate, this backroom group orchestrated Poulson's election victory in 1953. Feeding on the anti-Communist hysteria that characterized politics in Los Angeles and elsewhere and antic ipating the subsequent political housecleaning, Poulson asserted during the campaign that as mayor he would "launch an investigation of *all* suspected communists on the city payroll, removing those who refused to testify or who are shown to advocate overthrow of the government by violence."[45]

Despite the rightward political shift, the increasingly suburban lifestyle, and a saccharine culture dominated by the movie studio system, Los Angeles also experienced countercurrents, some subtle, others more pronounced. These changes inspired new collaborations, new constituencies, and new movements. In 1953, the same year Poulson was elected, and a year before the U.S. Supreme Court's *Brown v. Board of Education* decision outlawed school segregation, Buddy Collette, an accomplished jazz musician, led a successful effort to merge Local 767, the Black local of the American Federation of Musicians, with the all-White Local 46—one of the first integrated union locals.[46] Outside the studio system, director Herbert Biberman (one of the Hollywood Ten), producer Paul Jarrico, writer Michael Wilson, blacklisted actor Will Geer, and famed Mexican actress Rosaura Revueltas, along with a cast of local community residents, completed the film *Salt of the Earth* under great duress and political harassment. This film, which chronicled the real-life strike of Latino and Anglo mine workers in New Mexico, was shunned by distributors and had to attract its own audience by showings outside the commercial movie houses.[47] But *Salt of the Earth*—like Geer's theatrical productions at his playhouse in Topanga Canyon, the postwar Black cultural scene on Central Avenue, and a vital new art form of jazz and poetry readings in places like Venice and Echo Park—presented an alternative to the increasingly homogenized Cold War cultural fare that dominated Hollywood and other forms of mass culture.

In fact, L.A. emerged as a center for alternative cultural voices. For example, the work of progressive African American writer Chester Himes—especially his novels *If He Hollers Let Him Go* (1945) and *Lonely Crusade* (1947)—described the daily struggles, frustrations, and triumphs of the city's Black community as well as the ambivalent and sometimes hostile relationship among the civil rights, union, and left-wing movements. A vibrant mural movement, especially in Latino neighborhoods, also took root. Initially inspired by Mexican muralist David Siqueiros, who had lived briefly in Los Angeles during the 1930s, it extended through the mural projects of the New Deal's Works Project Administration during the Depression. *Muralistas* created a visual feast on post offices, libraries, and other public buildings and ultimately became a key element of the Latino cultural and political scene in East L.A. during the next several decades.[48] The progressive momentum that began with EPIC, but was submerged during the McCarthyite era, became visible once again in 1958, when Edmund "Pat" Brown was elected governor and Claire Engle was elected U.S. senator, replacing incumbent Governor Goodwin Knight (who ran for the Senate seat) and incumbent Senator William Knowland (who ran for governor). A new agenda, including a commitment to higher education for all Californians, fair housing, civil rights and civil liberties, and new forays into land use and environmental planning, was on the horizon.[49]

Latino politics also took a new turn during the late 1940s and 1950s. In 1947, organizer Fred Ross helped to establish the Community Service Organization (CSO), a Latino civic group affiliated with Saul Alinsky's Industrial Areas Foundation (IAF). The CSO helped to organize Ed Roybal's unsuccessful bid for a seat on the Los Angeles City Council and was the driving force behind his 1949 victory. Roybal, a social worker and community organizer, was the first Latino since 1881 to be elected to that body. During the 1950s, Roybal became a prominent participant in the protracted housing battles and community activism associated with the fights against the redevelopment of Bunker Hill and Chavez Ravine. These two working-class Latino communities near downtown were bulldozed to make way for new cultural centers and corporate offices as well as the new Dodger Stadium. Despite the defeats, these struggles forged a new Latino political identity and helped to build progressive coalitions. In 1959, Latino activists formed the Mexican American Political Association (MAPA) to mobilize Latino voters. By 1962, Latino activism had helped to secure Roybal's status as the first Mexican American in the U.S. Congress.[50]

Civil rights politics within the African American community also expanded during the decade. In the late 1940s and early 1950s, the Civil Rights Congress, a predominantly Black organization with ties to the Communist Party, was especially active. Its demonstrations and legal defense activities in Los Angeles, around issues of police brutality and discrimination, included a multiracial focus that provided support for Latino, Asian, and African American victims of discrimination and abuse. The CRC was also notable for handling cases that the more mainstream civil rights organizations like the NAACP did not or would not pursue. The demise of the CRC and the rise of a younger generation of civil rights activists (many of whom were inspired by the sit-in movement in the South and the boycott campaigns against retail outlets like Woolworth) signaled a transition from the defensive battles of the late 1940s and 1950s. By the end of the decade, a more assertive civil rights politics was emerging that would resonate over the next ten years.[51]

Dorothy Healey was part of the periodic shifts and fortunes of the region's progressive movements from the 1930s through the 1970s. As a teenager and Communist Party member in 1933, Healey organized with the Mexican and Japanese berry pickers in El Monte. As head of the Los Angeles branch of the Communist Party after 1946, she helped to build bridges between unions, civil rights movements, and progressive electoral coalitions. During the Red Scare, she was one of the original Smith Act defendants, tried, arrested, and jailed until the Supreme Court declared the law unconstitutional. In the mid- and late 1950s, Healey reemerged as an effective behind-the-scenes figure in the efforts to create new grassroots coalitions of progressive Democrats, such as the California Democratic Council and Californians for Liberal Representation. While the U.S. Communist Party never recovered from its association with the Soviet Union (particularly after the 1956 Khrushchev speech attacking Stalinism and the Hungarian uprising), the Los Angeles party under Healey's leadership was able, to a certain extent, to maintain its roots within the larger L.A. progressive community. A 1959 Municipal Program for Los Angeles, issued by the local party, was indicative of its desire to focus on local issues, although it continued to position its local agenda as secondary to its international perspective on Cold War issues, including support for the Soviet Union. Healey's subsequent disenchantment with the Soviet Union, culminating in her opposition to the Soviet invasion of Prague in 1968, ultimately led her to quit the Communist Party in 1973. However, she continued her political activism through participation in the New Left–oriented New American Movement as well as by hosting a current events program on KPFK radio (an alternative, listener-supported radio outlet). Through her continuing work, Healey became one of the few Old Left activists who helped to mentor a new generation of New Left activists and progressives. Like Upton Sinclair, Carey McWilliams, and Charlotta Bass before her, Dorothy Healey became a link between progressive movements and across political generations.[52]

THE 1960S:
SOCIETY DIVIDED, POLITICS RENEWED, DREAMS DEFERRED

Amid rising affluence, persistent poverty, and a war in Vietnam that threatened to tear the country apart, the 1960s made possible a personal and social transformation of many different Angelenos and of Los Angeles itself. New heroes like Cesar Chávez, Mario Savio, and Martin Luther King, Jr., appeared on the scene. It was a period of change, sometimes dramatic, eventually tumultuous.

At the *Los Angeles Times*, Ruben Salazar, an ad salesman turned reporter (and later columnist), personified the 1960s journey away from "acceptance of the American way of life," as he put it, and became a voice for a new progressive politics. Initially skeptical of those people who primarily identified themselves politically as Mexican American, Salazar spoke of this community as "like a fighting bull, but a fighting bull made of paper."

Cautious and thoughtful, Salazar gradually began to adopt a more anti-establishment perspective. "The word Mexican," he wrote later in the decade, "has been dragged through the mud of racism since the Anglos arrived in the Southwest." A one-year tour of duty in Vietnam further radicalized Salazar. By the late 1960s, in his column at the *Times* and in his new position as news director of Spanish-language KMEX-TV, Salazar sought to bridge the gap between the new generation of "brown power" activists and the older generation of civil rights groups and Roybalistas who had painstakingly created the progressive coalitions of the '40s, '50s, and '60s. All these activists finally came together on August 29, 1970, when twenty-five thousand people participated in the Chicano Moratorium, the largest demonstration ever by Los Angeles Mexican Americans. But the demonstration ended in tragedy at the Silver Dollar café, where Salazar and his TV crew had retired after recording the day's events. Sheriff's deputies, responding to a rumor about a "man in a red vest," opened fire with tear gas projectiles after hearing Salazar declare, "Let's get out of here." Salazar's odyssey through the 1960s and his untimely death came to symbolize, like so much else during the 1960s, the hopes of Progressive L.A. magnified, while its dreams were deferred.[53]

Los Angeles in the 1960s represented an unusual mix of urban decline and suburban expansion, to the point that L.A. appeared to lose any appearance of the classical "city," with a defined center and distinctive neighborhoods. A popular postcard of Los Angeles included a photo of a man in a suit with a puzzled expression, standing ankle-deep in the Pacific Ocean, looking at a map with the heading "Yes but . . . where *is* Los Angeles?!?" Below the photo appeared the words "Strange But True: Another common-but-rarely-talked about tourist problem is the inability to actually locate the 2nd largest 'city' in the U.S.A. The confusion is mostly caused by the fact that once you get close to it you discover that it's really a lot of *little* places trying to pass themselves off as one big one."[54]

Los Angeles' sprawling suburbs, with no center and lots of far-flung lit-

tle places, were fed by the region's increasing identification with the automobile and freeway culture. Reyner Banham called the Los Angeles freeway system a "single comprehensible place, a coherent state of mind, a
complete way of life." With the completion of the remaining parts of the
highway system in the region, including its last leg, the 10 Freeway to
Santa Monica, L.A. truly became a city of freeways.[55] Earlier, the construction of the Arroyo Seco Parkway and, to a lesser extent, the Hollywood
Freeway (the first freeways in the region in the late 1930s and early 1940s)
had been predicated on the notion of a multimodal transportation system
available to all transit users, with the parkway blending into a landscape of
open areas and green space. By the 1960s, however, the highway builders
were able to simply bulldoze their way through intact neighborhoods and
eliminate any transportation policy other than that of getting commuters as
quickly as possible from one end of the suburban maze to some other point
(and not necessarily a central point).[56] By doing so, the highway builders,
real estate speculators, and other entrepreneurs of this expanding and fragmented Los Angeles encouraged the flight of retail outlets such as supermarkets, centrally located industries, and jobs from what remained of the
city's core.

Los Angeles increasingly took on a split personality: the divorce of jobs
from housing; the absence of cultural centers; growing income disparities
between the Westside and the San Fernando Valley on the one hand and
South and East L.A. on the other. This split personality ultimately became
apparent with the explosive and unexpected events of the summer of 1965,
when Watts, one of L.A.'s oldest neighborhoods and by then almost entirely
African American, went up in flames.

The Watts riots revealed the region's increasing divisions. L.A.'s growing
African American and Latino populations (the African American population
alone had increased almost tenfold, from 75,000 in 1940 to 650,000 in 1965)
faced discriminatory practices by government and private businesses,
employers, banks, and landlords. This exacerbated the contradiction between
an ideology of opportunity and the reality of an urban divide based on race
and class. A growing civil rights movement in Los Angeles had made gains
in such areas as jobs, welfare, education, housing, and political action in the
early 1960s, but a clear backlash emerged that was ignored or, in some cases,
encouraged by local elites. This counterrevolution reached a peak in
November 1964, when more than two-thirds of the state's voters supported
the repeal of the Rumford Fair Housing Act, which had outlawed discrimination in the sale of homes. That challenged one of the core goals of the civil
rights cause. Less than a year later, the Watts riots effectively changed the

dynamics of politics and social action in Los Angeles and elsewhere, heightening recognition of this divided and unequal society while highlighting the urgency for change.[57]

The Watts riots were a critical moment in the fracturing of Los Angeles, but they also represented a transitional point in the evolution of Progressive L.A. Despite the overt hostility of the Cold War era, progressives in the 1950s had nevertheless laid the groundwork for a revival of political activism in the following decade. It began, quietly enough, with the growth of grassroots community organizing. Groups such as the Community Service Organization provided the training ground for a new generation of social activists, skilled in identifying issues and waging campaigns among constituencies thought to be unorganizable. The best known of those activists was Cesar Chávez, who had been mentored by Fred Ross through the CSO. Los Angeles' progressives supported Chávez's efforts to organize a union of farmworkers, primarily in central California. Unions, churches, and Latino community groups became the backbone of the consumer boycott, which was an essential ingredient in the union's early success. These actions were complemented by the rise of Chicano activism, embodied in such groups as Young Chicanos for Community Action, founded by David Sanchez in 1966 (soon tagged by sheriff's deputies as "the Brown Berets"), and the MEChA (Movimiento Estudiantil Chicano/a de Aztlán) student organizations that sprouted up on several L.A.-area college campuses.[58]

The African American community led a surge of organizing and mobilization following the Watts riots. This included the local chapter of the Black Panther Party, a group that had originated from a Community Alert Patrol and sponsored a wide range of community programs. The Panthers eventually got caught up in a spiral of violence and law-enforcement harassment that decimated the local organization. The group's offices and free breakfast program were raided by the police and FBI. Two of its leaders, John Higgins and Bunchy Carter, were gunned down on the UCLA campus by rival members of a Black nationalist organization.[59]

The era's powerful mood of reform and revolt influenced other communities and constituencies. Protests against the Vietnam War, for example, heightened the urgency for change. Students on college campuses and in high schools mobilized around these issues, not only at places like UCLA, but also at the California State University campuses and at community colleges like Pierce College in the San Fernando Valley. In the summer of 1967, student activists gathered at an old brownstone in Echo Park to establish the Students for a Democratic Society (SDS) summer school. This and other

L.A.-based New Left organizations joined with the growing youth and anti-war movements around the country. That summer, Los Angeles witnessed its largest antiwar gathering at Century City, where President Lyndon Johnson was staying at the Century Plaza Hotel. A police riot broke up the demonstration, with scores of protesters beaten and injured, while LBJ watched from his hotel room.[60]

A new generation of women activists joined with others who had participated in the progressive union, civil rights, and other battles of the previous decades to forge a new wave of feminism. This grassroots feminism took many forms, including the growth of consciousness-raising groups, women's rights organizations, and radical political and cultural groups that sought to uproot sexist language, politics, and economics. These groups provided an informal link to an earlier generation of middle-class women's advocacy groups, such as Women Strike for Peace (formed during the anti–nuclear testing campaigns of the late 1950s and early 1960s), Women for Legislative Action, and Women For. Together with the new feminists, these groups made feminist politics central to the Progressive L.A. agenda.[61]

It was clear what these various activists opposed—racism, sexism, the Vietnam War and the arms race, the urban-renewal bulldozer and unending sprawl. But it was not always clear what vision and agenda they held in common, a problem heightened by the mood of urgency that the Watts riots and the Vietnam War had provoked. In the late 1960s and early 1970s, activists reflected the diversity—and sometimes the confusion—of the period's progressive movements. These included an action-oriented environmentalism, a militant gay and lesbian movement, a burst of activism within the Latino and Asian communities, the growing Black power movement, reform stirrings within the labor movement, and a wave of "community development" efforts by neighborhood activists.

United Auto Workers' union leader Paul Schrade symbolized the effort to link these disparate strands of progressive politics. While the national AFL-CIO supported the Vietnam War effort, Schrade and a handful of other L.A. union activists sought to bring unions into the broader antiwar movement through such antiwar coalitions as the Peace Action Council. In the wake of the Watts riots, Schrade also helped to build bridges between the UAW and the city's Black and Latino communities. He supported the development of the Watts Labor Community Action Committee and the East Los Angeles Community Union (TELACU), which used union and federal funds to build low-income housing, set up job-training programs, and mobilize community residents around neighborhood improvement. Schrade was a key figure in Robert Kennedy's presidential campaign in 1968. Kennedy's brief campaign drew on both the energies and the frustrations of the civil rights, antiwar, and community organizing crusades. Activists like Schrade, Tom Hayden, Cesar Chávez, and others joined Kennedy's effort, even while other activists, frustrated by the limits of the electoral system, talked of "voting in the streets."[62] Kennedy's victory in the June California primary appeared to seal his status as the Democratic candidate. But suddenly, following a victory celebration at the Ambassador Hotel in Los Angeles, Kennedy was assassinated, with Schrade, farmworker union leader Dolores Huerta, and other activists at his side. Just as the Watts riots had anticipated a period of turmoil, the Kennedy assassination and other events of the late 1960s intensified the mood of political anger and frustration. The nation's racial and foreign policy crises appeared to have no end point, no light at the end of the tunnel, as one often-used Vietnam War metaphor put it. For Progressive L.A., the 1960s became an opportunity lost, never recognized, and not well understood.

THE 1970S:
FROM ECONOMIC DEMOCRACY TO TAXPAYER REVOLTS

Spawned by the protest movements of the late 1960s and early 1970s, a colorful collection of former antiwar activists, social justice organizers, and urban environmentalists in 1976 launched a campaign to demand a "lifeline" rate for low-income utility consumers of the Los Angeles Department of Water and Power. Using guerrilla-theater tactics, community and constituency organizing, and considerable media savvy, the group, known as CAUSE (Campaign against Utility Service Exploitation), forced the mighty DWP to adopt a lifeline policy. CAUSE went on to challenge oil company profits, the DWP's investment in the Palo Verde nuclear power plant, and a proposed gas company surcharge for advance payments to ARCO for its planned development of gas deposits on the North Slope of Alaska. CAUSE's victory in the lifeline issue, and its ability to shed light on backroom maneuvers by utilities and the oil companies, demonstrated a new kind of militancy among consumer groups.[63]

CAUSE reflected the diversity and potential reach of the social movements of the 1970s. These groups were concerned with basic issues of survival as well as quality-of-life matters. Even in the midst of a political backlash fed by antitax and antigovernment sentiment, the new social movements in Los Angeles spawned a new kind of politics and a renewed image of Los Angeles as a place of social ferment and experimentation.

Its reputation as a Mediterranean-type paradise already undermined by riots and other social strife, Los Angeles during the 1970s confronted a wave of economic and environmental dislocations, from the decline of major industries to its dubious distinction as the nation's smog capital. Yet in the 1970s, Progressive L.A. catalyzed new ideas and movements. Environmentalism became a dynamic new force. Its visionary wing was expressed in the growth of multipurpose ecology centers and in the establishment of alternative institutions such as food cooperatives. But environmentalism also presented a radical and pragmatic challenge to the dominant political and industrial status quo. Environmental organizers helped to launch crusades against nuclear power plants, led the successful initiative to establish the California Coastal Commission to protect the coast, and, in 1974, won a campaign finance reform initiative to limit the growing influence of money on mainstream politics.[64]

Spearheaded by a Los Angeles group known as the People's Lobby, this effort became a key element in Jerry Brown's successful run for governor in 1974. Brown, despite his participation in several activist causes during the 1960s, never fully embraced a progressive agenda. But a wing of Brown's administration kept the progressive flame lit, encouraging a wide range of innovative initiatives, such as the establishment of the California Agricultural Labor Relations Board (which gave a boost to Chávez's union-organizing efforts among farmworkers), support for farmers' markets in urban communities, and the development of alternative technologies and energy approaches.[65]

While Jerry Brown played a cat-and-mouse game with progressives, Tom Hayden's campaign for the U.S. Senate in 1976 crafted an explicit progressive vision for the state. Hayden, who had written the Port Huron Statement, the founding document of SDS, and participated in 1960s community and civil rights organizing, had become a celebrity as a defendant in the Chicago Seven trial and as husband to actress Jane Fonda. Hayden used his bid for the Senate to further consolidate a wide range of progressive activity, from environmental and tenants' rights activities to community economic development, into a statewide progressive network called the Campaign for Economic Democracy (CED). CED's slogan of "economic democracy" captured its progressive program and vision. Hayden's unexpectedly strong showing in the Democratic primary against incumbent Senator John Tunney laid the groundwork for Hayden's later success in running for office at the state level (first for the State Assembly and subsequently for the State Senate), where he became part of an informal (though not always united) progressive caucus that grew in strength and numbers in the 1980s and 1990s.[66]

Many of the 1970s' new ideas, movements, and progressive initiatives occurred outside the electoral arena. In the area of housing, for example, the struggle for rent control was fueled in 1978, when tenants received notices of rent increases shortly after the tax-cutting Proposition 13 had passed. Tenants who had been hit by rent increases organized meetings to demand that landlords share their property tax savings. Governor Brown established a renter "hotline," which received twelve thousand phone calls a day to register complaints about rent hikes. When heavy real estate industry lobbying defeated a statewide bill requiring landlords to pass on Proposition 13 savings to tenants, the battle shifted to the local level. Groups like the Coalition for Economic Survival, the Gray Panthers, and the Campaign for Economic Democracy organized tenants and kept the anger about post–Prop 13 rent hikes in the news. There was an upsurge of rent strikes, even in the politically moderate San Fernando Valley. Within a few years, Los Angeles, Santa Monica, West Hollywood, and other cities had adopted strong tenants' rights laws. Tenants became, for at least a decade, a potent political force, forging alliances with other progressive movements and helping to reshape the political contours of Southern California.[67]

Other movements grew or expanded in new directions during the 1970s. For example, the women's movement began to focus on new concerns, such as violence against women, reproductive rights and women's health issues, and cultural stereotypes. The Los Angeles Women's Center opened its doors in 1970 and, along with the Sisterhood Bookstore (started in 1972), soon became a gathering place for feminist activism. In 1975, a group of women artists and writers founded the Woman's Building in downtown Los Angeles, which provided the space and home for what emerged as a new cultural renaissance, including the Feminist Studio Workshop. Several local campuses initiated women's studies programs in the 1970s. And a new organization, Women against Violence against Women (WAVAW), organized the first of what became nationally known as the Take Back the Night marches, proclaiming that violence and sexual abuse against women needed to become part of the city's (and the nation's) political agenda.[68]

Progressive bookstores, publications, libraries, and foundations became both the memory and the catalyst for Progressive L.A. These included the Midnight Special Bookstore (opened in Venice in 1971), the *L.A. Weekly* (founded in 1978 as an alternative and progressive voice in its news and cultural coverage), KPFK radio (which provided alternative news and cultural views of Los Angeles), and the Southern California Library for Social Studies and Research (which became the historical archive for activists by gathering the little-known history of Progressive L.A.).

As for progressive foundations, Sarah Pillsbury helped to ignite new energies among Los Angeles activists by creating the Liberty Hill Foundation. Pillsbury, an heir to the Minnesota baking fortune, settled in Los Angeles in the early 1970s, attracted to the region's sense of possibility, and soon became a widely respected and successful producer of socially engaged movies. In 1976, Pillsbury helped start the new foundation, taking its name from the 1923 Liberty Hill episode involving Upton Sinclair and the dockworkers. The Liberty Hill Foundation, along with a handful of counterparts in other cities, was unique in how and to whom it distributed funds. Its Community Funding Board, composed of grassroots activists, made the decisions, providing crucial seed money for a wide range of grassroots movements. Liberty Hill's annual Upton Sinclair Award dinner also became a place where progressive actors, directors, filmmakers, and other participants in the entertainment industry joined with grassroots organizers.[69]

Like the Liberty Hill Foundation, the American Civil Liberties Union emerged as an umbrella organization that connected different parts of Progressive L.A. The ACLU often spoke of its one client, the Constitution, but in Southern California, the group also became an important player in the progressive struggle for social, economic, and racial justice. Beginning in the 1970s, under the leadership of director Ramona Ripston, the ACLU made its mark on a variety of issues. These included classic civil liberties causes such as police abuse in communities of color, "police spying" on progressive groups, opposition to the death penalty, voting rights, and academic freedom. But they also included issues not traditionally associated with civil liberties, such as reproductive rights, violence against women, the war in Vietnam, and the rights of immigrants.

The ACLU was a key ally of the civil rights movement, especially in its push to desegregate the schools and to establish stable, integrated communities. Activists like Joyce Fiske, who for more than thirty-five years was an indefatigable organizer both inside and outside the ACLU and in her neighborhood in the Pico-Fairfax area, helped to establish the organization's progressive reputation. Though Fiske, a one-time president of the ACLU board, was not a visible public figure, she was widely known among activists in many communities and causes. Fiske symbolized Progressive L.A.'s mosaic of movements during the 1970s. When she died in 1998, her memorial, which brought together many of those activists and participants in Progressive L.A., was a reminder, as one activist put it, "of how much Joyce and others had accomplished, and how much still needed to be done."[70]

THE 1980S:
A CITY OF IMMIGRANTS AND A WIDENING DIVIDE

In October 1989, police arrested one hundred gay and AIDS activists at the Federal Building in West L.A. who had been protesting government inaction on AIDS treatment—one of the largest mass arrests in L.A. history. This protest was part of a broader effort to respond to the AIDS crisis and to link the gay and lesbian movement to other progressive activism. Two key figures reflected the effort to build these political bridges: Mark Kostopolous, a postal worker and union organizer with a New Left background, who was the leader of L.A.'s ACT-UP chapter until his death in 1992; and Torie Osborn, a civil rights and antiwar activist, who turned the L.A. Gay and Lesbian Center into the world's largest gay organization and later became executive director of the Liberty Hill Foundation.

The Los Angeles ACT-UP group not only served as an effective and militant advocate regarding AIDS issues, but also participated in the defense of abortion clinics and in solidarity work in support of radical movements in Central America. In the late 1980s, figures such as Rolando Palencia (the son of a Uruguayan Tupamaro guerrilla leader) helped to push the gay and lesbian movement to reflect the city's racial and cultural diversity and link diverse constituencies around a common cause.[71]

Swelled by an influx of immigrants from Mexico, Central America, Asia, and other parts of the world, Los Angeles emerged in the 1980s as the nation's most multicultural city. By the end of the decade, more than a third of the residents of the region were foreign-born. The number of Angelenos who had been born in Asia, Latin America, and the Middle East increased more than sixfold between 1960 and 1990. The Los Angeles region, in fact, had become home to almost a quarter of the nation's immigrants.[72]

In response to the city's changing demographics, with its new immigrant neighborhoods, cultural identities, and social realities, Los Angeles' progressive movements incorporated new issues like Central American solidarity work and the rights of immigrants. A number of Latino leaders also served as bridges between movements and generations. One was Bert Corona, who was recruited to L.A. with a USC basketball scholarship, worked as a longshoreman, served as president of Local 26 of the International Longshoremen's and Warehousemen's Union during World War II, and then helped to organize the Community Service Organization and MAPA in the Mexican

American community. Corona and other activists were at the forefront of what became an ongoing mobilization against repeated threats to immigrants. Demonstrations, such as the massive turnout in March 1982 protesting federal immigration policies, coincided with a wave of organizing, activist leadership, and the formation of other ethnic-based organizations (such as the Asian Pacific Legal Center, the Korean Youth and Community Center, and the Korean Immigrant Workers Advocates).[73]

This shift also extended to the labor movement, where new leaders emerged such as María Elena Durazo (who was elected president of Local 11 of the Hotel Employees and Restaurant Employees Union in 1989). Unionism was still largely a defensive movement during the 1980s, as witnessed by systematic anti-union policies of the commercial building industry and its janitorial service subcontractors. But this new generation of labor organizers began to challenge the practices of what had become a largely moribund movement that had abandoned its mission of organizing. "Don't mourn for the movement; organize!" became the rallying cry of this new force in labor, centered in the expanding immigrant workforce and communities of Los Angeles.[74]

The cry for justice also underlined a new kind of community-based environmental justice movement in Los Angeles and in communities around the country. This progressive alliance of environmentalists and communities burdened by a proliferation of environmental hazards emerged around struggles to stop the siting of trash and hazardous waste incinerators in communities like South Central and East L.A. One of those battles, the fight to stop the LANCER project—a proposed sixteen-hundred-ton-per-day solid waste incinerator at 41st Street and Martin Luther King Boulevard—reflected this new environmental justice coalition. Mayor Tom Bradley at first supported the project as a way to alleviate the growing problem of landfill capacity, due in part to the objections of Bradley's Westside supporters regarding the expansion of the Lopez landfill. The city's Bureau of Sanitation, in conjunction with major industry, legal, and political interests, came up with a plan to construct three of these huge incinerators—with the first to be built in South Central, on the assumption that low-income Blacks and Latinos did not care about environmental questions. Later, incinerators at sites on the Westside and in the San Fernando Valley could be built because any future opposition would be characterized as "racist." The elected officials and Bureau of Sanitation managers assumed that activists in different parts of the city would not join forces. Instead, groups in South Central mobilized, allying with groups throughout the city to stop the project. These alliances helped to promote a potent progressive environmental movement and ultimately forced Bradley to pull the plug on LANCER.[75]

The defense of neighborhoods by environmental justice groups like Mothers of East L.A. and Concerned Citizens of South Central extended to concern about Los Angeles' landscape and seascape. Hundreds of high school students and other beach users protested government failure to clean up Santa Monica Bay. This effort eventually led to the establishment in 1988 of the Heal the Bay organization and also forced the city of Los Angeles and its water and sanitation bureaucracies to reduce pollution in the bay. Similarly, environmental activists in the Coalition for Clean Air sued the federal government and ultimately forced the South Coast Air Quality Management District to develop a more far-reaching and vigorous plan to clean the region's air.[76]

While new movements proliferated, the 1980s also became a time of growing economic inequality and overt expressions of racism. The decade saw the rise of a movement to slow down the closing of factories as a result of the rapid dismantling of the region's manufacturing base. The destruction of hundreds of thousands of decent-paying jobs, and the Reagan administration's war on social spending, led to growing homelessness, malnutrition and hunger, and pressures to lower wages in such areas as janitorial work. By the middle 1980s, for example, the Liberty Hill Foundation was processing dozens of proposals to provide basic survival services that were formerly provided by the government. Groups such as the Los Angeles Regional Food Bank became major de facto service providers.[77]

The loss of jobs, the environmental burdens, and the collapse of an affordable housing market led to a deterioration of social and economic conditions in low-income communities. Meanwhile, the crack cocaine epidemic took hold in places like South Central and East L.A., creating a level of daily despair in the inner city not experienced since the 1930s. The policy response—the war on drugs and programs like Operation Weed and Seed— sought to criminalize an entire community instead of treating addiction and substance abuse as medical and social problems. A handful of groups— among them, the Community Coalition for Substance Abuse Prevention and Treatment, founded by longtime South Central activist Karen Bass— emerged to organize low-income communities, including recovering addicts, and to demand treatment and policies that would address the causes and triggers of drug and alcohol use.[78]

The 1980s also witnessed a new wave of community development organizations, such as the Coalition for Women's Economic Development and the Esperanza Community Housing Corporation (founded by Sister Diane Donaghue, who learned her organizing skills with the Industrial Areas Foundation, or IAF). Among other leaders in this area, two longtime activists, Denise Fairchild and Jan Breidenbach, forged the dozens of separate nonprofit neighborhood developers into a broader movement for community development through such umbrella organizations as the Local Initiatives Support Corporation and the Southern California Association for Non-Profit Housing. The Jobs with Peace campaign sponsored a citywide referendum in 1984 calling for the federal government to cut the Pentagon budget and to funnel that money instead into job-creating community economic-development programs.

Another progressive response to the widening economic divide was the successful statewide campaign for a "moral minimum wage" conducted in 1987 by three Los Angeles–area affiliates of the IAF. Based in seventy-three churches, mostly in low-income neighborhoods, the leaders of the IAF groups—the United Neighborhood Organization (based in East L.A.), the South Central Organizing Committee, and the East Valley Organization (based in the San Gabriel Valley)—saw their constituents' living standards decline as wages stagnated and housing costs skyrocketed. Their solution was to mobilize a grassroots campaign to increase the state minimum wage from $3.35 to $4.25 an hour, the highest in the nation at the time. By building on the IAF's strong and racially mixed congregation-based leadership and bringing in allies from labor and church groups and some elected officials, this impressive campaign ended in victory, representing an annual raise of eighteen hundred dollars for each of the state's nearly 1 million low-wage workers.[79]

By the end of the decade, with another recession taking root and further exacerbating the widening economic, demographic, environmental, and cultural divides in Los Angeles, the new organizing initiatives of the 1980s essentially had cut their teeth on protecting limited gains and fighting various scourges—AIDS, hunger, homelessness, unemployment, crack cocaine, and environmental degradation, among others. In some respects, Progressive L.A. could be seen as a holding action, ensuring that a tradition of social action and political gains would not entirely erode, while laying the groundwork for a new generation of activism. It envisioned Los Angeles as a place of possibility, rather than one of division and turmoil, which, once again, would soon turn into rage.

THE 1990S:
A LIVING WAGE

Almost by accident, Richard Riordan, a wealthy Republican businessman elected mayor in 1993, was partly responsible for the rebirth of the city's union movement. This rebirth began with the campaigns of unions such as the Hotel Employees and Restaurant Employees Union (HERE), the Service Employees International Union (through its Justice for Janitors campaign), and UNITE (Union of Needletrades, Industrial and Textile Employees, supported by progressive Asian, Latino, and Jewish groups fighting to end the exploitation of garment workers in modern-day sweatshops). They focused on organizing the growing and primarily immigrant low-wage workforce in the tourism, office, and garment economies, constituencies long neglected by the labor movement.

Riordan, a champion of lean-and-mean government, helped to inspire progressive union mobilization by his plans to privatize much of the city's municipal workforce, handing over contracts for garbage collection and cleaning services to private firms that paid lower wages and provided few or no benefits. For the city's progressive activists, Riordan's push to contract out municipal services raised a larger question—shouldn't firms with government contracts, some of which also received government subsidies, have some responsibility to pay decent wages? They answered that question with a proposed living wage law, sponsored by City Council member and 1960s veteran activist Jackie Goldberg, that required firms with municipal contracts to pay employees wages above the poverty line and to provide health benefits. Spearheaded by Madeline Janis-Aparicio of the Tourism Industry Development Council (later the Los Angeles Alliance for a New Economy) and Anthony Thigpenn of Action for Grassroots Empowerment and Neighborhood Development Alternatives (AGENDA) and the Metro Alliance, the Living Wage Coalition built a powerful grassroots alliance of unions, religious groups, and community organizations. Despite opposition from Riordan and the business community, the coalition gained overwhelming support within the City Council, enough to override the mayor's veto in 1997. This victory became part of a national living wage movement. Activists in more than one hundred cities—including Boston, Minneapolis, Chicago, Milwaukee, San Jose, and Baltimore—waged similar campaigns, winning victories in a number of places. While the Los Angeles living wage campaign was part of a new kind of community-labor alliance, it also signified a major new direction for Progressive L.A. Such issues as immigrant status, worker dignity, and social and economic justice paralleled the emerging demographic and political shifts in the region and the rise of a new generation of movement leaders.[80]

Despite these critical, though still only baseline, victories, the polarization of the region into a "First World" of prosperity and a "Third World" of disappearing jobs and declining neighborhoods had intensified. The civil unrest of April 1992—called the "Los Angeles riots" by the national media—indicated that life in the city's poorest neighborhoods had become intolerable. The city's business and political establishments, unprepared to respond in any coherent way, were shocked by the civil unrest. But they assumed that some demonstrable response was needed to avoid embarrassment and prevent another outbreak. Mayor Bradley recruited business leader Peter Ueberroth (who had organized the 1984 Los Angeles Olympics) to coordinate the city's response. This was called Rebuild L.A. (later RLA), organized at first as a top-down, private-sector vehicle to induce blue-chip corporations to invest in the city's low-income neighborhoods. In its first few years, RLA made little headway. Few businesses made more than token investments, banks made only a few loans, few jobs were created, and most of the buildings damaged in the civil unrest were not rebuilt.

But as RLA's high-profile, media-focused approach began to fade, the group's new leadership explored relations with the wide variety of grassroots activists who wanted to rebuild Los Angeles with a different approach and vision. On the other side of the city's racial and class divide, progressives forged new alliances to take advantage of the opportunities created by yet another crisis point in the city's governance. Progressive leaders of Black, Asian, Hispanic, Jewish, and other constituencies forged groups such as the MultiCultural Collaborative to address racial tensions and develop a forward-looking agenda. They pushed the city's political, business, and philanthropic leaders to address real concerns and to work with grassroots organizations. Their activism provided progressive elected officials, sympathetic foundation staff, and a few civic-minded business leaders with more possibilities for linking up with progressive movements in order to rethink the strategy of how to rebuild Los Angeles from the bottom up.

The civil unrest and its aftermath also helped to energize a new set of progressive initiatives. The Labor Community Strategy Center, led by Eric Mann, organized a Bus Riders Union, which waged a campaign to challenge the city's two-tiered transportation system. With the help of the NAACP Legal Defense Fund and attorney Connie Rice, the bus riders won a legal challenge against the Metropolitan Transportation Authority (MTA), not only to rescind a rate hike but to require the MTA to add new buses and expand bus service for the overwhelmingly low-wage and minority riders who depended on buses. In the wake of federal "welfare reform," community groups such as the Community Coalition, the Association of Community Organizations for Reform Now (ACORN), the Los Angeles Coalition to End Homelessness and Hunger, and Crystal Stairs (which worked with child-care and family home-care providers) began mobilizing to reshape riot-torn communities. They demanded that the "welfare-to-work" program provide opportunities for jobs at decent wages, that food programs be developed to ensure food security for those who were continually subjected to being hungry, that liquor stores in poor communities be replaced by genuine initiatives for community economic development, and that affordable child care be made available to all who needed it.

Immigrant-rights advocates also continued their efforts to mobilize immigrants, in part through dramatic campaigns to force the federal Immigration and Naturalization Service (INS) to speed up the process of granting citizenship, by mounting an impressive voter registration campaign among the newly naturalized citizens, and by mobilizing through demonstrations, such as the campaign against the anti-immigrant Proposition 187, which passed in 1994. By the end of the decade, the efforts of immigrant coalitions like the Coalition for Humane Immigrant Rights of Los Angeles (CHIRLA) and labor-organizing campaigns like Justice for Janitors had helped to shift political dynamics around the immigration issue. Impressive new coalitions, such as the unprecedented alliance between the labor movement, church groups, and immigrant-rights organizers, seized the imagination of Progressive L.A.

The renewed energy around immigration issues was complemented by the maturation of the environmental justice movement, which initially had formed out of neighborhood struggles. Environmental justice research and organizing groups, such as Communities for a Better Environment and the Labor Occupational Safety and Health groups, saw themselves as part of a broader progressive movement. New organizations—such as the Metro Alliance, the Los Angeles Alliance for a New Economy, AGENDA (Action for Grassroots Empowerment and Neighborhood Development Alternatives), the Surface Transportation Policy Project, the Community Food Security Coalition, and the Urban and Environmental Policy Institute at Occidental College—also began to identify broader regional solutions not only to rebuild, but also to reenvision Los Angeles. This Los Angeles, they argued, could become a more livable, economically just, and environmentally healthy place. By the end of the decade, with Los Angeles potentially primed for major change, the role of progressive social movements appeared more dynamic than ever.

ANOTHER HISTORICAL MOMENT?

It seemed possible that the first years of the twenty-first century could constitute another historical moment, another opportunity for social movements and progressive ideas to come together to carry on Progressive L.A.'s quest for a more just and livable city. In advance of a conference on the past, present, and future of Progressive L.A. in 1998 at Occidental College, conference organizers posed this question: If Upton Sinclair were alive today, trying to recapture the spirit of Liberty Hill and the EPIC campaign, what issues would he focus on? What constituencies would he seek to mobilize and coalesce?

Sinclair, the conference organizers argued, would surely have had his pick of issues in Los Angeles, since major social, economic, and environmental problems cried out for new solutions and new political forces. He would then, the argument was made, be able to build on an extraordinary level of activism around workplace issues, economic development, environmental problems, neighborhood improvement, education, racial and ethnic tensions, and other issues. But the conference organizers also warned that the fragmentation of Progressive L.A. organizations and activists across the metropolitan area meant that the new century could witness a patchwork of progressivism with no unifying theme, agenda, or movement. The history of Progressive L.A. in the twentieth century—dynamic movements, important policy breakthroughs, and a wave of social action, but an inability to extend itself beyond the political moment to establish a more cohesive and continuing alternative to the dominant forces in the region—remained an invaluable, though ambiguous, legacy.

The new century had already begun to present significant challenges. These included the September 11, 2001, terrorist attacks and their economic fallout, which particularly hit the membership of some of the core progressive unions (such as the Hotel Employees and Restaurant Employees Union); a new set of anti-immigrant policies; and secession movements to break up and refragment Los Angeles. But the lessons of the past century also suggested that progressive movements have enormous potential to forge a powerful political force.

2 Charlotta Bass

*A Community Activist for Racial
and Economic Justice*

Individuals who participate in social movements often reflect the differences in temperament and strategy and the complex histories of those movements. By analyzing the political evolution of key individuals, we can understand how people shape movements as well as how movements shape the beliefs and values of their participants. This understanding is especially important when both movements and individuals, such as those involved in Progressive L.A., are situated at the margins of conventional histories and mainstream political discourse.

Indeed, the history of L.A.'s progressive movements and some of its leading participants during the past century is largely untold and misunderstood, but a few key figures, such as Carey McWilliams, Upton Sinclair, and Dorothy Healey, have become reasonably well known. These key figures had a contemporary, Charlotta Bass, who was one of the most significant progressive leaders in Los Angeles for over forty years. Yet Bass remains an invisible figure to many activists and scholars. Telling her story provides a snapshot of Progressive L.A. at a critical time of transition—and highlights the continuities within this historic mosaic of movements.

Bass played three key roles in L.A.'s progressive community. From 1912 to 1951, she was the editor and publisher of the *California Eagle*, the longest-running Black newspaper in the city at the time. Bass was also a committed activist, organizer, and bridge builder. She moved between liberal and radical political circles whose activities sometimes intersected, but whose relationships were often fraught with tension and suspicion. A Republican for much of her life, she was later close to the Communist Party, but she also worked with groups such as the NAACP and the Congress of

Industrial Organizations (CIO). Bass was also a candidate for several elected offices, becoming for a brief period a controversial candidate for Los Angeles City Council and vice president of the United States on the Progressive Party ticket in 1952. Bass used these campaigns to raise issues and educate the public as an extension of her work as journalist and activist. Because she was associated with the Left—and often worked closely with Communists and other radicals—Bass was subject to Red-baiting and harsh criticism. While her color and gender compounded the obstacles she had to face, she learned to negotiate a range of difficult situations. She became an advocate who was constantly in motion. With her own positions at times in flux, she nevertheless continually sought to create new kinds of coalitions and to help to establish new pathways for change.

The fact that Charlotta Bass's name and story are not widely known may well reflect the gender, race, and political blind spots of historians and the mainstream media. Most recently, for example, Kevin Starr's history of California during the 1940s, *Embattled Dreams*, omits any reference to Bass.[1] This absence is particularly striking because Bass, who died in 1969, was in the forefront of many of the key struggles discussed in chapter 1, including housing, immigration, labor, women's rights, and civil rights. Like many progressives of her era, the views she expressed were typically controversial, decades ahead of where the nation and public opinion were at the time. She was an important coalition builder among L.A.'s progressives, finding common ground among a diverse group of activists seeking to make Los Angeles a more humane and livable city for everyone. Understanding Bass's life and work, then, can help us to overcome one important type of historical amnesia associated with Progressive L.A.: the neglect of the intersection of race and community politics so central to the historical—and contemporary—Los Angeles experience.

A REPUBLICAN AND A RADICAL

Little is known about Bass's early life. Even her date of birth is uncertain. Born Charlotta Spears in Sumter, South Carolina, in 1879 or 1880, she moved to Rhode Island after high school and began working in the newspaper business.[2] Bass migrated to Los Angeles in 1910 on the advice of her physician, like many of those who came to the region, though her specific ailment is unknown. Soon after arriving in the city, she took a job selling subscriptions to the small African American newspaper the *Eagle*. Just before he died in 1912, the paper's founder, John J. Neimore, asked Bass to take over the paper. Changing the name to the *California Eagle*, Bass in

1913 hired Joseph Blackburn "J. B." Bass, who eventually became the editor of the paper as well as Bass's husband.[3]

From the beginning of their association with the paper, this husband-wife team used the *California Eagle* as a vehicle for advancing a range of social justice causes. Like most Black newspapers of that period, the *Eagle* served as a source of both information and inspiration for the Black community, which was largely ignored or negatively portrayed by the White press. After J. B. Bass's death in 1934, Charlotta Bass continued and expanded the paper's political advocacy, highlighting many of her issues and causes. Bass also used her weekly column and her editorial page contributions to draw attention to social and political conditions, as well as to promote campaigns to reform what she considered a fabric of injustice. She wrote her last column for the *Eagle* on April 26, 1951, and sold the paper soon after.

In addition to using the *Eagle* to support political work, Bass was active in electoral politics, both as a candidate and in others' campaigns, identifying less with specific parties than with her own principles and views about community, race, and politics. Like most African Americans prior to the Depression, Bass was a supporter of the Republican Party, although she would back Democratic or independent candidates when she felt they demonstrated a stronger commitment to social and particularly racial justice. "While our nationality is American, our race Black, Religious denomination Baptist, and our political creed Republican," she wrote in one 1929 column, "we reserve and cherish as our inalienable right the privilege of thinking for ourselves."[4] Core principles and issues outweighed party loyalty and even racial loyalty. This led her, for example, to support Franklin D. Roosevelt in the 1932 presidential election, even as she maintained her Republican Party affiliation.[5]

Still a registered Republican, in 1945 Bass entered the electoral arena herself, with a nonpartisan run for a seat on the Los Angeles City Council, representing the 7th district, which was at the time 45 percent African American.[6] Her campaign focused on the need for full employment with job security and decent wages, fair and adequate housing, improved public health-service delivery, upgraded transportation, additional recreation and child-care facilities, and lower utility rates.[7] Despite receiving 34 percent of the vote and forcing the incumbent Carl C. Rasmussen into a runoff, Bass was defeated, due in part to Rasmussen's mean-spirited and radical-baiting campaign. Increasingly critical of the two-party system, Bass went on to run on the Progressive Party ticket for Congress in 1950, challenging Sam Yorty, who won the race, served in Congress, and later went on to become the mayor of Los Angeles.[8]

In 1952, Bass was selected by the Progressive Party as the first Black woman to run for vice president. At the Progressive Party's national convention, Bass was nominated by Paul Robeson, with W. E. B. DuBois seconding the nomination.[9] During the campaign, Bass extended her arguments, promoting an explicitly radical agenda that included support for a national housing program, a national health insurance plan, and increased funding for public schools.[10] The Progressive Party's slogan in 1952—"Win or lose, we win by raising the issues"—reflected Bass's own orientation toward electoral politics as a forum (sometimes successful, sometimes marginalized) for political education.[11]

Bass's move from the Republican Party to the Progressive Party reflected a political evolution that also characterized her evolving role as a political activist. An early example was her role in founding the local chapter of the Universal Negro Improvement Association (UNIA) and her subsequent break with the group. Organized in 1920, the Los Angeles chapter of the UNIA, an affiliate of the national organization founded and led by Marcus Garvey, was committed to pan-Africanism and economic nationalism. The group's philosophies were attractive to hundreds of Black Angelenos who faced increasing discrimination when the city's Anglo population expanded just prior to the 1920s.[12] Bass and her husband were founding members of the chapter and she served as the group's first "Lady President."[13] But many of the members of the L.A. chapter, including Bass, were more attracted to UNIA's commitment to Black economic self-sufficiency than to the separate UNIA goal of building an independent Black nation.[14]

Bass left the UNIA in 1921 in a dispute with the national organization over financial irregularities and its unwillingness to give the local Los Angeles chapter greater autonomy.[15] Her departure from the UNIA coincided with her increasing interest in moving beyond a narrower version of nationalism to embrace non-Black allies in the quest for Black empowerment and her developing ties with a number of multiracial organizations.

Bass had her share of political critics, many of whom came from within the African American community, including those who distrusted her because of accusations about her presumed ties to the Communist Party. In the midst of the Red Scare and the McCarthy era in the late 1940s and 1950s, many individuals and organizations sought to distance themselves from Communism. Organizations such as the NAACP, the ACLU, and numerous labor unions purged themselves of suspected Communists, and many former Communists disavowed their previous ties. Those who continued to support Communism and/or Communists were increasingly isolated.

Reflecting the era, the Black editor of a rival Black newspaper, the *Los*

Angeles Tribune, warned that Bass was "suspected of getting [her] convictions by mimeographed dispatch weekly from one of the lesser hierarchy of Stalin. . . . Mrs. Bass, as we know, is a political chameleon who already appears to have a pink tinge at present."[16] Such sentiments were reinforced by the California State Un-American Activities Committee's decision in 1945 to call Bass to testify at a hearing and to label her a Communist. Later, the U.S. government revoked her passport and thus her ability to travel abroad.[17] A Black sorority, Iota Phi Lambda, rescinded Bass's honorary membership due to the accusations about Communist Party affiliation.[18] She even encountered hostility from the NAACP, which she joined soon after its establishment in Los Angeles. In an undated article, Bass recounted how an NAACP membership campaign organizer from northern California tore up Bass's membership card as a result of suspicions that she was a member of an organization declared to be an enemy of the government. Bass responded, "I have no membership card in any organization that I am afraid or ashamed to show. If fighting segregation, discrimination, and housing restrictions, and seeking to build a better social climate for my people constitutes a crime, I plead guilty."[19]

Her troubles with the NAACP evidently subsided over time, as evidenced by an NAACP membership card dated 1965 found in her papers, which are housed at the Southern California Library for Social Studies and Research.[20] In 1948, Bass explicitly denied that she was a member of the Communist Party and demanded retraction of this accusation made by another newspaper.[21] Despite her denial, the FBI considered Bass to be a Communist and a subversive. Agents maintained surveillance of her activities, read each issue of the *Eagle*, and made regular reports to FBI director J. Edgar Hoover.[22]

Bass was disturbed but undeterred by such attacks, and in her last column for the *Eagle*, in 1951, she directly addressed them:

> For many years the reactionary forces in this community have tried
> to crush me and *The California Eagle*. . . . Among them, I regret to say,
> are some of my own people, whom I have personally helped over the
> years to become successes in business, in the professions, and in political
> office. They have joined forces with the enemy of their own people
> and the enemy of democracy. Their fate is not difficult to foretell.[23]

While Bass maintained these commitments and refused to reverse her position regarding Communist affiliation, the *Eagle* began to lose readers in the mid- to late '40s due to these attacks, and financial losses resulted. Bass eventually had to sell the *Eagle* and thus lost her most powerful source of advocacy.[24]

Bass's changing political perspectives, evidenced early on by her departure from the UNIA, can also be seen in her evolving positions on Communism. In a January 1942 column of the *Eagle*, Bass, still a registered Republican, observed, "Perhaps the greatest single deterrent to the full development of a healthy Negro economic life, aside from our sweeping mass poverty, was the 'pink decades' of the twenties and thirties. An entire generation of Black youth floundered during these years under the shoals of Marx and Joe Stalin."[25]

This critique of Communism's influence among Black Americans contrasts with her 1945 assertion that "the only threat by Communists is to point the way to an open door to freedom, the kind promised by the Four Freedoms, to all enslaved minorities."[26] Already by 1943, eighteen months after Bass's critical commentary at the beginning of the war, the *Eagle* had begun to run ads for the Communist Party.[27] Bass argued that her changing views were due to the political dynamics of World War II and the new alliance of the United States and the Soviet Union. In applauding the reinstatement of the Communist Party on the California ballot, Bass wrote in July 1942, "This newspaper [*The Eagle*] once felt that no good could come from the infiltration of Communism in the American political scene. The changing of our views on this matter is reflected also in the change of policy of the great state of California and follows logically in the development of true national unity aimed at victory for the anti-Fascist world."[28] Bass connected persecution of Communists, such as the purging of the CP from the ballot, to broader threats to political and social freedom. Later in this same article, and in several other articles she subsequently published, Bass linked the fight against anti-Communism to that against domestic racial discrimination and the war against fascism abroad. By doing so, she hoped to expose the perceived hypocrisy of U.S. policy (where discriminatory practices still occurred), in order to effect changes in such policy.[29]

It is not clear from her writings whether Bass ever joined the Communist Party. However, she was quite explicit about her opposition to the Red-baiting epitomized by the California State Un-American Activities Committee and by the House Un-American Activities Committee (HUAC), its congressional counterpart. Whether she actually joined the CP, her active participation in groups with large numbers of CP members and leaders, such as the Civil Rights Congress, indicated her comfort in working with CP members and CP-influenced groups, and her defiance of an increasingly virulent anti-Communism.[30]

The issue of membership in the CP has often been used by historians and politicians to question whether activists' politics were dictated by the Party, as opposed to being more organically connected to their own beliefs and actions. Bass's long trajectory of activism and deep ties to diverse constituencies within the African American community underlined the point that she controlled her own agenda and was willing to make significant political shifts (i.e., from Republican to radical). Whether using the *Eagle* to promote Black businesses on Los Angeles' Central Avenue, speaking to the Black Baptist church congregation to which she belonged, working with decidedly non-Communist groups such as the post-1940s NAACP, or serving on the board of the Civil Rights Congress, Bass consistently identified her commitment to social justice and community empowerment as being the core of her beliefs.

Throughout her life, Bass remained rooted in collective Black struggle, whether through her UNIA activism, her promotion of multiracial alliances, or her role as community advocate, particularly for individuals whose rights were violated. As a result, many in the Black community strongly identified with her as a widely respected leader. She continually linked her advocacy to broader political principles and social justice activism, but she generally did not use explicitly ideological rhetoric in her columns or speeches. Instead, she relied on appeals to reason and to the most immediate and direct community concerns. Undaunted by attacks from inside and outside the Black community, she continued her strong social justice advocacy even after selling the *Eagle* and after her 1952 campaign for vice president. For health reasons, she moved to Lake Elsinore, a small town near Los Angeles, and purchased a home. She turned the garage into a community reading room and a voter-registration site for local African Americans. In addition to continuing her civil rights activism, Bass also joined protests against apartheid in South Africa, and on behalf of prisoners' rights in the state of California, until she suffered a stroke in 1966 and was placed in a Los Angeles nursing home. Bass died three years later from a cerebral hemorrhage.[31]

While she was involved in countless campaigns for social justice in Los Angeles, Bass's involvement in four sets of specific issues best reflect her general outlook and underline the contemporary relevance of her approach and activities. These include her leadership in the fight for the rights of Black women workers; multiracial organizing against police brutality and an unfair criminal justice system; the battle to protect the rights of immigrants (the foreign born); and the struggles for fair and adequate housing. Her activities in these four issue areas in turn reflected her commitment to coalition building among diverse constituencies and her recognition of the importance of fighting on multiple fronts. They also indicate how she used the *Eagle* as both a source of information and a movement-building vehicle.

GENDER AND RACE DISCRIMINATION:
THE LOS ANGELES NEGRO VICTORY COMMITTEE

World War II produced massive changes in Los Angeles. As the West Coast center for wartime industries, the area attracted migrants from all over the country looking for work. African Americans flocked to the region following Roosevelt's June 21, 1941, signing of Executive Order 8802 in response to pressure from activists such as A. Phillip Randolph to integrate the war industries.[32] Locally, Bass joined with Reverend Clayton Russell of the People's Independent Church, an activist Black congregation in South Los Angeles, as coleader of the Los Angeles Negro Victory Committee to ensure that Blacks fully participated in the region's defense industry.[33] She used the pages of the *Eagle* to help to organize members of the Black community to demand their right to work. One of the Victory Committee's campaigns sought to ensure the rights of African American women to obtain jobs in shipbuilding enterprises. Acting on behalf of women who complained directly to Bass and the *Eagle* about discrimination by the United States Employment Service (the agency responsible for wartime hiring), Bass and Russell organized a meeting in July 1942 at the Independent Church of Christ. Bass herself describes "a spirited meeting." "For the first time in Los Angeles," Bass wrote, "Negro women, led by a Negro preacher, decided that they were going to fight untidily [sic] for food, clothing and the comforts of life which were due them."[34] Bass then recalled what happened next: "The strategy adopted was to meet at the U.S. Employment Headquarters, at 11th and Flower Streets, Monday, at 8:00 a.m., and register for employment. A deluge of Negro women flooded the employment office and their quiet determination brought results. It was the lifting of the discrimination ban against Negro women in the war industries."[35]

While Bass's advocacy on behalf of these workers was rooted in the struggle for Black rights, she was also committed to gender equality. Unlike many African American women of her day, Bass was not especially active in the club movement.[36] She nevertheless maintained an involvement in women's causes through the war industries campaign, in her own support for women's suffrage, and later as a member of the Sojourners for Truth and Justice, an early Black feminist organization.[37] The *Eagle* periodically featured a "Negro Women in History" page and Bass often appealed directly to Black women in her columns and editorials.[38] Her gender-based activism was expressed through the *Eagle* and was tied to other struggles. The campaign on behalf of Black women workers was part of a larger strategy to pressure the government to ensure African American access to employment. Another aspect of this campaign involved monitoring discrimination and working conditions in the industry as a whole. Bass always involved herself and the *Eagle* in efforts to improve working conditions in the city, often through supporting union activism. For example, during the strike against the American Tobacco Company, one of the earliest interracial strikes in the country, Bass used the *Eagle* to rally local support for striking employees.[39] She also strongly supported A. Phillip Randolph and the Pullman porters, numerous longshore union strikes, and various local CIO campaigns for workers' rights.[40]

While Bass was committed to struggling on behalf of Black women workers, she did so by organizing around multiple issues and movements. For Bass, this provided a means for connecting distinct struggles, thus prefiguring contemporary coalition-building efforts and challenges.

COMMUNITIES OF COLOR: THE SLEEPY LAGOON CASE

Evidence of Bass's activism on multiple fronts was most visible in the pages of the *California Eagle*. She used her weekly column, "On the Sidewalk," and her editorial-page contributions to highlight current campaigns against injustice and to assess conditions in her own and other communities. Bass's activism is also documented in the many speeches she made, including those delivered on the campaign trail, and in her connection to numerous activist organizations such as the Civil Rights Congress and the Sleepy Lagoon Defense Committee.

On August 2, 1942, teenager José Díaz was found dead on a ranch near a reservoir called Sleepy Lagoon, in East L.A. Sheriff's deputies immediately rounded up several hundred Mexican American youths as suspects and threw them in jail. Many were beaten and terrorized, until twenty-three of them were eventually indicted for the murder. Evidence against the defendants was largely confined to the clothes they were wearing (long, baggy pants and jackets, or "zoot suits," as they were called) and racist assumptions about the presumed criminal nature of Mexican American youth.[41] This case was part of a larger environment of wartime hysteria that sought to root out "enemies within." It followed the issuing of Roosevelt's Executive Order 9066, which interned Japanese Americans on the basis of their presumed security risk. Both instances underlined the vulnerability of minority residents in Los Angeles in times of crisis.[42]

Bass and the *Eagle* played a visible role in supporting the Sleepy Lagoon defendants. In addition to serving as a sponsor of the Defense Committee,

Bass used the paper to inform Black readers about the injustices suffered by the defendants. Additionally, the *Eagle* reproduced a pamphlet detailing the story of the case and aided in the legal appeal. For Bass, "the case represented in all its horror the use of all the powers of local government to smear and terrorize an entire racial group."[43] In separating the *Eagle* from the main-stream press, and the *Los Angeles Times* and Hearst papers in particular, she noted, "A sensation-mongering, circulation-mad metropolitan press was a prime factor in fanning the flames of race hate and suspicion before and during and after the long 'Sleepy Lagoon' trial."[44] Bass asserted that the proper role of the *Eagle* was to advocate for marginalized communities that had suffered through the type of characterizations found in the mainstream press. This advocacy role extended beyond the Black community to include Mexican Americans, situating Bass as one of the city's earliest advocates of a Black-Brown coalition.

The county grand jury became another arena in which Bass sought to connect African American and Mexican American struggles. One of the cases she reviewed as a member of the grand jury involved several Mexican American youth charged with burglary. A number of Bass's White counter-parts on the grand jury voiced their belief that Mexicans were naturally pre-disposed to commit crimes. This, they said, was enough evidence to indict the suspects. As she recounted later, Bass listened to such comments at length before interjecting:

> Ladies and gentlemen of the jury . . . I consider what I have just heard an outrageous attack on our Mexican American citizens, and as a member of another minority group, a personal attack on me. For I am sure what you have said about the Mexican people, in your sub-conscious mind, is precisely what you feel about my people. Do you realize that the very land you claim and live on was once the property of these Mexicans you now despise? Did you buy it? . . . Like the Mexican people who have contributed so much to art and science I am not ashamed of my African background. But as I look at you I am ashamed and afraid that your ignorance and prejudice will be your undoing unless you wake up and together all of us, you and I—Mexican, Negro, Asian, European, and African—create a world in peace dedicated to the real brotherhood of man.[45]

Bass's willingness to use her access to power (grand jury service) and resources (the *Eagle*) on behalf of Mexican American youth reflected a broad commitment to racial justice and coalition building. This commit-ment was equally demonstrated by her participation on the board of the Civil Rights Congress (CRC). While the CRC focused primarily on the fight for the rights of working-class African Americans, it also advocated on behalf of Mexican Americans and other people of color.[46] In Los Angeles, the CRC's work was largely dedicated to fighting police brutality by publicizing complaints and providing legal support for victims. Through the connection between Bass and the CRC, many such cases, including those involving non-Blacks, found their way onto the pages of the *Eagle*.

IMMIGRANT RIGHTS: THE COMMITTEE FOR THE PROTECTION OF THE FOREIGN BORN

Bass's involvement in two organizations, the American Committee for the Protection of the Foreign Born and the Los Angeles Committee for Defense of the Bill of Rights, illustrates another focus of her activism: immigrant rights. In the 1940s and 1950s, immigrant rights was not a popular cause. Although World War II had made Americans aware of the plight of Jews in Europe, there was considerable resistance during and after the war to allowing large numbers of Jewish immigrants into the United States. The war had strengthened feelings of hatred toward Japanese Americans, many of whom were interned in camps during the war out of fear that they were not loyal citizens. These fears were projected onto other Asian residents of the city, who were primarily immigrants. Immigrants from Puerto Rico, Mexico, and other Spanish-speaking countries were treated with considerable ambivalence, and often outright hostility, and were subject to racist stereotypes and social segregation.

Despite these prevailing attitudes, Bass remained a strong advocate for the rights of immigrants throughout her life. She became most active in her support of the rights of immigrants in her final year with the *Eagle*, when she publicized cases of political persecution of even longtime residents who had not received citizenship. This was during the Red Scare, and Bass's defense of immigrants was linked to her support for the rights of radicals and dissenters to express unpopular views without facing repression or deportation.

In a 1950 column, for example, Bass highlighted the case of José Estrada, who had immigrated from Mexico to the United States in 1905 and, forty-five years later, faced deportation for "un-American activities." In her article Bass pointed out that Estrada deserved protections afforded all Americans. "He is married to a native Texan and has ten American-born children," Bass wrote. "Three sons served in the armed forces during World War II. . . . Each spent over three years fighting, one receiving the Purple Heart."[47] Her decision to focus on Estrada's "American-ness," as illustrated by his ties to this country and the patriotic actions of his children, was in keeping with her argument about the contradictory nature of American policy during the war: discriminatory practices toward Blacks at home while the country was fighting a war for freedom and democracy abroad. Bass shared this view with many Black activists and Black journalists who participated in the "Double V" campaign during and after World War II—the name stood for victory against fascism abroad and victory against racism at home.[48] She was particularly concerned about the portrayal of activists during this period as anti-American for daring to speak up and point out those contradictions in wartime.

Beyond the pages of the *Eagle,* Bass sought to protect immigrant rights by serving in the late 1950s and early 1960s as honorary cochair of the American Committee for the Protection of the Foreign Born, and prior to her death in 1969, for the Los Angeles Committee for Defense of the Bill of Rights.[49] Both organizations were particularly active in supporting cases of radical activists facing deportation or denaturalization proceedings under the Alien Registration Act of 1940 (known as the Smith Act) and the Immigration and Nationality Law of 1952 (known as the McCarran Act). Bass wrote a letter on behalf of the protection committee to the Los Angeles City Council, focusing on the treatment of immigrants:

> In order to lead a free world to the coveted goal of peace, the employ-
> ment, education, and religious rights of all Americans of whatever
> racial, political, or religious faith must be protected as long as they
> don't threaten the security of our government. I am afraid, however,
> that the rights of many of our good foreign born American citizens,
> as well as those of many other loyal Americans have been infringed
> upon.[50]

This sentiment echoed many such declarations of Bass's support for the protection of the civil rights and civil liberties of foreign-born Americans. She often listed the foreign born, along with "Negroes, the Jews, the Mexican people, the Asian," as populations particularly vulnerable to denial of basic constitutional rights.[51]

The American Committee for the Protection of the Foreign Born came under criticism for limiting its immigrant-rights advocacy to those, primarily Whites, who were being politically persecuted.[52] While some of this criticism may apply to some of Bass's own advocacy, particularly to her prioritization of politically oriented cases that were then featured on the pages of the *Eagle,* she nevertheless tied such struggles to a broader agenda for civil rights for other groups, including the more generic cause of rights for all immigrants.

SEGREGATION PRACTICES:
THE FIGHT FOR FAIR AND ADEQUATE HOUSING

Bass was a longtime advocate for fair and adequate housing, a key civil rights issue of the 1940s and 1950s. Through the pages of the *Eagle*, through her work with a variety of community organizations, and in her electoral campaigns, she was deeply engaged in housing issues, fighting against racial restrictions and their resulting overcrowding and slum conditions while supporting public housing and rent control programs. In the housing issue, as in others, Bass engaged in cross-racial alliances and used the *Eagle* to educate and mobilize the Black community.

Despite its reputation as a "northern" city, Los Angeles was highly segregated. Racially based restrictive covenants were prevalent throughout the city and had enormous impact in fostering residential segregation. Written into property deeds, these covenants restricted sale of property to Whites only (and often just White non-Jews). As a result of these restrictions, housing for Blacks, Mexicans, and others remained isolated and segregated in a small number of areas of the city. As populations expanded with increased migration, overcrowding and slum conditions grew as well. Landlords capitalized on patterns of segregation by overcharging residents and creating what amounted to slum housing conditions.

Mobilization against these housing practices grew significantly among communities of color during the 1940s. New forms of individual resistance and political action took root, largely ignored by the White press and also largely absent in historical accounts of the housing issue in this period. African American residents, especially, organized to push for changes in this more pernicious form of segregation and, as a kind of individually oriented civil disobedience, even intentionally violated the laws that allowed restrictive practices.

Already by the early 1940s, racial restrictions in housing had become a dominant theme for Bass and in the pages of the *Eagle*. In an August 5, 1943, editorial, for example, Bass wrote: "While we emphatically support the demand for increased emergency housing in the Negro districts of Los Angeles it is certainly obvious that the FUNDAMENTAL housing necessity in Los Angeles is the total destruction of property restrictions. Today it is a fact that Negroes are confined to a ghetto area comprising only FIVE PERCENT of the residential area of the city."[53]

Often, when individuals and families purchased and occupied homes in violation of restrictive covenants, they were subject to harassment by neighbors. Some even faced eviction when brought to court by real estate agents eager to obtain their property. As early as 1914, Bass actively involved herself in the defense of Black homeowners' rights in Los Angeles. When Mrs. Mary Johnson appealed to the *Eagle* for help after literally being kicked out of her newly purchased home by White neighbors, Bass "discussed the situation with some club women, and that evening a brigade of a hundred women marched to the Johnson home."[54] The women were ultimately successful in getting the sheriff to help Mrs. Johnson back into her home.

Over the years, Bass became involved in a number of similar episodes where she would respond to a request for help by mobilizing support for individual residents. This role of community advocate defined Bass as much as any other.

Bass combined direct engagement in support of residents battling restrictions with use of the *Eagle* to publicize such cases and mobilize community support. The Lawses' case of the 1940s, described in chapter 1, was perhaps the most famous of these. Throughout the duration of their seven-year battle to occupy their home free of harassment, the Lawses benefited not only from Bass's leadership in the Home Protective Association, but also from continuous coverage on the pages of the *Eagle*.[55] In writing about the case, Bass again made the point of connecting this struggle to America's effort in World War II, highlighting the fact that members of the family were jailed for occupying their home, despite being employed in the defense industry and having a son-in-law overseas fighting with Allied forces.[56] After the war, Bass, the Home Protective Association, and the *Eagle* also pushed for desegregated housing for veterans.

For Bass, a focus on Black resistance to restrictive covenants did not mean that housing was exclusively an African American issue. "Since the question of restrictive covenants concerns such minorities as Orientals, Mexican-Americans, Indians, the Jewish, Italian and Negro people," Bass wrote in her autobiography, "our discussion of the Negro people's struggle against restrictive covenants applies to the struggle of all minority groups."[57] In the early 1940s, for example, Bass used the *Eagle* to alert the Black community to the struggle of primarily Mexican American families to pressure the city to alleviate slum conditions in the Chavez Ravine area near downtown L.A. Bass's consistent battling against all racial bias prefigured the multiethnic issues that emerged as part of the politics of Progressive L.A. three decades later.[58]

In the electoral arena Bass championed the cause of decent and fair housing in her own campaigns for City Council, Congress, and the vice presidency. But she also publicized other candidates' records on the housing issue. In 1929, under the banner headline "Defeat Harry F. Burke for Councilman in the 8th District," the *Eagle* ran a story about a City Council candidate's leadership of the White Home Protective Association, one of many such associations that formed in the wake of World War II to "protect" White communities from encroachment by non-Whites. The White Home Protective Association in particular was devoted to renewing racial restrictive covenants.[59] Thanks in part to the *Eagle*'s opposition, Burke was defeated.[60]

The *Eagle* also urged readers to attend a City Council meeting to support a resolution condemning racial property restrictions in a new Watts housing area.[61] When the resolution was defeated the *Eagle* published a record of how each member of the council voted.[62]

In addition to the battle against restrictive covenants, Bass was active in bringing more public housing to the city. She supported progressive efforts by the city's housing authority to gain federal support for this effort. Bass also explicitly connected the fight for public housing to the fight against racism. In the pages of the *Eagle* she supported the call for twenty thousand units of public housing and demanded that they be desegregated. "Since the inception of the Public Housing program in this community, racists and real estate interests have tried to prevent Los Angeles from obtaining needed units, rented on a democratic basis according to need," she wrote in one 1950 editorial.[63]

Finally, Bass openly supported rent control as an important part of the solution to the housing crisis. In March 1950, the City Council considered a proposal to lift existing rent control on residential hotels. Bass saw this as a threat to the primarily working-class residents who lived in these units. "Millions of families are victims of high rents and low wages," Bass wrote in the *Eagle*. "Now if rent control is taken off, the heartless property owners or landlords will make life miserable and children homeless for millions of local and migrant families. What we need is regulation not de-control."[64]

As with other issues, Bass advocated access to public information as well as regulation of the activities of private individuals and businesses. She firmly believed in the right and the responsibility of government involvement. But by 1950, the concept of activist government, to Bass's dismay, was under attack, and rent control was lifted on a March 31 vote of the Los Angeles City Council.[65] This rent control vote anticipated the growing counterattack against progressive policies in housing and other civil society issues.

THE BASS LEGACY

Charlotta Bass was obliged to sell the *California Eagle* in 1951, an event that anticipated and ultimately reinforced the decline of significant grassroots movements within the Black community, as well as of other multiracial organizing and movements in Los Angeles. Both Bass and the *Eagle* had symbolized a level of activism that was crippled by the anti-Communist attacks and reactionary mobilization that took place during the 1950s. A political vacuum emerged, not just in the Black community but citywide. A period of political denial followed, including a failure to recognize the simmering tensions associated with the daily conditions of life for African Americans, such as segregated housing, poor jobs, and inadequate education.

Following the 1965 Watts rebellion, new organizing in communities of color began to occur, led by such groups as the Black Panther Party and La Raza Unida. But these groups also witnessed, similar to what Bass and her contemporaries had experienced, a level of hostility and government-sponsored suppression. So another set of movements and individual organizers were undermined, creating another political hiatus in the late 1970s and 1980s. With movements struggling to survive, once again Los Angeles exploded, with the period following the April 1992 civil unrest leading to a renewal of an activism that was at once multi-issue, multiracial, and more connected—the kind of activism that Charlotta Bass embodied.

Bass's legacy is both positive and long-lasting. To begin with, her work over a lifetime of advocacy and coalition building helps to situate the protracted nature of the challenges faced by those seeking to create a more just and livable city. Employment discrimination, police brutality and an unfair criminal justice system, the denial of equal protection for immigrants, and unfair and inadequate housing continue to plague Los Angeles and other cities. The lingering nature of these issues underlines their complexity. Yet Bass's steadfast fifty-plus-year commitment to addressing these issues, and her successful strategies of community-based advocacy, coalition building, and cross-constituency organizing, offers instruction and inspiration. It was her activism and the actions of hundreds, if not thousands, of her contemporaries that ultimately laid the groundwork for the progressive activism that continued, despite reversals, to reemerge in the years following her death.

PART II

Reemerging Movements

Los Angeles in the Wake of the 1992 Civil Unrest

Introduction

The intense, explosive events in Los Angeles from April 30 to May 2, 1992, revealed underlying divisions in the city and also led to a renewed attention to the urban crisis in the nation as a whole. After twelve years of the Reagan-Bush administrations and two sharp recessions, the social and economic safety net had frayed badly. Use of the emergency system of food banks and soup kitchens, for example, had reached unprecedented levels, with the working poor vying with the unemployed and homeless for such services. "Livability" and "democratic participation" factors had also declined. Environmental policies enacted during the 1970s had been weakened and in some cases eliminated. Political and civic engagement, as measured by voter turnout, union membership, community activity, and other forms of democratic participation, continued to decline. And Los Angeles had become, once again through an explosive event, the place that identified the depth and breadth of the social, racial, environmental, and economic problems that plagued cities and regions across the United States.

During the 1960s and early 1970s, in response to the violent unrest in the inner cities, there briefly emerged new urban innovation and community-based development strategies that sought to address a range of poverty, quality-of-life, and participation issues. But the challenges of the early 1990s seemed at once more complex and intractable. The economic restructuring, rapid demographic changes, decline of livable neighborhoods, and continuing erosion of civic engagement and political participation of the previous two decades overwhelmed minimal initiatives, such as Rebuild L.A., that quickly came and went. And even as the 1990s brought economic growth, the problems identified by the 1992 civil unrest remained largely unaddressed.

However, while policy elites proved to be incapable of sustaining any new initiatives to address the problems of the cities, and attention to L.A.'s moment of crisis began to fade, a new generation of community, labor, environmental, and immigrant-rights groups took root in Los Angeles. Many of these groups recognized that the 1992 events represented a pivotal moment in their own organizing and policy focus and were able to significantly expand their agendas and organizing reach. These groups, occasionally linked though often acting separately on behalf of their communities, workplaces, or issue-based constituencies, became the basis for a reconstituted Progressive L.A.

This section describes the economic, political, demographic, social, and environmental changes that led up to and followed the 1992 civil unrest and the reemergence of the new social movements that became the basis of a renewed Progressive L.A. The section is divided into two chapters, which provide an economic, social, environmental, and political snapshot of those changes. Chapter 3, "The Continuing Divide," identifies the major economic and demographic changes of the past two decades, the issues that have resulted from those changes, and their impact on the development of new social movements. Chapter 4, "Stresses in Eden," discusses changes in housing, food and nutrition, the urban environment, transportation, education, and other social indicators of quality of life in the region.

The 1990s, including the events and changes that led to the civil unrest and the subsequent response to those events, were a critical time in the evolution of Progressive L.A. These chapters elaborate why that is so.

3   The Continuing Divide

The Demographic and Economic Transformation of Los Angeles

> Los Angeles cannot permanently exist as two cities—one amazingly prosperous, the other increasingly poorer in substance and in hope.
>
> MAYOR TOM BRADLEY, FIFTH INAUGURAL ADDRESS, 1989

TWO ERUPTIONS

At two critical moments—in 1965 and 1992—Los Angeles erupted in civil unrest. After both eruptions, local and national political leaders expressed shock. L.A. was seen as somehow different from the industrial cities of the East and the Midwest, with their entrenched patterns of racial segregation and bleak ghetto neighborhoods. In fact, in 1964, one year before the Watts riots, the Urban League, a civil rights group, had ranked L.A. first in livability criteria for African Americans among sixty-eight American cities. The report noted that "the opportunity to succeed [in L.A.] is probably unequaled in any other major U.S. city."[1] Likewise, in the decade prior to the 1992 civil unrest, Los Angeles was one of the few cities with a majority White population that had elected a Black mayor. Los Angeles was basking in the success of its hosting of the Olympics in 1984 and was increasingly touted as a model world city for its ties to the dynamic and growing Pacific Basin region.

But the 1992 civil unrest, which left over forty dead and caused a billion dollars worth of damage, should not have been such a surprise. The region was by then mired in a deep recession, facing a widening gap between rich and poor. If the same indicators used in the 1964 Urban League report—such as housing, employment, and income—had been updated to 1992, L.A. would have been seen as among the most troubled major cities in the nation. And the conditions underlying the riot—a division between the suburbs and the central city, the loss of decent-paying blue-collar jobs in the service economy that was replacing the industrial one, growing income inequality, and the demographic transformation of the region through Latino and Asian immigration—continued to shape the Los Angeles region.

Compounding these social and economic conditions was the persistent racism of the Los Angeles Police Department, long a grievance of the city's communities of color. The LAPD's harassment, racial profiling, and brutality have also been constant reminders of the city's ethnic and income divide. The immediate spark for the 1992 events, outrage over the Rodney King beatings and the acquittal of four police officers charged with using excessive force during his arrest, confirmed the "expectation of unequal law enforcement" that the U.S. Commission on Civil Rights had identified, as early as 1963, as "the attitude and opinion of the great majority of Los Angeles Negroes."[2]

Yet the 1992 civil unrest, far more than the 1965 events, was exacerbated by L.A.'s increasingly complex ethnic realities. What were once majority African American neighborhoods now were mixed with new Latino and Asian enclaves. Widespread unemployment—brought about by a combination of the nationwide recession and regional factory closings—had intensified ethnic and racial tensions. Unlike the 1965 events, the 1992 civil unrest was not just about relations between Black and White.

Some of the most intense confrontations of the 1992 civil unrest occurred in the Pico-Union neighborhood—home to Blacks, Latinos, Koreans, and Whites, predominantly the working poor—a few miles from the downtown financial district. Ethnic tensions had risen as the area's demography had changed with the arrival of Latino and Asian immigrants. In South Los Angeles, a historically Black area, the number of Latinos had reached roughly the same level as the number of African Americans, although they often lived in distinct enclaves within the same neighborhood. Both of these groups had uneasy relationships with some of the Korean merchants who operated small markets and retail stores in the area. In particular, the shooting of an African American teenager by a Korean store owner, on March 16, 1991—between the time of Rodney King's arrest and the trial verdict—had pushed Black-Korean mistrust to a boiling point. When the Rodney King verdict sparked rage, underlying tensions between ethnic groups fanned the flames. Korean-owned stores were the most prominent targets for arson and property destruction, though businesses owned by all ethnic groups, as well as government buildings, were destroyed.[3]

Arrests during the civil unrest also reflected the complex ethnic demographics of those neighborhoods torn by rioting. About half of the people arrested were Black and half were Latino. Those convicted of serious charges were almost all young (80 percent were between the ages of eighteen and thirty-four) and male (88 percent). Following a decade or more of plant closings and the loss of good-paying jobs in South L.A. and the South Bay area, these young men faced exceptionally high unemployment rates (up to 50 percent in the case of African American men). As a result, many were disaffected, with less to lose than most community residents and with more time to be on the streets during the chaotic days in 1992.[4]

When the disturbances ended and the smoke finally cleared, Los Angeles faced daunting challenges. These included not just the physical reconstruction of razed buildings and areas, but also the need for economic development and community revitalization, so that neighborhoods weren't rebuilt complete with preexisting disparities. The initial response of Los Angeles' business, civic, and political elites was to launch a private sector–led rebuilding effort, Rebuild L.A., that ultimately fell far short of its goals.

Progressive activists in L.A. had a different, though somewhat overlapping, agenda for change. Community leaders argued, for example, that these neighborhoods already had a surplus of liquor stores but no supermarkets, lots of check-cashing outlets but few full-service banks. It was sometimes possible to find work, but few jobs provided health insurance or a decent wage. Police reform was also high on the priority list. So was the cultivation of understanding between ethnic and racial groups, particularly among activists engaged in union and community organization, community development, environmental justice, and similar efforts. The civil unrest had brought those issues and the need for change to the fore: the challenge now was to make it happen.

LOS ANGELES:
IMAGE AND REALITY

What is Los Angeles? Pauline Kael called it "a mock paradise" in 1974; Morrow Mayo termed it "a commodity; something to be advertised and sold to the people of the United States like automobiles, cigarettes and mouthwash" in 1933. "Call [it] any dirty name you like . . . but the fact remains that you are already living in it before you get there," said Clive James of the place, and Ann Magnuson said it was defined by "cheap pedicures, perpetual sun, guilt free careerism, seeing Vincent Price at the 7-Eleven, having a back yard, no cockroaches, true love, and Disneyland." It is "a city of several cities, divided by color, culture, and cash," according to Bob McEnery. And yet it is also, as a local activist at the Progressive L.A. conference in 1998 said, "a city of the future, a place of possibility."[5]

Caught on videotape, the Rodney King beatings and the subsequent civil unrest became two of several spectacles—the 1984 Olympics, the 1994

Northridge earthquake, the O. J. Simpson trial, the annual Academy Award shows—that have helped to define Los Angeles in the eyes of others. When these images fade into the background, L.A. becomes more complex, subject to multiple interpretations. There is Los Angeles as a physical location, with its mountains, its beaches, its dry river bed that can become torrential with winter floods, its four- and eight-level freeway interchanges, its inversion layer, and its abandoned interurban tracks that once formed the most extensive rail system in the country. There is L.A. as social reality, with its ethnic and linguistic diversity, both melting pot and cauldron, a place where—for several generations—people have arrived from elsewhere to start anew, seeking opportunity and, in some cases, a new identity.

And there is the physical and political geography of Los Angeles—its huge size and concentric circles of governance at the municipal, county, and regional levels. In the year 2000, the City of Los Angeles was the second most populous city in the United States, with 3.7 million residents.[6] The city covers 469 square miles, stretching from the San Fernando Valley in the north to a southern tail that embraces part of the port and the South Bay, and from the hilly, Pacific Ocean–facing Westside to flat East L.A. It has a mayor and 15 City Council members, each representing almost 247,000 constituents.[7] (In comparison, Chicago, with a population of 2.89 million, has 50 members on its governing body, the Board of Aldermen.)

Los Angeles County is a state masquerading as a county. More people live in L.A. County than in forty-one of the fifty states in the United States. Its economy of $294 billion in annual gross product is the same as New Jersey's, greater than that of forty states. While 39 percent of the county's population resides in the City of Los Angeles, eighty-seven other cities are also situated within the county's borders. Fifteen of them have populations over 100,000, including Long Beach (with 450,000 residents), Glendale, Santa Clarita, Pomona, and Torrance.[8] Some of the smaller cities are simply overgrown suburbs, glorified subdivisions, or even company towns incorporated by local manufacturers.[9] The county has a five-member Board of Supervisors. With each supervisor representing around 2 million residents, a ratio more like that of U.S. senators or state governors than is typical for local-government officials, political accountability within the county barely exists.

As many as six counties—Los Angeles, Orange, Ventura, Riverside, San Bernardino, and Imperial—constitute what has sometimes been characterized as the Greater Los Angeles Region. Orange County, long perceived to be a conservative bastion, is still home to a large number of affluent residents but has been as transformed by immigration as any part of the

region. Ventura County, north and west of Los Angeles, maintains significant remnants of its agricultural heritage while also hosting commuter suburbs and some of the L.A. region's newer, high-tech firms. Riverside and
San Bernardino Counties make up the Inland Empire, the eastern flank of
greater Los Angeles, where cheaper land has given rise to fast-growing suburbs and warehouse and transportation hubs. Imperial County, south and
west of Riverside, is primarily rural desert country, where major agricultural landholdings are made possible by imported Colorado River water,
and it has the highest unemployment rate in the state due to the seasonal
nature of its agricultural workforce. Partly due to its water conflicts with
urban Southern California, Imperial County sees itself as a politically, economically, and culturally distinct area, though it is sometimes included as
part of the Southern California region in various demographic assessments.
And while San Diego County, south of Orange County, is a member agency
of the large Southern California water wholesaler, the Metropolitan Water
District, it has also assumed a distinct political, economic, and cultural identity and has long considered itself competitive with and separate from
greater L.A.[10]

While these counties form an economic region, there is no political juris-
diction or institution to provide coherence in terms of governance. A few
intergovernmental agencies, serving significant parts of the region, tran-
scend city and county boundaries, but these are limited to specific functions
and missions. For example, the Metropolitan Transportation Authority
(MTA) operates some but not all of the buses and rail lines within L.A.
County, while the Southern California Association of Governments (SCAG)
has a hand in transportation planning. The South Coast Air Quality
Management District (SCAQMD) and Metropolitan Water District (MWD)
have significant influence over resource and planning decisions involving
air pollution and water use, which, in Southern California, constitute crucial
development decisions, but these agencies refuse to address the land-use
implications of those decisions, such as whether and where to build housing.

The size, political fragmentation, and large number of special districts
and intergovernmental bodies have posed a special challenge to progressives seeking to build alliances and change policy. There are elected and
unelected officials to influence and geopolitical boundaries to cross; plus,
the sheer size of the region makes it hard to conceive of it as a distinct place
that people can work together to change. "Thinking Big," a one-time motto
of the *Los Angeles Times*, suggests the problems of size, distance, and lack
of connection and accountability that greater Los Angeles has come to
represent.[11]

A CENTURY OF GROWTH

What a difference a century makes. In 1900, Los Angeles was a modest-sized town, home to 102,479 people. Fewer than one of every thousand residents of the United States lived in the Los Angeles region. By the year 2000, following the arrival of waves of new residents from other parts of the United States and from abroad, Los Angeles was at the heart of a vast urban region. One in seventeen Americans lived in greater L.A.[12] Government policies—the channeling of water, defense spending, port construction, subsidization of roads and suburban homes—helped to prime a sequence of industries—agriculture, oil, film and television, real estate, heavy manufacturing—that transformed the region from a sparsely populated patchwork of small towns, farms, and desert into one of the world's largest urban areas. Although government had much to do with the area's economic and physical transformation, there was very little government involvement in planning the region to make it more governable or livable. Outlying counties and cities grew more rapidly than downtown Los Angeles and other older settled areas, fueling a boom in residential and infrastructure construction. Southern California thus became famous (or notorious) for its sprawl, traffic congestion, and environmental pollution.

By 1940, on the verge of World War II, the City of Los Angeles had 1.5 million residents, while the region had 3.3 million. Much of the region was devoted to farming. With rich agricultural land, and one of the world's prime citrus belts from Pasadena to Riverside, places like Arcadia, Walnut, Pomona, and of course Orange County were still aptly, rather than nostalgically, named. World War II was the catalyst for dramatic change. The federal government poured money and resources into Southern California. Military bases, research institutions like the Jet Propulsion Laboratory and the California Institute of Technology, and defense contractor manufacturing facilities were founded or expanded by this funding stream, which continued to flow throughout the Cold War. Fueled by the industrial triad of aerospace, autos, and shipping, alongside a residential real estate dynamo that converted orange groves to subdivisions, L.A. became a very different place than it had been before the war. Between 1940 and 2000, the population of L.A. city more than doubled, the county's population tripled, and the region's population grew fivefold, to more than 16 million.[13]

In the last decade of the twentieth century, greater Los Angeles grew more slowly than in prior periods. Between 1990 and 1998, two hundred thousand more people actually moved *out* of Los Angeles County than moved in or immigrated.[14] The outflow was primarily a reaction to the lin-

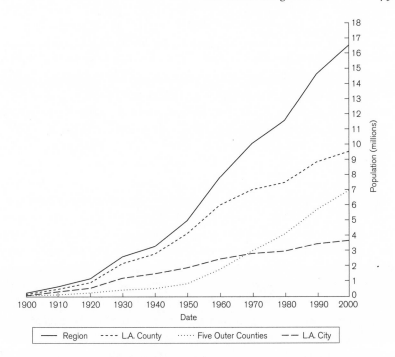

FIGURE 1   Los Angeles region population growth. (Source: U.S. Census Bureau, data from 1900 to 2000 decennial censuses.)

gering recession and the 1992 civil unrest, but it tapered off by the middle of the decade. One million births to county residents outweighed the exodus, even as the local birthrate dropped over this period.[15] Nevertheless, local planners and officials predict significant and continuing population increases. SCAG, for instance, anticipates an additional 8 million residents in the region by 2025,[16] so dealing with a growing population remains one of the Los Angeles region's primary challenges.

It was not inevitable that the region would grow by sprawling, but that's what occurred, fostered by real estate interests seeking cheaper land and abetted by politicians who sponsored the roads and other infrastructure that made sprawl possible.[17] In 1940 almost half (45 percent) of the L.A. region's people still lived in L.A. city and just 15 percent resided outside L.A. County in the towns, farms, and deserts of the five outlying counties. By 2000, these ratios had nearly reversed. The city held just 22 percent of the region's population, while 43 percent lived outside L.A. County.[18]

Though the region continues to sprawl and expand outward, with the highest growth rates scattered among far-flung suburbs,[19] the core L.A. population centers have not been abandoned. Unlike many cities in the Northeast and Midwest, where population decline, White flight, and bank redlining have led to the hollowing out of central urban areas, the L.A. region has grown on the edges *and* at its center.[20] To be sure, Central L.A. suffers from all the classic urban-center ills—clustering of poverty, loss of commercial vitality, and so forth—but these stem from a lack of investment and from disparities in power, not from wholesale population flight.

THE SIGNS OF DIVERSITY

Los Angeles in many ways is a city of signs, including the famous 50-foot-tall, 450-foot-long Hollywood marker; the neon signs first introduced in the 1950s and 1960s, including the towering marquees that lend L.A.'s strip malls a tacky charm; and the ubiquitous billboards, whose politically savvy owners have managed to stave off significant regulation. Signs also represent neighborhood designations won by tenacious homeowners associations, as well as murals providing their own cultural markers and social history. In traveling across Los Angeles, one is struck by the spectrum of languages in its signs and markers: Spanish, English, Farsi, Arabic, Cantonese, Mandarin, Hebrew, Armenian, and Vietnamese lend a cosmopolitan air to the messages of advertising, information, art, and boosterism. Over 40 percent of residents of the City of L.A. are foreign born. Like the signs that label it, Los Angeles is becoming harder to read but more intriguing.

Since 1960, L.A. has been transformed from the Whitest large city in the country to its most diverse. By the twenty-first century, Los Angeles had no majority ethnic group. Latinos represented the single largest ethnicity, followed by Whites, Asians, and African Americans.[21] For decades, native-born Whites and African Americans had migrated to the L.A. area from the Midwest, South, and East, drawn by the promise of jobs in factories and on farms, the climate, and advertisements of neat, affordable bungalows. Over the last third of the twentieth century, international immigration, primarily of Latinos and Asians, replaced internal migration as the "feeder" of Los Angeles.

By 2000, over a third of the residents of L.A. County were foreign born, and at least another third were children of immigrants.[22] The Los Angeles region held some of the world's largest communities of Koreans outside of Seoul, of Jews (including Israeli immigrants) outside of Israel and New York City, of Mexicans outside of Mexico City, and of Armenians and Iranians outside their native countries; and it had the second largest community of Arabs in the United States. The broad ethnic categories of the census were inadequate for describing the mix of ethnic, national, and subnational origins that make up L.A.'s "Latino," "Asian," "White," or "Black" populations. Two-thirds of Latinos in the City of Los Angeles are of Mexican origin. Immigrants brought Mexico's diversity to L.A., with individuals and families from different states within Mexico, as well as that country's many indigenous groups, adding to a complex of regional dialects, cuisines, cultures, and occupational niches. Over six hundred thousand city residents are from other Latin American countries, primarily Guatemala and El Salvador. Major Asian communities in greater L.A. include people of Chinese, Korean, Japanese, Vietnamese, Cambodian, and Filipino descent.[23]

East L.A. continues to be the center of Latino L.A., and South Los Angeles holds a significant share of Los Angeles' African American community. There is still a Chinatown near downtown in the City of L.A. But as members of the middle class from these communities have moved to suburban areas, and immigration has boosted the numbers of Latinos and Asians living in greater Los Angeles, new residential clusters of people of color have emerged in the region. As might be expected, Los Angeles' growing ethnic diversity has not translated into a seamless process of integration. Instead, ethnic dispersal, with new concentrations of non-White residents, can be found throughout the region. These "ethnoburbs," as some social scientists have labeled them, serve as bridges between historical ethnic neighborhoods and the broader region.

The city of Santa Ana, in Orange County, became majority Latino in 1984. By 2000, Santa Ana—the ninth most populous city in California and the county seat of what was once a nearly exclusively White Orange County—had the seventh highest percentage of Latino residents (76.1 percent) of any American city with over one hundred thousand people.[24] What's more, Santa Ana has the highest percentage of Spanish speakers in the country. Seventy-four percent of residents told the Census Bureau that Spanish was their primary language. Ruben Martínez, the owner of Martínez Books and Art Gallery on Main Street in Santa Ana, tracked the same trends, though his documentation was based on language and literature rather than census reports. When Martínez first opened his shop in 1992, 75 percent of sales were English-language books. By 2001, 85 percent were Spanish-language books, a sign that Latino roots in Santa Ana had deepened beyond mere residency and that a cultural transformation was accompanying demographic change.[25]

North of Santa Ana, in L.A. County's eastern San Gabriel Valley, Los Angeles' Asian communities have an equivalent impact on the region's linguistic and cultural landscape. By 1990, the San Gabriel Valley was home to the United States' largest suburban Chinese population, which continued to

TABLE 1. *Total Population and Major Ethnic Groups by Percentage in the Los Angeles Region, 2000*

	Total Population	Latino	White	Asian	African American
City of L.A.	3,695,000	46.9%	29.7%	10%	11.2%
L.A. County	9,519,000	44.6	31.1	11.8	9.5
Orange County	2,846,000	30.8	51.3	13.6	1.7
San Bernardino County	1,709,000	39.2	44	4.7	9.1
Riverside County	1,545,000	51	36.2	3.7	6.2
Ventura County	753,000	33.4	56.8	5.3	1.9
Imperial County	142,000	72.2	20.2	2	4
Six-county Southern California Association of Governments region	16,514,000	40.6	38.9	10.2	7.3

SOURCES: U.S. Census Bureau, *Profile of General Demographic Characteristics*, Census 2000 Summary File 1 (SF 1), 100 percent data for Imperial, Los Angeles, Orange, Riverside, San Bernardino, and Ventura Counties (Washington, D.C., 2001).

grow over the next ten years. The City of Monterey Park, for example, located just east of the City of L.A., was home to sixty thousand residents in 2000, 61.8 percent of whom were Asian and 41.2 percent ethnically Chinese.[26]

Chinese residents of Monterey Park tend to be younger, wealthier, and more likely to speak English than their counterparts in L.A.'s downtown Chinatown. But this surface statistical assimilation does not mean that San Gabriel Valley ethnoburbs are just bedroom communities for L.A.'s Chinese residents. Many more businesses and services catering to Chinese communities, such as Chinese medical clinics, have located in the suburbs rather than in the old Chinatown.[27] If Los Angeles remains a set of suburbs in search of a city, as it has been frequently derided, then the Los Angeles region, through places like Santa Ana and Monterey Park, is also helping to redefine suburbs as more diverse than suburban communities are commonly thought to be.

The African American population of greater Los Angeles has not grown as rapidly in recent years as the region's Latino or Asian communities, and middle-class African American residents have stayed closer to downtown

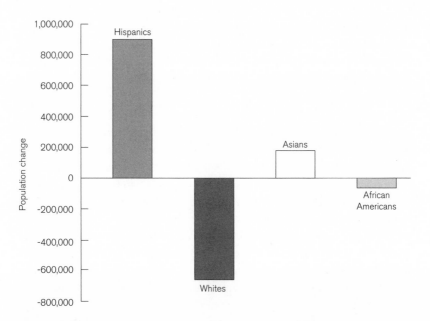

FIGURE 2   Los Angeles County demographic change, 1990–2000. (Source: U.S. Census Bureau, data from 1990 and 2000 decennial censuses.)

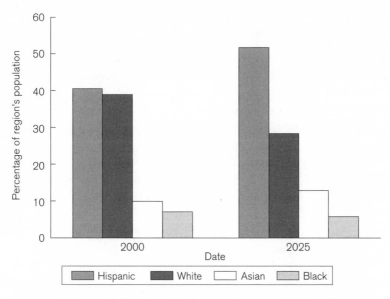

FIGURE 3   Projected demographic change, six-county Los Angeles region, 2000–2025. (Source: Southern California Association of Governments, *Population Growth in the SCAG Region, 1950–2025* [Los Angeles, 2001], 7–8.)

than their Asian or Latino counterparts. As a result, L.A.'s greatest concentrations of Black residents still live in a central band that starts west of downtown and stretches south and east toward Long Beach. New majority–African American ethnoburbs did not coalesce in the 1980s and 1990s. In fact, between 1990 and 2000, some independent cities in South L.A. that historically had been majority Black became evenly split between African American and Latino residents (Inglewood) or became majority Latino (Compton).[28] Meanwhile, a significant number of African Americans moved out of Los Angeles city and its inner suburbs in search of cheaper housing, safer streets, job opportunities, and other amenities. For example, San Bernardino, a city of 185,000 sixty miles east of L.A., was 16 percent Black in 2000, and as much as 28 percent Black in some of the town's zip code areas.[29]

These demographic shifts have been accompanied by the incorporation of a series of new municipalities. The proliferation of new suburbs was, at least in part, an effort by the region's more affluent residents, disproportionately White, to wall themselves off from the poor, from immigrants, and from L.A.'s public schools. Between 1978 and 2000, approximately thirty new cities were formed in the six counties. Although the White share of the region's population dropped from 61 percent to 39 percent during this period, all of the new cities had a White majority upon incorporation.[30]

REWEAVING THE TAPESTRY

In June 2000, more than twenty thousand people packed into L.A.'s downtown sports arena. Many were recent immigrants, waving American flags and the flags of their native countries. The crowd was there for a gathering that would have seemed implausible just a few years earlier: a mass rally *for* immigrant workers' rights, *in* Southern California, *headlined by* national labor leaders.

Six years before that memorable L.A. Convention Center rally, California voters, led by what appeared to be powerful anti-immigrant forces in Southern California, had approved Proposition 187, a draconian anti-immigrant measure, which was designed to force children of undocumented immigrants out of public schools and to punish their parents with up to five years in prison for using false identification to get a job.

Was this the same Los Angeles? And the same question could be asked about the union movement, which had traditionally displayed a nativist and anti-immigrant attitude that dated back more than one hundred years. Recently, the union movement and labor organizing in L.A. had become as diverse as the city. From janitors to city employees to film actors, unions in

L.A. had changed along with the region. Unions began to make inroads among the emerging Latino majority population. For example, when Gigante, Mexico's third largest supermarket company, launched its first stores in Southern California in 1999, the United Food and Commercial Workers (Local 770) immediately focused on the chain, which is unionized in its home country but chose to open as a nonunion shop in the United States. UFCW launched an organizing drive at Gigante and ultimately convinced the company to stay neutral in an election, which UFCW won in 2001. There has also been a significant level of workers' rights education and organizing in Asian communities, focused on L.A.'s sweatshop garment sector. Some unions have even conducted their meetings in multiple languages. In the region's burgeoning informal economy, labor rights groups and unions have helped to win some dignity for street vendors and day laborers of all ethnicities.

The successes and evolution of the Korean Immigrant Workers Advocates (KIWA) offer an example of L.A.'s changing immigrant workforce, and the possibilities of labor and political organizing in a diverse metropolis. KIWA was founded in March 1992, a month before the civil unrest that heightened tensions between Korean shop owners and Black and Latino residents of South and Central Los Angeles. The aftermath of the civil unrest exposed divisions within the Korean community, as a conservative Korean businessowners' group sought to deny relief money to workers in stores shut or destroyed by the unrest. KIWA brought together Korean and Latino workers to demand a share of the assistance.[31] When seventy-two Thai immigrants were freed from an El Monte "slave shop" garment factory in 1995, where they had labored for seventeen hours a day, KIWA helped workers to win over $2 million from retailers and manufacturers that did business with the now notorious slaveshop owners. Through the late 1990s and into the twenty-first century, KIWA continued to assist Asian and Latino workers, targeting Korean-owned businesses, first restaurants and then grocery stores. Their tactics reflected a need for cross-ethnic alliances, exposed the diversity of the immigrant experience, and gave lie to the myth that ethnic groups will always protect their own rather than expanding the circle of justice. KIWA's success, in turn, inspired the development of other new ethnic-based immigrant rights groups, such as the Pilipino Workers Center and the Thai Community Development Center.[32]

Still, the climate facing all immigrants in Los Angeles and in California, particularly vitriolic in the early and mid-1990s, remained hostile, a problem compounded by the policy environment and anti-immigrant sentiments after September 11, 2001. Nevertheless, thanks in part to the immigrant rights movements and their supporters, Proposition 187 never took effect in

California, having been whittled away by lawsuits and the eventual settlement facilitated by a new Democratic governor and attorney general. The shift that took place within organized labor perhaps most directly illustrated the progress toward the inclusion of immigrants and immigrant rights. For decades, unions, led by the national AFL-CIO, had maintained their nativist approach regarding immigration, wary that employers would hire illegal immigrants at lower wages rather than U.S. citizens, thereby displacing union members or suppressing their wages. These employer strategies had been utilized effectively in a number of sectors, including within the janitorial workforce. Policy goals of limiting immigration quotas, especially from poor countries, and cracking down on undocumented workers and their employers went hand in hand with labor's fears.[33]

Labor leaders in Los Angeles, who had experience organizing in immigrant communities, viewed the national union movement's priorities as misplaced. Immigrants weren't a threat; as the most exploited of American workers, they deserved justice and representation and were an untapped pool of potential members who could help to rebuild organized labor in this country. But to fully welcome immigrants into the union fold, labor would have to do two things: clean its house of lingering anti-immigrant biases and policy stances and work for changes in the status of immigrant workers. For as long as employers could hold the threat of deportation over workers' heads, immigrant workers would face significant barriers in their ability to join unions.

The Los Angeles County Federation of Labor and service-sector unions with a tradition of organizing immigrant workers were among the leaders in lobbying inside the AFL-CIO for a new position on immigration and immigrant workers. In February 2000, the AFL-CIO announced a bold switch in its stand on immigration. Its new priorities were to "criminalize employer exploitation of immigrant workers and allow undocumented immigrants who are in the United States and contributing to their communities an opportunity to become U.S. citizens."[34]

It was in this spirit that unions, along with a variety of community groups and religious organizations, led the June 2000 rally in downtown L.A. for amnesty for illegal aliens. Over the next year it seemed that the stars were aligning for a full national discussion on improving the legal status of undocumented immigrants. Political changes in Mexico in particular set the stage for discussions on the possibility of normalization or amnesty for many undocumented residents in the United States, including hundreds of thousands in Southern California. The terrorist attacks of September 11, 2001, significantly dampened the dialogue on immigration and amnesty, but more narrow immigrant justice efforts progressed, even in this far more hostile environment.

In California, for example, the equal opportunity–oriented system of community colleges, the California State Universities, and the University of California campuses had long been economic and cultural stepping-stones into the middle class and political leadership. But immigrant children, even those who had lived in California nearly all of their lives, were forced to pay out-of-state tuition. With such costs four times greater than in-state rates ($10,700 versus $2,800 at CSU, for instance), immigrant high school students from low-income families were priced out of a chance at higher education. In 2000, State Assemblyman Marco Firebaugh, who represented majority Latino communities in southeast Los Angeles, introduced a bill to make immigrant children who were in the process of applying for citizenship eligible for in-state tuition as well as state scholarship funds. The legislation, which had been crafted by a number of the immigrant-rights groups, passed, but it was vetoed by the Democratic governor, Gray Davis. The next year, Firebaugh, backed by the growing immigrant-rights movement, tried again. Even after the terrorist attacks, pressures from students, parents, and immigrant-rights organizations were enough to convince the governor to sign the measure. Passage of this bill, just weeks after September 11, indicated that Los Angeles, and its progressive movements, spoke the language not just of diversity but of the people from many places who had now made Los Angeles home.

ECONOMIC DIVIDE

In 1992 General Motors shut down its Pontiac and Chevy production factory in Van Nuys in the San Fernando Valley. For the region, the closure of the plant was as symbolic as the civil unrest that same year. Automobiles had helped to define the Southern California way of life and shaped its landscape. Ford had opened the region's first auto plant in 1914. Between World War II and the 1960s, the local auto manufacturing industry was second only to Detroit's, rolling out half a million cars every year.[35] In the postwar years, Southern California became an industrial powerhouse, as defense contractors and other heavy industrial sectors opened factories. These plants were quickly unionized—although often with significant labor-management conflict—and thus provided decent-wage jobs that anchored L.A.'s cluster of growing residential suburbs and its middle class.

By the 1980s, impacted in part by competition from imports and the restructuring of the U.S. auto industry, most auto manufacturers had aban-

doned the region. GM's Van Nuys plant was soon the only one left. Over
the course of four decades, GM had built 6 million cars at the Van Nuys site,
but in the early 1980s the company announced plans to relocate the plant's
production to Canada. For the next ten years, while the city's political and
business elites were busy celebrating L.A.'s arrival as a "world city" (which
to them meant glitzy downtown office buildings filled with bankers and
lawyers, and high-tech parks that looked like college campuses), a coalition
of workers and community members successfully pressured GM into temporarily keeping the factory open. But eventually the company prevailed.[36]

GM's decision was part of a steady drumbeat of bad news about factory
closures and laid-off workers in the steel, tires, auto, and aerospace industries. Los Angeles' economic base had already begun to shift away from
heavy manufacturing as well as the residential real estate sector that had
housed the post–World War II entry of working-class residents into middle-
class neighborhoods. Economists called these closures "deindustrialization,"
but the workers used other words to express their outrage.

Los Angeles' economy became increasingly defined by the cluster of
industries that served or profited from international corporations (e.g.,
finance, consulting, accounting, commercial real estate), as well as those
whose products were ever more oriented toward global markets (e.g., the
entertainment industry, which had shifted from a solely domestic audience
to an international one as well). The factory work that remained in L.A. was
primarily the kinds of unskilled, low-wage jobs, such as those in clothing
and food processing, that barely paid enough to live on, rarely provided
health insurance, and typically were not unionized.

The most significant consequence of these changes was the widening
divide of the region's economy, revealing the gap between the working poor,
an eroded middle class, and the region's wealthiest professionals, managers,
and business elite. At the same time, a nationwide economic slowdown that
coincided with the end of the Cold War and a reduction in federal defense
spending wreaked havoc on Southern California's aerospace and related
defense industries in the early 1990s. As then mayor Richard Riordan put it
shortly after taking office in 1993, California had boomed when the state
had been "subsidized by people around the world to build things to kill
people."[37] With the end of the Cold War, the L.A. region, home to a cluster
of defense contractors and military bases, underwent significant job loss
that rippled through much of the economy. The unemployment rate jumped
from 5.9 percent in 1990 to 8.2 percent in 1991, reaching a high of 9.8 percent in 1992 and 1993.[38]

Ordinary Angelenos experienced these trends in very personal ways.

When the L.A. regional economy took a nosedive in the early 1990s, leading to massive layoffs, people were pushed out of jobs and couldn't pay rent; retail stores that depended on their consumer dollars closed down. Between 1969 and 1990, per capita income in the L.A. region rose each year. Then, during the 1991 to 1993 recession, per capita income declined. L.A. had lost ground, with not enough high-wage jobs to go around.

Between 1990 and 1994 the number of manufacturing jobs in the Los Angeles–Long Beach metropolitan area fell 23 percent. Durable-goods manufacturing jobs, the higher-wage and traditionally unionized segment of the manufacturing sector, fell 32 percent in this brief period. Just two major industries, the higher-wage motion pictures industry and lower-wage apparel manufacturing (whose wages were 52 percent below the average salary in Los Angeles County), added workers during the early 1990s.[39]

It would be easy to attribute the 1992 L.A. civil unrest to the recession. There is, in fact, some truth to the idea that the economic downturn influenced those events. But even after L.A. recovered from the recession, it was not out of trouble. Recovery did increase *average* incomes and lift some Angelenos out of poverty, but the long-term trends that were the roots of the unrest—the widening economic divide, the increase in low-wage jobs, the crises of access to affordable health care and housing—remained.

Between 1997 and 2001, L.A. County's unemployment rate fell from 6.8 percent to 5 percent (in the City of L.A., it was about a point higher).[40] The tight labor market, combined with a rise in the federal and state minimum wage, trickled down to some extent to those at the bottom of L.A.'s economic ladder. But most of the fruits of the economic expansion benefited upper-income Angelenos. Year after year, through good times and bad, the region's economy had been diverging onto two tracks. If you had the training, education, and connections to work in the upper end of the services, finance, or entertainment industries or the conceptual (engineering and design) side of manufacturing, times were good. But if, like increasing numbers of Angelenos, your background didn't mesh with these sectors, and you worked in the lower tiers of "light" (nondurable goods) manufacturing, laboring, or services, L.A. hardly seemed like a "world-class" city.

The frequently used term *deindustrialization* didn't accurately characterize Los Angeles. In fact, the region was still the number-one manufacturing region in the United States, but the nature of those jobs had shifted. As late as the early 1980s, two-thirds of L.A. manufacturing jobs were in higher-paid, often unionized industries such as autos, tires, electronics, and aerospace. Even during the 1990s expansion, L.A. continued to hemorrhage high-wage jobs in "heavy" manufacturing (e.g., durable goods, such as cars

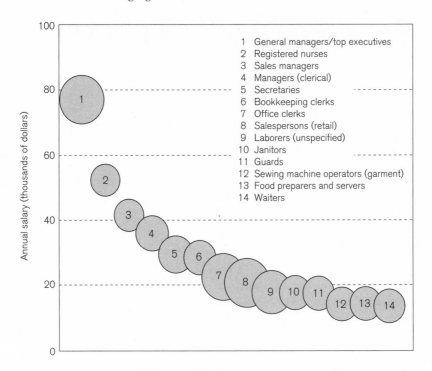

FIGURE 4 Average annual salaries of the fourteen most common jobs in Los Angeles County. The size of the circle represents the number of people employed in the occupation (ranging from around 50,000 to 110,000), while the circle's height on the graph indicates the average annual salary for the position. Note: The salaries given for the highest-paying (executives') and lowest-paying (waiters') jobs graphed are too low. Waiters' tips are not factored in. And many executives make more money than the salary survey's top category, so the salary graphed for executives is the median annual wage rather than the mean annual wage. (Source: California Employment Development Department, *Occupational Employment and Wage Data for Los Angeles–Long Beach MSA [Los Angeles County]* [Sacramento, 2002].)

and airplanes), while adding more low-wage jobs in sweatshops and other "light" factory sectors. By the year 2000, nearly half of regional manufacturing employment was in lower-wage sectors, exemplified by garment, furniture, toy manufacturing, and food processing.[41]

If you didn't want to make sausages or sew clothes, you could look for work in the booming retail and office-work sectors of the area economy. From the early 1970s to the late 1990s the percentage of those employed in services rose from 19.7 percent to 32.5 percent, while all other sources of employment—including the region's second leading job source, trade (encompassing retail, wholesale, and international trade jobs), remained relatively steady.[42]

Unfortunately, many of the most widely available jobs did not pay a "living wage": a salary with benefits that would allow a worker to support a family (or even him- or herself). According to one estimate of the cost of living in Los Angeles, it took an annual wage of $19,311 for a single adult to make ends meet in the L.A. region, $42,485 for a single parent, $35,207 for a two-parent household where one person works, and $51,547 for a household with two working parents. By this reckoning, only eight of the fifteen most common occupations in L.A. County paid (on average) enough to adequately support even a single person.[43]

MARCHING DOWN WILSHIRE

> They may be the invisible underclass of California's booming
> economy, but without them the offices of Los Angeles' rich and
> powerful would be reduced to dust and filth. . . . in a brilliant
> propaganda coup, [the striking janitors] have guaranteed them-
> selves extensive media coverage by refusing to clean the toilets
> at the downtown headquarters of the Los Angeles Times.
>
> *The Independent* (London), April 6, 2000

The nearly two-decades-long campaign waged in L.A. and other parts of the country for "Justice for Janitors" illustrated many of the challenges and opportunities faced by low-wage workforces and progressive movements. When Rodney King was growing up, his father was a janitor. In those days the janitorial workforce was primarily African American, and the salaries were often enough to get by on, thanks in part to union representation. Membership in the local janitors' union peaked at around five thousand in 1978 and wages for union members reached twelve dollars an hour in 1982. Starting in the 1980s, however, the janitorial services industry extensively restructured, including a shift from union representation to medium-sized, nonunion contractors. Contractors pushed for labor-related cost-cutting strategies, while converting union jobs to far lower-paying nonunion jobs (sometimes as low as three to four dollars an hour). At the same time, increasingly toxic cleaning products were introduced, designed in part to serve as labor-saving strategies. Thus, the loss of union jobs and, for many, health benefits, coincided with an increase in occupational hazards and exposure to more toxic substances.[44]

The janitorial workforce also changed. As janitors retired or left the industry, fed up by falling wages and increased health hazards, contractors replaced them with Latino immigrants, largely Mexican at first, then increasingly of Central American origin. Many of these immigrant janitors settled in the Pico-Union neighborhood near downtown. They walked to jobs in high-rise buildings in the downtown area and bused to office towers in Century City, catching buses in the afternoon and the middle of the night. A majority of the new immigrant workforce was female. A union organizer described the owners' labor-force rationale as "be cheap" and keep them "controllable."[45]

But where the cleaning-services companies and their clients saw a quiescent, exploitable workforce, others sensed the potential for mobilization. Local 1877 in Los Angeles of the Service Employees International Union (SEIU), which had lost more than half of its janitor members during the 1980s, decided, in conjunction with the national Justice for Janitors (JfJ) initiative of the international union, to scale up efforts to organize the now largely nonunion janitorial workforce. After an initial campaign in Denver, JfJ focused on Los Angeles as its first major test. Faced with the difficulties of organizing workers in an industry with two levels of "bosses," the contractors and the building owners, the campaign moved beyond a building-by-building organizing approach to take on the entire industry and try to organize its largely recent-immigrant, Latina workforce.[46]

The JfJ campaign raised traditional wage and benefit demands but broadened them to craft an appeal based on worker dignity. It utilized street protests and guerrilla theater to attract media attention, win support from civic leaders, and shame employers, including the cleaning contractors, and some of the wealthy law firms, banks, and other blue-chip tenants that occupied the buildings the janitors cleaned each night. In Los Angeles, JfJ first went after the gas company, a high-profile, quasi-public utility vulnerable to political pressure. To increase the pressure on its next target, a small private company, the union tracked its owner to his favorite restaurant and his golf course: a move emblematic of the movement's "no justice, no peace!" approach.

The going wasn't easy at first. In June 1990, with janitors engaged in a general strike against the building owners and contractors in Century City, a high-rise, commercial district that epitomized the commercial development strategy that city leaders and business had pursued in the 1980s, dozens of those attending a rally in support of the strike, including pregnant women, were assaulted by police. But the workers vowed to redouble their efforts, and video footage of the police violence convinced SEIU's sister local in New York City to pressure one of the key contractors (whose New York operations were unionized) to agree to terms with the union's Los Angeles counterpart. Worried about the potential for the strike to spread, the contractor came to terms with the L.A. local soon afterward. This victory helped to convince the international union that the Justice for Janitors campaign could be expanded throughout the country.[47]

By 2000, with some union contracts up for renewal and the nonunion workforce still a considerable percentage of the overall workforce, the Los Angeles union decided to launch a countywide strike. In many ways, the terrain had changed, favoring the janitors. The strong economy made the contractors' initial refusal to grant a three-year, dollar-per-hour salary increase seem heartless in a robust economy.[48] The public response, in turn, was overwhelmingly supportive of the janitors. Not a day went by without an article or column in the *Los Angeles Times* about how the struggle of the primarily Latino janitors reflected L.A.'s class and ethnic divisions. The Republican mayor, Richard Riordan, who had refused to sign a living wage ordinance three years earlier, told the building owners they should pay up. L.A.'s Cardinal Roger Mahoney held a mass for the strikers, while Rabbi Steven Jacobs conducted a labor-oriented Passover Seder. Several members of the L.A. City Council were arrested for civil disobedience in support of the janitors. Some members of the state legislature sat on the janitors' side of the table during bargaining sessions. Members of Congress addressed rallies. Senators Ted Kennedy and Dianne Feinstein and Vice President Al Gore came to town and spoke for their cause.

On Friday, April 7, 2000, the janitors of SEIU Local 1877 marched down Wilshire Boulevard from downtown Los Angeles through Beverly Hills to Century City, roughly an eight-mile walk. Ten years earlier, another such march had culminated in the confrontation where police had set upon the marchers in Century City, beating and injuring scores of demonstrators. This time L.A. city attorney (and soon to be mayor) James Hahn walked in the front row of the parade, flanked by a dozen other elected officials, as well as Jesse Jackson and a host of ministers, priests, and rabbis. But that was not the only thing that was different about the April march down Wilshire Boulevard.

As the janitors left downtown, observers—few had known in advance about the march—started coming out of their buildings or leaned out of windows giving a thumbs-up sign. After a couple of miles, people watching from the sidewalk started to cheer. Then, as the march reached Beverly Hills, people on the sidewalk—first one, then a couple, then several—did something that had never been seen before. People darted into the street and handed the janitors cash. Office workers also emerged from high-rise buildings to raise a fist in support or flash a sign of victory. As SEIU official Eliseo Medina remarked, "In the past we were used to getting only one finger, so this [victory sign] was a welcome change."[49]

A little more than two weeks after that memorable march on Wilshire, L.A.'s janitors won a considerable wage increase of about 26 percent, spread over three years. The janitors who worked in unionized buildings, including almost all of the downtown and Century City buildings, saw their hourly pay rise from just under eight dollars to just over ten dollars. Janitors in nonunion buildings saw an even greater percentage increase.

This victory for economic justice was in the best tradition of Progressive L.A. In a sense, progressive movements in Los Angeles had come full circle. Organizing among recent immigrants had revitalized the labor movement, which in turn fought for just treatment of immigrant workers and communities, and for all of Los Angeles. The struggle for a more just Los Angeles in turn became one of the cornerstones for establishing a different kind of economic, political, social, and cultural fabric designed to overcome L.A.'s continuing divide.

MAGICAL DIVIDES: ONE CITY . . . OR MANY?

"Some man wrote me a letter. 'To Mrs. Young . . . I saw your interview on television [during the riots]. As far as I'm concerned, you're a dumb shit bimbo talking about having fun during the riots at the Polo Lounge. . . .' I mean, oh my God, if he had only left his number, so I can call and explain that in no way did I mean to be so flippant. . . . It was like people hanging out together, like safety in numbers. No one can hurt us at the Beverly Hills Hotel 'cause it was like a fortress."

ELAINE YOUNG, REAL ESTATE AGENT,
QUOTED IN ANNA DEVEARE SMITH, *Twilight: Los Angeles, 1992*

In 2001, according to *Forbes* magazine, thirty-nine of the four hundred richest individuals in America, including twenty-two billionaires, lived in Los Angeles or Orange County. For the most part, these ultrarich Southern Californians maintained primary residences in a limited number of tony L.A. neighborhoods and upper-income coastal communities. The City of L.A. headed the list with twenty-two superrich residents, seven in the gated Bel Air section alone. Eight lived in Beverly Hills, three in Newport Beach, and one each in Malibu, Laguna Hills, Laguna Beach, Pasadena, Palisades, and an unspecified location in Orange County.[50]

A divorce proceeding that same year pierced the veil concealing the lifestyles of L.A.'s rich and famous. According to court records, the three-year-old daughter of Kirk Kerkorian, owner of MGM movie studio and MGM Mirage Casino, racked up such monthly expenses as $14,000 for play

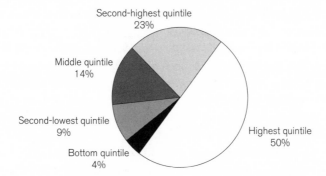

Second-highest quintile
23%

Middle quintile
14%

Second-lowest quintile
9%

Bottom quintile
4%

Highest quintile
50%

FIGURE 5 Income distribution in the Long Beach–Los Angeles metropolitan area, 1999. (Source: Neeta Fogg and Paul Harrington, *Growth and Change in the California and Long Beach/Los Angeles Labor Markets* [Center for Labor Market Study, Northeastern University, 3 May 2001].)

dates and parties and $436 for bunny care. If true, this meant that Kyra "spent" 45 times as much as the average Angeleno on food eaten at home; 86 times as much on food eaten out; and 283 times as much on parties, play dates, movies, theaters, and outings as the average L.A. resident spends on all entertainment.[51]

This kind of income divide grew enormously in Los Angeles during the 1990s. Between 1990 and 2000, the number of families in L.A. with incomes of $150,000 or greater jumped 79 percent. Households in L.A. County with a net worth of at least $5 million (excluding the value of their primary residence) rose 37 percent from 1995 to 2000. And the number of local billionaires nearly tripled from 8 in 1997 to 22 in 2001. Meanwhile, between 1990 and 2000, median household income fell in the City of Los Angeles and in L.A., Orange, Riverside, and San Bernardino Counties. By the decade's end, the number of people living below the federal poverty line in the L.A. region had increased by 650,000—almost the population of San Francisco.[52]

Income inequality was greater in L.A. than in the state of California or the United States as a whole. The richest fifth of the population of the Los Angeles–Long Beach metropolitan area earned $13 for every $1 earned by the poorest fifth—compared to a national ratio of $10.6 to $1.[53] Inequality of wealth and purchasing power was greater, since a disproportionate percentage of the stock market gains of the 1990s had gone to the region's wealthiest. In 2001, the combined net worth of the fifty wealthiest Angelenos was $76 billion. That's greater than that of the region's 9 million poorest residents![54]

Los Angeles' outrageous inequality paralleled all the region's fault lines, including ethnicity, immigration status, and geography. The median household income of Anglos and Asians in L.A. County ($47,000 and $42,000) was higher than that of Blacks and Latinos ($28,000 and $27,000). Poverty was twice as common among Asians as among Anglos, a reflection of the diversity of their immigrant experience. Immigrant families on the whole were poorer than families headed by U.S.-born parents, with an especially large gap between the median income of native-born households ($53,000) and recent-immigrant households ($21,800).

Income, wealth, and poverty also varied widely by geographical area within the region. In general, the eastern, inland, and flat areas were poorer, typified by the crowded neighborhoods of East L.A., the Central L.A. city area, and the older areas of San Bernardino, Riverside, and the desert beyond. Coastal and foothill zones, where views and natural amenities have boosted real estate prices, tended to be upper-income areas. Some of the starkest contrasts were between different parts of Los Angeles. Consider four L.A. communities—East L.A., South Central, Eagle Rock, and Bel Air—as samplings of the city's residential areas.

Although there are rich and poor people within each racial and ethnic group, the demographics of a neighborhood usually indicates something about its economic condition. East L.A. and South Central L.A. are among the poorest parts of the city. East L.A. is over 90 percent Latino. South Central, the historical center of Black life in L.A, is about evenly split between Latino and African American residents. Eagle Rock is a middle-income neighborhood adjacent to Pasadena and Glendale, with a mix of homes and businesses. Around 40 percent of its residents are Latino, 30 percent White, and 30 percent Asian. Bel Air, one of L.A.'s richest neighborhoods, is approximately 85 percent White, the epitome of the wealthier areas of L.A.'s Westside.[55]

Residents of the 90033 zip code in East L.A. and the 90059 zip code in South Central got by on incomes of $4,600 to $5,400 per person. Residents of Eagle Rock (zip code 90041) made three times as much; Bel Air residents twelve times more. L.A.'s income gap translated into political influence. In general, wealthier areas and individuals enjoy greater access to those in positions of power. For example, residents of the 90033 zip code in East L.A. gave just 18¢ per person in campaign contributions during the 2000 federal election and the 2001 Los Angeles mayor's race. Donations from Bel Air averaged $234 per person in the same election cycles: over a thousand times more. The vast majority of Los Angeles mayor James Hahn's appointments to official city commissions in his first months in office in 2001 came from affluent sections of the Westside and the San Fernando Valley, adding to the

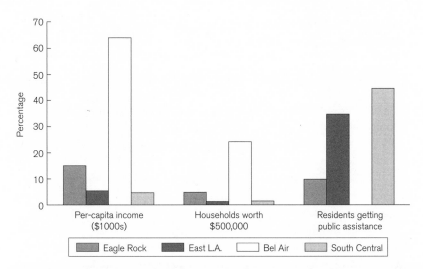

FIGURE 6   Inequalities of wealth: four Los Angeles zip codes. (Sources: U.S. Census Bureau, Summary File 3 [SF 3], sample data for zip codes 90033, 90041, 90059, and 90077 [Washington, D.C., 2002]; United Way of Greater Los Angeles, *Los Angeles County Zip Code Data Book* [Los Angeles, 1999].)

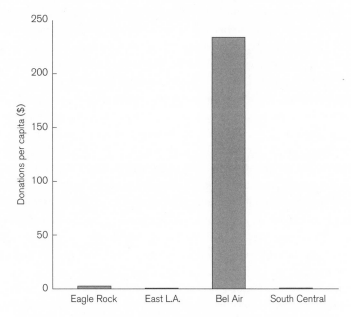

FIGURE 7   Per capita campaign contributions, 2000 (federal) and 2001 (mayoral) elections: four Los Angeles zip codes. (Sources: Los Angeles City Ethics Commission and Center for Responsive Politics, www.opensecrets.org.)

reality and the perception that L.A. is run at the behest of the city's wealth-ier neighborhoods.[56]

BRIDGING THE DIVIDE

Before May 1997, Pablo Morales, an immigrant from Guatemala, earned $5.45 an hour at his job as a janitor at Los Angeles International Airport (LAX). With the City of L.A. outsourcing most janitorial jobs at the airport, the zoo, and other public facilities, Morales and his colleagues were part of the vast pool of working poor having to get by on minimum-wage salaries. (If they were lucky enough to be part of the legal economy, since the pay for many immigrants working off the books was often below the legal mini-mum.) For Morales, getting by meant living in a garage in the city of Compton with his sister, her husband, and their two children. The garage was unfurnished, so the extended family slept on cardboard. Morales did not make enough money to afford a car, instead catching a bus before dawn for the two-hour ride to LAX.

By early 1999, Pablo Morales's salary had risen to $7.39 an hour. The contractor at the airport had started providing health insurance as well. With the extra money, Morales and his sister's family could afford to rent an eight-hundred-square-foot apartment, furnished with beds and furniture rather than cardboard boxes. Morales, the primary breadwinner, had bought a used car to get to work.[57] Morales's jump in income did not come about because of the rising tide of a growing economy. He was instead the benefi-ciary of a new law, inspired by a new social movement.

Despite the wide economic and political disparities that existed in L.A., lower-income workers were not without a voice. In the 1990s, L.A.'s social- and economic-justice advocates, including its newly energized labor move-ment emboldened by a growing, diverse membership, decided to focus on local and regional policies that had underwritten high-status cultural build-ings and supported hotels and offices for corporate executives while allow-ing vast numbers of workers to languish in low-paying jobs, overcrowded housing, and dangerous neighborhoods. As the centerpiece of this justice agenda, unions linked with religious leaders, community groups, and other progressive activists to press the City of Los Angeles to adopt a living wage ordinance that would require private contractors that do business with the city or receive public subsidies to pay their workers more than the mini-mum wage: a "living wage" that would better allow workers to support their families.

During the mid-1990s, this progressive coalition, convened under the auspices of the Los Angeles Alliance for a New Economy (LAANE), faced off against the business community and Richard Riordan, L.A.'s Republican mayor. Building their case on the commonsense proposition that public spending shouldn't be subsidizing poverty jobs that leave workers dependent on government programs, the labor and community alliance was able to convince the Los Angeles City Council to unanimously pass a living wage ordinance in March 1997. In May of the same year, the council overrode the mayor's veto. The adopted living wage ordinance required L.A. city contractors and companies receiving $25,000 or more in city funds or subsidies to pay $7.25 an hour with health coverage, or $8.50 without health benefits. These wage floors have since increased.

Soon after the living wage ordinance was passed in L.A., activists and unions in the nearby coastal city of Santa Monica decided to push the concept one step further. Much of Santa Monica's economic development efforts had aimed at stimulating tourism in the beachfront areas. The direct and indirect aid Santa Monica had provided to coastal businesses had not trickled down to thousands of luxury-hotel workers along the coast, who earned an average annual salary of $14,250 and received no heath benefits, proof that the "tale of two cities" bifurcation of the region's economy was a reality even in affluent Westside beach communities.

Santa Monicans Allied for Responsible Tourism (SMART), a clergy-community coalition that had formed to investigate labor abuses in the hotel industry, took the lead in developing a new kind of living wage law. While all previous successful efforts across the nation had placed obligations only on companies with a specific financial connection to local government, the Santa Monica proposal sought to require all large, private employers in a "coastal zone" (basically, a few large hotels) to pay a minimum, set living wage that was considerably higher than the requirement in adjacent Los Angeles. Workers and their allies argued that the general investments and support that Santa Monica had pumped into the tourism industry in that zone justified the requirement. In 1999, the Santa Monica City Council tentatively agreed, launching a study of SMART's proposal.

To head off regulation, the big coastal zone hotels devised a backdoor way to kill the proposal: they sponsored a weak living wage initiative of their own to preclude stronger rules down the road. Despite the ingenuity displayed by the hotels, SMART was able to mobilize enough grassroots awareness to defeat the hotels' initiative. Then, in May 2001, Santa Monica adopted an innovative living wage ordinance based on SMART's proposal. In 2002, the hotels once again sought to undermine the new law, through an initiative to repeal the council's action. After the hotels had spent over four hundred thousand dollars to qualify the initiative for the ballot, and a significant amount on a campaign that, among other messages, compared the targeting of large hotels to discrimination against Jews and other minorities, Santa Monicans narrowly voted to repeal the ordinance.[58]

While living wage laws do not apply to all workers, they do improve the lot of thousands of workers while building the case that public investment should create good jobs. In this sense they bear the seeds of broader efforts to transform local government's development efforts and bridge the gap between the two tiers of L.A.'s economy.

To live and work in L.A. continues to be an enormous challenge for low-income residents, including immigrants and those employed in the low-wage sectors, who make up a larger and larger percentage of the workforce. In relation to its economy and demographic changes, Los Angeles is increasingly a tale of two cities. But living and working in L.A. have been made easier and more viable by the growing strength of its social and economic justice movements. The victories these movements have helped to secure for inclusion and economic justice are themselves in the best traditions of Progressive L.A., and they ultimately have created some of the foundations of a more just and livable city.

PHOTOGRAPH 1 Job Harriman, circa 1911. Harriman, a labor lawyer and Socialist leader, was nearly elected mayor of Los Angeles in 1911. (Courtesy of University of Southern California, on behalf of the USC Specialized Libraries and Archival Collections.)

PHOTOGRAPH 2   Dora Haynes, 1919. Haynes led the campaign to win women the right to vote in California elections and organized the Los Angeles chapter of the League of Women Voters. (Reprinted with the permission of the John Randolph Haynes and Dora Haynes Foundation.) ˙

PHOTOGRAPH 3   Writer and political activist Upton Sinclair an-
nounces his candidacy for governor of California, 1933. (Courtesy
of University of Southern California, on behalf of the USC Specialized Libraries and Archival Collections.)

PHOTOGRAPH 4 International Ladies Garment Workers' Union organizer Rose Pesotta being arrested during a 1941 strike. Pesotta led the predominantly Latina workforce in the garment industry in one of the few industrywide strikes in Los Angeles' history. (Reprinted courtesy of the Herald Examiner Collection/Los Angeles Public Library.)

PHOTOGRAPH 5   The alleged leaders of the so-called Zoot Suit riots appear before the grand jury, 1943. (Reprinted courtesy of the Herald Examiner Collection/Los Angeles Public Library.)

PHOTOGRAPH 6   The Laws family awaits trial for buying a house in violation of a restrictive covenant, 1945. This case triggered a grassroots crusade for civil rights and better housing. (Reprinted courtesy of the Southern California Library for Social Studies and Research, Los Angeles, CA.)

PHOTOGRAPH 7 Amigos de Wallace rally, 1948. Former vice president Henry Wallace was running for president, on the Progressive Party ticket, on a platform that challenged the Cold War, the arms buildup, and racial segregation. (Reprinted courtesy of the Southern California Library for Social Studies and Research, Los Angeles, CA.)

PHOTOGRAPH 8   Rally to free the Hollywood Ten, 1949. The Hollywood Ten was a group of screenwriters, producers, and directors who were convicted of contempt and jailed for their refusal to "name names" before the House Un-American Activities Committee. (Reprinted courtesy of the Southern California Library for Social Studies and Research, Los Angeles, CA.)

PHOTOGRAPH 9   Dorothy Healey, longtime chairwoman of the Communist Party's Southern California District, in jail, 1949. (Courtesy of University of Southern California, on behalf of the USC Specialized Libraries and Archival Collections.)

PHOTOGRAPH 10   Charlotta Bass, activist and editor-publisher of the *California Eagle*, 1950. (Reprinted courtesy of the Herald Examiner Collection/Los Angeles Public Library.)

PHOTOGRAPH 11   Edward Roybal, 1956. Roybal was the first Latino in the twentieth century to be elected to the Los Angeles City Council; he was also the first Latino congressman from California in the twentieth century. (Courtesy of University of Southern California, on behalf of the USC Specialized Libraries and Archival Collections.)

PHOTOGRAPH 12   Augustus Hawkins, 1961. Hawkins was a California assemblyman and later the first African American congressman from California. (Courtesy
of University of Southern California, on behalf of the USC Specialized Libraries and
Archival Collections.)

PHOTOGRAPH 13   L.A. City Councilman Tom Bradley debates Mayor Sam Yorty
in 1973. After losing the mayor's race to Yorty in 1969, Bradley won the 1973 rematch, becoming Los Angeles' first African American mayor. (Reprinted courtesy of
the Herald Examiner Collection/Los Angeles Public Library. Photograph by Sergio
Ortiz.)

PHOTOGRAPH 14   Pete Beltram, far left, president of the United Auto Workers Local 645; Cesar Chávez, second from left, founder of the United Farm Workers; and Maxine Waters, California assemblywoman (and, later, congresswoman), march in support of workers at General Motors plant in Van Nuys, 1983. (Reprinted courtesy of the Herald Examiner Collection/Los Angeles Public Library. Photograph by Mike Sergieff.)

PHOTOGRAPH 15   Justice for Janitors rally, 1989. The Justice for Janitors movement helped reinvigorate the organizing thrust of the labor movement. (Reprinted courtesy of the Herald Examiner Collection/Los Angeles Public Library.)

PHOTOGRAPH 16   Los Angeles public school students rally against Proposition 187, 1994. Although Proposition 187—the initiative intended to deny the use of public facilities, including schools and hospitals, to undocumented immigrants—was approved by voters, it was struck down by courts and had the effect of politically mobilizing Latinos. (Reprinted courtesy of the Security Pacific Collection/Los Angeles Public Library. Photograph by Gary Leonard.)

PHOTOGRAPH 17   Los Angeles City Councilwoman (and, later, State Assembly-woman) Jackie Goldberg (right) celebrates after passage of the Los Angeles living wage ordinance, 1997. Goldberg became one of the most effective advocates for the range of social movements that constituted Progressive L.A. (Reprinted courtesy of the Office of Assemblywoman Jackie Goldberg.)

PHOTOGRAPH 18 Los Angeles City Councilman (and, later, State Assemblyman) Mark Ridley-Thomas, 1999. In the 1990s, Ridley-Thomas became a strong voice for neighborhood development, environmental justice, and affordable housing. (Reprinted courtesy of the Security Pacific Collection/Los Angeles Public Library. Photograph by Gary Leonard.)

PHOTOGRAPH 19 Members of the Association of Community Organizations for Reform Now (ACORN) rally at Los Angeles City Hall, 2000. (Reprinted courtesy of Los Angeles ACORN.)

4　Stresses in Eden

Los Angeles on the Edge

LIVING IN LOS ANGELES

To live in Los Angeles can be an enormous stress and burden, given its geographic expanse, its economic divide, and its conditions of daily life.

Consider Arturo and Claudia Ramos, both in their late twenties. He is a waiter at a hotel in Santa Monica, where he earns, with tips, a little more than twice the state minimum wage—about $23,000 a year. They have two children—a six-year-old daughter and an infant son. Claudia worked part-time as a waitress until their son was born. They now live in a tiny one-bedroom apartment in Hollywood. They pay $675 a month in rent and another $80 monthly for gas and electricity. Each year, $9,060 goes for rent—about 40 percent of their household income. All four members of the Ramos family sleep in the same small room. Jesus's crib is nestled in one corner, Teresa's bed sits in another corner, and the parents' bed rests in a third corner. The sixty-unit building has no place, inside or outside, for the children to play. Arturo often has to fix leaky faucets and the toilet because the manager claims the handyman is unavailable.

Arturo works the 6 A.M. to 2 P.M. shift and travels forty miles round-trip every day to work—about an hour each way at a minimum, and far longer if he has to experience any of L.A.'s notorious freeway crawls or "sig alerts"—because rents in buildings closer to his job are even higher. Even with this sacrifice, after paying for food, gas, car repairs, and clothing, the family has nothing left, is frequently in debt, and has had problems paying the rent. They've received several eviction notices for late payment, but Arturo persuaded the landlord to let them remain after they borrowed money and paid what was due. Arturo is thinking about getting a second job, but that would mean he would rarely see his children.[1]

It's not just those at the lowest end of the economic divide who face daily life stresses in Southern California. Sally and Howard Edwards are both in their mid-thirties; she is a receptionist at a hospital in Glendale, he is a fire-fighter in Los Angeles. Their combined income is almost seventy thousand dollars, putting them in the top 20 percent of households in L.A. County, where the median household income is about forty-two thousand dollars. They have two sons—a six-year-old and a five-year-old. For nine years after they were married, they lived in the same apartment in Pasadena. They spent several years looking for a house to buy. They wanted to live in a community with good schools and at a reasonable commuting distance from their jobs. They almost gave up before they found a two-bedroom house in Palmdale, at the northern edge of Los Angeles County, for $210,000. Payments for the house, insurance, and property taxes absorb more than a third of their income. The commute from Palmdale to their jobs takes each of them at least an hour, sometimes ninety minutes. Since they both get home from work between 6:30 and 7 p.m. each night, they have to pay someone to pick up their kids from school, take care of them, and give them dinner. To make ends meet, and to save enough to buy the house, several years ago they stopped taking a yearly vacation, stopped going out to eat in restaurants, and stopped going out to movies.

These realities of daily life constitute a part of Los Angeles' livability crisis, including, as in the case of the Ramos and Edwards families, a serious and growing lack of affordable housing, a skewed transportation system, and a disconnection between jobs and housing. Clearly, Los Angeles is still a stressful place to live, when ordinary people can't afford to live there, when their commute to work consumes a major part of the day, when they are transit-dependent in a region that has come to be synonymous with what Reyner Banham calls the "auto-ecology" of Los Angeles, or when their neighborhoods lack good schools or are short of places to play, access to health care, or places to buy fresh food.[2]

Los Angeles at its best is a city of linked, vibrant neighborhoods, with homes, stores, and civic buildings in a diverse palette of architectural styles across the Southern California landscape. The victims of residential segregation have historically been left out of the idealized Southern California image of an orange tree–flanked bungalow. Even so, successive generations of migrants from across the United States and from other countries have at least partially succeeded against the odds in creating neighborhoods where families can raise children, workers find steady employment, entrepreneurs start small businesses, and residents become engaged in the community.

L.A.'s neighborhoods have survived and occasionally even thrived despite the problems plaguing the region.

But the families who live in Los Angeles face pressures large and small that conspire against livability. Spiraling housing costs. Outdated transportation planning still closely wedded to the losing cause of adding more highways to fight traffic gridlock. Troubled and underfunded public schools. Distrust between law enforcement and some communities that the police are charged to protect. Food insecurity just miles from what had been some of the world's richest agricultural land. A toxic legacy of industrial waste mixing with a sea of vehicular emissions. A shortage of parks and a desperate need for urban oases.

This chapter documents the problems of living in Los Angeles. It also identifies the environmental and social justice movements and their policy agendas to address these issues. The problems of living in Los Angeles represent a challenge for Progressive L.A.'s quest not only to improve the quality of life in the region for all its residents, but also to establish a sense of place and more just conditions for its diverse communities.

WHERE CAN WE LIVE, HOW CAN WE LIVE?
THE CRISIS OF AFFORDABLE HOUSING

In the 1950s, when the bulldozers removed the last of the small family homes that had dotted Chavez Ravine just north and west of downtown Los Angeles to make way for construction of a new icon for Los Angeles, Dodger Stadium, the city's political and economic leaders, its newspapers, and many of its baseball-loving residents welcomed this L.A. version of urban renewal. The razing of a Latino neighborhood in Chavez Ravine followed the redevelopment of the adjacent Bunker Hill area, which had destroyed another Latino working-class neighborhood to make way for the elite-sponsored Music Center (and subsequent commercial and high-rise developments).

These two episodes were skirmishes in a protracted battle waged over subsidized housing and the fate of working-class neighborhoods that stood in the way of the corporate elite's redevelopment plans. Ironically, Los Angeles had started removing families from Chavez Ravine in the 1950s, with the original intent of building affordable housing developments in place of single-family homes. But as the 1950s progressed, the city's conservative forces likened the proposed project to Socialism—and pulled the plug. With the defeat of public housing and the uprooting of the Bunker Hill and Chavez Ravine neighborhoods, the cause of affordable housing was set back for decades.[3]

More than four decades after the bulldozers had gutted the homes of Chavez Ravine, another sports stadium extravaganza—the construction of the Staples Center in downtown Los Angeles—also destroyed homes and forced low-income residents to relocate to less desirable and less secure places.[4] The Staples Center development revealed an accelerating shortage of affordable housing.

Indeed, as measured by the mismatch between high numbers of low-income residents and the small amount of affordably priced housing available, the Los Angeles metropolitan area has experienced the largest affordable-housing gap in the country.[5] Making matters worse, up through 2001 the City of Los Angeles dedicated almost no local financial resources to improving its housing situation.[6] In 2000, New York City, with twice L.A.'s population, spent more than fifty times the amount on housing that Los Angeles did: $265 million versus just $5 million.

Major housing developers in Southern California like to argue that new subdivisions are the answer to affordable-housing needs. But if one compares maps of the L.A. region from the end of World War II and the start of the twenty-first century, one might assume, following the logic of those developers, that Los Angeles would have housing to spare, given all the conversion of agricultural and marginal land to subdivisions. It's symptomatic of the region's poorly planned growth that despite decades of massive residential development, Los Angeles' housing stock didn't increase and diversify enough to meet the needs of an expanding population.

Two trends stand out as prime culprits. Sprawling development patterns have meant that most new housing has been built in outlying areas. In the late 1960s and early 1970s, about half of new housing permits issued in the region were for construction in L.A. County. By the late 1990s, just 25 to 30 percent of new housing starts were in L.A. County, even though almost 60 percent of the region's residents still lived there.[7] Over the same period, the number of new apartments fell precipitously: from 270,000 units in the 1980s to only 56,000 in the 1990s.[8]

As a result, each year the housing crisis gets worse. The Southern California Association of Governments (SCAG) has estimated that the City of Los Angeles needs eight thousand units annually just to keep up with population growth. The housing squeeze, especially in central areas and the lower end of the price range, has left many Los Angeles residents with two bad choices. They have to either spend a huge percentage of their incomes on housing in the city or nearby suburbs or move to cheaper areas inland, as the Ramos and Edwards families have done.

By the late 1990s, rising house prices meant that many middle-class people, such as elementary school teachers, electrical engineers, and police officers, couldn't afford to buy a house in Los Angeles.[9] In 2000, two-thirds of American families owned their own homes. The homeownership rates in California (57 percent), L.A. County (48 percent), and the City of L.A. (39 percent) were much lower.

At the same time, rent levels in Los Angeles broke the budgets of low-income workers such as nursing aides, secretaries, janitors, and garment workers. The average rent of $1,220 per month for a two-bedroom apartment was far beyond the reach of minimum-wage earners (who would have to work 151 hours a week to afford that amount).[10] Renters had to go without health and child care to scrape together rent payments. Two out of five renter households paid more than half their income in rent.[11] Many renters were also forced to accept substandard housing. About one out of seven apartments—more than 125,000 units—was substandard, while 30 percent of all households lived in overcrowded conditions.[12]

CREATING NEW FOUNDATIONS

On December 8, 2000, thirty-one-year-old Juan Pineda, from Guatemala, a father of two children, was crushed to death when a two-story slum apartment building in Los Angeles' Echo Park neighborhood collapsed. Another thirty-six low-income tenants—mainly immigrant garment workers, day laborers, and their children—were injured. More than one hundred residents were left temporarily homeless. For years, tenants had complained about the building's numerous health and safety violations, including a faulty foundation, but city housing inspectors allowed the absentee landlord to get away with only minor repairs.[13]

Those who often can't afford even this sort of crowded, run-down housing—the most unfortunate ones of all—slip in and out of the ranks of the homeless. In 2000, there were 84,000 homeless people in L.A. County on any given night. Around 240,000 people were homeless for part of each year, but there were just 13,652 beds in homeless shelters in the whole county.[14]

In January 2002, a little more than a year after the Echo Park building collapsed, Mayor James Hahn announced plans for a $100 million annual Housing Trust Fund—the largest in the country—to expand the city's supply of affordable housing. A dedicated annual Housing Trust Fund was the brainchild of Housing L.A., a broad coalition of labor unions, community organizations, and housing groups. Hahn's announcement was the culmination of their two-year grassroots campaign, which was, according to State

Assemblywoman Jackie Goldberg, a former L.A. City Council member, "the most important progressive victory in the city since the Living Wage law was adopted in 1997."[15]

During Mayor Richard Riordan's two terms, the city used none of its own funds to subsidize affordable housing. Tenants' groups, nonprofit housing developers, and homeless advocates had little success in getting city officials or the local media to make housing a priority. Housing advocates were able to achieve a dramatic turnabout in the city's political priorities by forming coalitions with religious groups, community groups, and unions, including those that represented the working poor, who bore the brunt of the housing crisis, as well as the building trades, whose members built some of the housing.[16]

The Housing L.A. coalition recruited Cardinal Roger Mahoney and L.A. County Federation of Labor head Miguel Contreras as cochairs, and it engaged rank-and-file members of endorsing organizations to successfully elevate housing issues during the 2001 mayoral and City Council elections. To gain the support of L.A.'s fragmented business community, the coalition pointed out that many major employers faced problems in recruiting workers because of the region's high housing costs. Two influential business lobby groups endorsed the general idea of a trust fund but opposed the coalition's proposal to fund part of it with a "linkage" fee on commercial developers.

In the months before the 2001 elections, Housing L.A. invited every candidate to a series of housing tours, which made tangible the city's grim housing realities, contrasting slums, tiny apartments, high rent, peeling lead paint, and vermin with well-designed, affordable buildings sponsored by nonprofit developers in the same neighborhoods. Eventually each mayoral candidate supported the concept of a municipal Housing Trust Fund, and continued pressure from the coalition kept the idea alive in the face of budget pressures that followed the September 11, 2001, terrorist attacks. At the press conference announcing the adoption of the trust fund, held at a housing construction site, carpenters temporarily stopped hammering to allow the assembled reporters to hear the speakers' remarks. "Keep working," Hahn told them. "We need the housing."[17]

WALKABLE NEIGHBORHOODS AND PLEASURE RIDES: CHALLENGING THE FREEWAY CULTURE

John Grant, a lawyer with the United Food and Commercial Workers Union, in Los Angeles, tells a story about a union member that suggests why transportation is such an overwhelming concern for people who live and work in Los Angeles. The member, a supermarket clerk, lived in Downey, at the Los Angeles County–Orange County border. The store where she worked was about twenty miles to the east, in Central Los Angeles. Her family owned one car, but it broke down, forcing the clerk to take two buses to get to her job. The first ride followed a north-south route on Crenshaw Boulevard; from there she transferred to a bus that traveled along an east-west axis on Florence Boulevard. The route resembled a triangle more than a direct line and took up to two hours. The Crenshaw line was often so crowded that she couldn't catch the first bus that came by. Compounding her problems, the stop where she caught the second bus had been the site of two recent rapes. As a result of the dangers, especially at night, and the unpredictability of the bus service, the UFCW member refused to work a mandatory "overtime" shift that lasted until 8 P.M. When she refused, she was fired.

The union was able to get the worker reinstated, but her story highlights the transportation hurdles that many Angelenos have to negotiate, particularly low-income residents, who are the most dependent on public transit. For Los Angeles, as everyone knows, has long been car country, even as the car commute from home to work, let alone trips to other places such as shopping or child care locales, has become increasingly stressful.

That debate over transportation policy—the relative importance of cars, mass transit, and walking—came into play with the development of the Arroyo Seco Parkway in the 1930s and 1940s. It was the first grade-separated, limited-access, high-speed divided road in the West. Built in three major stages, from 1938 to 1953, the 8.2-mile highway, stretching from Pasadena to downtown Los Angeles, sought to combine parkway design with engineering inventiveness and technological innovation. The parkway concept in particular was associated in part with the idea of a "pleasure drive," where the parkway would blend into the surrounding areas and highlight the Arroyo corridor's rich array of parks, its celebration of the outdoors, its environmental amenities, and its historical and cultural sites.

But already by the 1940s, the parkway concept was being reframed to fit into a high-speed commuting system. As early as its groundbreaking ceremony in 1940, the Arroyo Seco Parkway was touted as the "first freeway of the West" (it is better known today as the Pasadena Freeway or 110 Freeway). This shift had two major consequences. On the one hand, it thoroughly undermined proposals made by various public transportation advocates during the 1930s and 1940s to establish a linked transportation system that included parkways, trains (including a rail system along the median strip of a parkway), buses, and even a bike-commute system from Pasadena to Los Angeles (an idea that had been pursued at the turn of the twentieth century by Pasadena's mayor).[18] At the same time, as the parkway gave way to the freeway, the goals of the "pleasure drive" and connection to place became even more problematic. The parkway was originally built to carry 27,000 automobiles per day at forty-five miles per hour. Today the freeway carries over 120,000 cars per day at speeds almost always exceeding the official limit of fifty-five miles per hour—except of course during commuting times, when it slows down to a crawl.[19] Drivers complain about the freeway's limited capacity, terrible congestion, and dangerous ramps. According to a UCLA–Occidental College study, the number of accidents on the Pasadena freeway is significantly greater than for any other freeway in metropolitan Los Angeles. Even in its earlier days, one motorist described the challenge of merging into traffic on the curving roadway as follows: "You wait at a dead stop for an opening in traffic, and then, with teeth clenched, you push the accelerator all the way to the floor saying 'Go, Go, Go,' afraid to look back and see if anything was gaining on you."[20]

In the 1950s, with the parkway concept having become a historical curiosity, Los Angeles (as well as other metropolitan areas) embarked on a highway construction frenzy, financed by the Federal Interstate Highway Act, that divided neighborhoods, reconfigured cities, and promoted suburban sprawl. L.A. already led the country in its myriad manifestations of car-centered growth, culture, architecture, politics, and residential development. Even its first major transportation system, the fabled interurban Red Cars and Yellow Cars, which provided Los Angeles with the most extensive rail system in the country through the 1930s, had established a sprawling land-use pattern that preceded and later became synonymous with the car commute. By the late 1940s, the interurban system was in deep trouble, abandoned by the Pacific Electric Company, which had shifted toward bus operations. The dominant auto-based system not only encouraged new suburban residential development at the urban edge, but also led to a shift of supermarkets away from the urban core to the suburbs, the rise of gated communities, and the making of an environment of strip malls, drive-throughs, and fast-food outlets. The car and the freeway became the very symbols of L.A., with the region's patterns of long-distance commutes, daily episodes of air pollution, traffic congestion, carved-up neighborhoods, and endless, monochrome suburban vistas and sprawling development.[21]

By the 1970s, however, many Angelenos began to challenge—or at least rethink—the primacy of L.A.'s affair with the automobile. While most Angelenos still depend on their cars for the vast majority of local trips (there are over 6 million cars registered in L.A. County alone),[22] controversies around transportation in Los Angeles have galvanized public debate about transit: pricey rail lines, feisty bus riders, and internecine struggles among agencies, advocates, and riders: all claim to want to reduce the region's auto addiction, but they have contrasting strategies and priorities. As a result, the needs of residents who don't rely on cars, or can't afford to own them, have slowly come into focus, with new visions of how Los Angeles can become a more livable place.

As the L.A.-area population continued to grow in the 1980s and 1990s, the region's transportation infrastructure was under increasing stress. It wasn't just that there were more people. Mismatches intensified between where residents chose to or could afford to live and the locations of employment opportunities. Job losses were highest in densely populated and growing areas like South L.A. and North Orange County; job gains were highest in areas with less dense or less rapidly growing residential clusters, including San Bernardino County and eastern Ventura County.[23]

As a result, more people needed to travel farther to work. Vehicle miles traveled in greater L.A. doubled between 1980 and 1999, while the population rose just 44 percent in that period.[24] The average speed on the region's crowded highways was reduced to thirty-four miles per hour and was expected to decline even further, to eighteen miles per hour, by 2020.[25] Despite some increases in local job opportunities, residents of the Inland Empire's outer suburbs had the longest commutes. By 2001, 40 percent of commuters from San Bernardino and Riverside County, most of them bound for L.A. or Orange County, traveled an hour or more each way to work, and 11 percent had daily commutes totaling four to six hours.[26] Some residents of L.A. County experienced even worse congestion in central areas. They wasted an average of fifty-six hours per year stuck in traffic, compared to thirty-eight hours for Riverside and San Bernardino County dwellers. Even so, L.A. congestion grew "only" 81 percent from 1982 to 2000, as compared to an astounding 533 percent increase in the Inland Empire.[27]

In response, L.A. County turned to transit. In the 1980s and 1990s, the county spent two-thirds of its transportation resources on transit, while the rest of the region used two-thirds of transportation dollars to build highways. The initial enthusiasm for transit was focused on the subway, seeking to mimic other metropolitan transit strategies such as Washington's Metro and San Francisco's BART systems. After enormous cost overruns and related fiascoes about location and neighborhood impacts, the Metropolitan Transportation Authority (MTA) opened its Metrorail subway system in

1990, expanding the system throughout the next decade, including a regional system of commuter trains, the Metrolink. But, in one short, troubled stretch that turned most L.A. voters against subterranean lines, MTA broke the world record for per-mile tunneling and construction costs.

L.A.'s new rail system was a welcome break from past efforts to build new roads to reduce congestion on other roads, which had also been designed to reduce congestion, and so on, ad infinitum. But the rail systems, like the freeways before them, mainly linked suburbs with the center, serving middle- to upper-middle-income travelers. Left out of the loop were those who needed to travel within older metropolitan areas and who did not have access to a car.[28] They were primarily poor and Latino and walked and rode buses.

In the early 1990s, the MTA allowed overcrowding in buses up to 140 percent of capacity. MTA raised bus fares even though most riders were poor. It spent just 30 percent of transit funds on the buses that carried over 90 percent of MTA users. It relied mainly on older diesel buses that polluted lower-income neighborhoods with carcinogenic exhaust. Seizing on the overt discriminatory nature of how funds were allocated for the two transit systems, activists associated with the Labor Community Strategy Center established a coalition called the Bus Riders Union (BRU). The BRU used theater and protests to bring its message to people on crowded buses or waiting at bus stations. The BRU turned up the heat at MTA meetings and adopted a hard-line position opposing all new rail projects as long as bus service was languishing, in the process crossing swords with a number of environmental and transit advocates who supported expansion of light rail. But most significantly, it took the innovative step of linking up with the NAACP Legal Defense Fund and attorney Connie Rice to sue the MTA, under Title 6 of the Civil Rights Act of 1964. The suit successfully argued that MTA's actions adversely impacted minorities, since most bus riders were Latino, Black, and Asian. As a result, in 1996, MTA signed a consent decree requiring it to invest over $1 billion to improve bus service, the largest civil rights award in U.S. history.[29]

MTA responded by increasing spending on buses (while continuing to extend light rail service), but the agency and some L.A. political leaders dragged their feet on fully implementing the consent decree, appealing it all the way through the legal system until the Supreme Court finally turned down a chance to hear the case in early 2002.

There were other transportation struggles during the late 1990s and early in the current decade, many involving similar questions of impacts and equity. Neighborhoods near Los Angeles International Airport stalled LAX expansion, forcing a plan to expand traffic at other regional airports. Trade and transport of goods increased, with the Inland Empire becoming a transshipment and warehousing hub, bringing an economic boost but increasing traffic, noise, and pollution along trucking and rail corridors. Residents in central areas, where increased traffic resulted in the deaths of a number of pedestrians, began to demand that transportation planners prioritize safe, walkable neighborhoods. Latino activists called for the creation of the kind of public plazas and shopping and strolling-friendly streets common in Latin American cities. Whether these efforts and visions could overcome the vast concrete legacy of a century of auto-oriented development was one of the critical questions facing L.A. at the start of the twenty-first century.

On June 15, 2003, thousands of bike riders and pedestrians made their way onto the Pasadena Freeway to walk and ride along the winding route of the historic Arroyo Seco Parkway. In an unprecedented step, the California Department of Transportation had closed the freeway to automobiles for four hours. The bikers and pedestrians were participating in ArroyoFest, an event designed to encourage rethinking of transportation strategies, changes in the watershed, development of open space and park sites, and, perhaps most important, the connection among the diverse neighborhoods of the Arroyo Seco corridor. There was talk of MTA's new high-speed bus system, the light rail system (the Gold Line) that would soon open and serve the entire Arroyo corridor, and even a bike commuter roadway that would be as quick as commuting by car. There were also proposals to transform the freeway back into a parkway, to lower speed limits, to redesign landscape and hardscape, and to restructure reliance on the automobile to create a multimodal system (car, rail, bus, bike, pedestrian). ArroyoFest, part festival, part community mobilization, symbolized the obstacles to and opportunities for rethinking the region's auto-ecology.[30]

THE URBAN ENVIRONMENT

In 1991, Southern Pacific Railroad put up for sale nearly fifty acres of land adjacent to Chinatown, near downtown Los Angeles. At first sight the area, known as the Cornfield, hardly fit the stereotype of an environmental treasure, having been used for a century as a railroad freight depot and switching yard. However, the Cornfield, located at the edge of the L.A. River as it made its way through downtown Los Angeles, had a rich earlier history. It was associated with farming (thus the name) and was the location of the Zanja Madre, the major canal of the pre-Anglo irrigation system that had served the Catholic Mission. By the 1990s, when the land was put on the market, the Cornfield was considered abandoned land, but its proximity to downtown made it a choice location. A group of high-powered developers made a bid for the property and seemed to have everything going their way. The developers, who included one of the owners of the railroad, were close to Mayor Richard Riordan and were already touting a number of big deals, including the construction of the Staples Center at the southern end of downtown. Their plan was to develop a warehouse and light industrial project, get some additional subsidies and capital by declaring the site a brownfield,[31] and waive any environmental review in order to expedite the development process.

For a while the developers' plans seemed to have momentum. In 1999, the City of Los Angeles helped to secure $11.5 million in brownfield loans and subsidies from HUD. The city also gave a waiver on the Environmental Impact Review (EIR) process. Things were on a fast track and not many were paying attention at first. But since open space and neighborhood park land were so scarce in L.A., the Cornfield became attractive to an array of activists, including L.A. River advocates, Chinatown community organizers, Latino groups (several Latino neighborhoods are east of the Cornfield), and other urban environmentalists. The Cornfield thus became a test case for a new community-based environmentalism, since the warehouse plan had bypassed any significant input from the local community, including the desire to use the yards for park space, housing, good jobs, and schools.

As a consequence, community and environmental organizations joined together and sued over the environmental review process. They convinced many of the candidates in the 2001 mayor's race to support them and convinced the federal government to withhold the brownfield cleanup funds. After many months of protest, negotiations, and arm twisting, in 2001 the developers agreed to sell the site (to the state of California), with an opportunity for the new community and environmental alliance to help to design the plan that could potentially include park space and recreational facilities.[32]

The vicissitudes of the Cornfield-site issue held lessons for a new kind of community-environmental alliance. The point that especially came into focus was that an unjust distribution of environmental burdens, such as contamination, and benefits, such as parks, reflects the city's income and race divisions and disparities. It was an example of how the power of wealth and inside influence conflicts with community visions of land use, and how this clash of interests gets played out in discussions over control of land. Finally, the Cornfield debate was evidence that environmentalism isn't just about animals and plants, air and water; it also can shape public-health decisions and revitalize neighborhoods.

Los Angeles' environmental split was a legacy of twentieth-century development: a climate and natural beauty that attracted millions contrasted with the realities of air pollution and sprawl. The way the region developed imposed a lingering toxic burden on L.A. residents. The oil extraction and heavy manufacturing that boomed here in the first half of the twentieth century, concentrated near the port zone and in south and east L.A. County, peaked before environmentalists had fought successfully for meaningful controls on factory emissions and waste disposal. As heavy industry declined in the 1970s and 1980s, the light manufacturing that took its place included a number of businesses that used toxic components and operated in poorly regulated, little-monitored areas of the economy (furniture, toy, and jewelry manufacturing, to name a few).

Meanwhile, the rapid, uncontrolled physical transformation of Southern California, based on real estate speculation and automobiles, created significant air pollution problems and bypassed opportunities to preserve greenbelts, river corridors, and other natural amenities. Though greater L.A. is vast, it is situated on sensitive natural ecosystems: an "island on the land" in Carey McWilliams's phrase.[33] The region's environmental profile included a blend of government policy and market manipulation, engineering marvels and astoundingly short-sighted land use promoted by development-oriented elites. The environmental outrages that flowed from poorly planned growth triggered a counterreaction that demanded a more thorough and equitable stewardship of the air, water, and land.

Smog, the visible and signature symptom of L.A.'s environmental malaise, declined in the 1990s and the early part of the twenty-first century, thanks in part to the struggles of clean-air advocates. Nineteen ninety-nine was the first year since the advent of monitoring with no declaration of a "stage 1 episode," a one-hour average smog concentration of 0.20 parts per million or above (two to three times the state and federal clean-air limits). In contrast, there were 101 stage 1 episodes in 1980 and 41 in 1990.[34] Despite the progress, the Los Angeles–Orange–Riverside metropolitan region still had the worst ozone problem in the nation.[35] An upsurge in smog levels in the summer of 2003 pointed out the need for more aggressive pollution control efforts.

Smog wasn't the only form of air pollution plaguing Los Angeles. L.A. County ranked among the dirtiest 10 percent of U.S. communities in cancer and noncancer health risks from airborne pollutants, such as particulates and nitrous oxide.[36] Like many environmental burdens, the impacts of smog and airborne contaminants were unevenly distributed throughout the region.[37] Greater L.A.'s prevailing winds blew car exhaust and other emissions east from coastal areas, to accumulate in the inland valleys. Ten to 15 percent of children in the Inland Empire suffered decreased lung capacity. Children in Mira Loma, which had the region's heaviest air particulate pollution (a third higher than in downtown L.A.), had 5 percent less lung capacity than their peers in less-polluted areas.[38]

Water rivals air as a key L.A. environmental indicator. Set between ocean and desert, Los Angeles is dependent on imported fresh water. Since the early twentieth century, the city and the broader Southern California region have developed by importing water from distant sources, beginning with the completion of the Los Angeles Aqueduct from Owens Valley in 1913. Importation of water created conflicts with areas where those water supplies originated and allowed L.A. to avoid responsibility for establishing a water-use ethic based on wise management of local demand and resources.[39]

L.A.'s own water resources—river systems, freshwater lakes, and coasts and beaches—also paid the price of poor planning. Industrial emissions and runoff from roads and suburban lawns damaged rivers, wetlands, and coastal waters and placed L.A. County in the dirtiest 30 percent of U.S. counties in terms of toxic water contamination.[40] In 2000, despite improvements in sewage treatment, contaminants in the region's coastal waters after winter storms exceeded health limits 58 percent of the time.[41] Overall, 25 percent of water bodies in L.A. County became impaired in some way by pollution.[42]

The region's land and built environment bore the marks of pollution and toxic materials. There were twelve Superfund sites in L.A. County, and numerous smaller contaminated plots of land.[43] Toxic lead paint brought contamination inside people's homes. Los Angeles County had the third highest number of lead-contaminated homes in the country. Roughly eight out of every ten buildings in the county were built prior to 1978, the year lead was removed from indoor paint.[44] As a result, more than two thousand children in the county—ranging from one to six years in age—are reported each year for lead levels in their blood that could cause neurological damage, decrease learning ability, or cause other health and behavior problems.[45]

Cumulatively, L.A.'s environmental burdens gave Los Angeles much of its reputation as a sprawling dystopia. But, as the fight over the Cornfield site and other environmental battles revealed, Los Angeles was also the place where a new form of community-environmental politics had begun to emerge.

In 1930, a detailed and imaginative planning document commissioned by the Los Angeles Chamber of Commerce, known as the Olmsted-Bartholomew Report, proposed a wealth of parks, playgrounds, and parkways centering around the Los Angeles River, which would have dramatically transformed the city and the region.[46] For a number of reasons, including competing demands for the land from powerful developers and other commercial and industrial interests, L.A. officials never seriously considered adopting the report's recommendations.

Fast-forward seventy years to the Baldwin Hills area, where residents in a predominately African American neighborhood organized around their vision of a large park in the face of proposals for luxury homes and a power plant.[47] Determined not to squander any more opportunities, the Baldwin Hills residents, like their counterparts all around L.A., worked to reverse Los Angeles' status as a park-poor city. Los Angeles had less neighborhood park space per person than nearly every major city in the country.[48] Three-quarters of L.A.'s youth lived more than a quarter mile from the nearest park, while the city spent far more to maintain parks in neighborhoods with wealthier, older residents than it did on establishing new parks where they were needed most.[49]

Faced with such enormous challenges, environmental activism expanded significantly in the last decades of the twentieth century. Public pressure forced some limits on toxic air and water emissions and unregulated growth. Los Angeles was one of the first cities where a new environmental justice movement forged alliances between local environmental activists and mainstream environmental organizations regarding the toxic hazards faced by low-income neighborhoods. Toxic contamination in Los Angeles was most severe in parts of south and east L.A. County, especially near abandoned and currently operating industries clustered near the port areas and along railway lines, as well as in freeway corridors with heavy truck use and diesel exhaust. Residents of these areas were disproportionately low-income Latinos and African Americans, clustered there because land prices were more affordable and as a result of past residential discrimination.[50] These communities had traditionally lacked the political connections of wealthier, Whiter areas. As a result, they had less experience and success in fighting eyesores and egregious polluters.

But that changed. Groups like Communities for a Better Environment (CBE) gave residents of neighborhoods impacted by toxic threats tools to monitor and combat pollution. CBE and other grassroots environmental groups targeted major polluters, such as oil refineries, and opposed new, dirty power plants. Larger environmental organizations listened to L.A. residents and worked with local activists to target lingering sources of pollution and health risks. A campaign to phase out diesel buses, especially diesel school buses, illustrated how community priorities catalyzed successful environmental advocacy. Diesel exhaust had been listed in California as a known carcinogen since 1986. By 2000, 70 percent of L.A.'s cancer risk from breathing the air could be attributed to diesel.[51] But most buses used by large public fleets, including those of the MTA and the Los Angeles Unified School District, still ran on diesel fuel. This placed a huge toxic burden on bus riders and residents of neighborhoods crisscrossed by bus routes.

In February 2001, two environmental groups released a study showing that diesel exhaust levels on school buses in Los Angeles were more than eight times higher than average levels in California and twenty-three to forty-six times higher than levels considered to be a significant cancer risk, according to federal guidelines.[52] These findings gave ammunition to a coalition of environmental, community, and health groups working to phase out diesel school buses. In April 2001, the region's Air Quality Management District adopted a rule requiring school districts to buy clean (nondiesel) buses when they replaced aging fleets. The antidiesel fight also extended to transportation corridors like the 710 Freeway and the Alameda rail corridor, where ambitious plans to move goods just in time from port to warehouse ignored the toxic threats to low-income neighborhoods.[53] In these and other struggles, the focus on the urban environment not only broadened the agendas and community focus of the environmental movement, but extended and deepened the Progressive L.A. focus on livability as a core social justice issue.

SEEDS OF CHANGE:
HEALTHIER FOOD, HEALTHIER COMMUNITIES

In the summer of 1992, shortly after the civil unrest, a group of UCLA graduate students decided to undertake a yearlong research study to document the problems—and possible solutions—confronting the areas most heavily impacted by the riots. Food issues, the students discovered to their surprise, registered as a major concern *and* as an opportunity for community action. Neighborhood residents, for example, identified food markets as their number-one retail need.[54]

One year later, the UCLA students released *Seeds of Change: Strategies for Food Security in the Inner City*, a report that identified a wide range of food security problems in the core areas of Los Angeles.[55] Twenty-seven percent of the residents surveyed in one neighborhood experienced hunger an average of five days a month, establishing a continuous pattern of dropping in and out of hunger. A food price survey indicated (as similar studies in other cities had also shown) that low-income residents paid more for the same food items found in equivalent stores in middle-income communities.[56] At the same time, low-income residents spent a far higher proportion of their overall income on food (36 percent compared to 12 percent of the budget for a middle-income family). Lack of access to fresh food and affordable, better-quality food was another significant concern. Since the 1960s, supermarkets had abandoned low-income neighborhoods in Los Angeles. The average number of residents or customers who potentially could be served in a supermarket service area was 50 percent greater in these central areas than in middle-income neighborhoods in the suburban San Fernando Valley. The problem of access was compounded by the nearly universal reliance on automobiles for food shopping at full-service markets and the substantially lower average car ownership in low-income areas.[57]

The *Seeds of Change* study also identified warning signs about the food that people were eating. Food was becoming increasingly processed, reconfigured, and supersized, subject to the influences of a fast-food culture. An obesity epidemic in Los Angeles and throughout the country was emerging, directly linked to poor diet and lack of exercise.[58] The problems associated with lack of exercise in L.A. were magnified by its dearth of open and recreational space and of recreational opportunities in its schools, and by heavy reliance on cars for short-distance trips. But the problems associated with high-salt, high-fat, and high-sugar diets reached into all communities. In food-insecure, low-income communities, overweight kids were also hungry. There was not enough to eat, and the foods that were available filled people's stomachs but didn't nourish them.

At the same time that the UCLA researchers were beginning their research, representatives of the Vons Corporation and staff from Rebuild L.A., the private sector–led initiative aimed at revitalizing Los Angeles following the 1992 civil unrest, held a press conference to announce Vons's plans to build at least twelve new supermarkets in the inner city. Vons's commitment was matched by Ralphs, Smart and Final, and Food 4 Less. The food retailers promised as many as thirty-two new supermarkets within a five-year period. This expansive promise was to be the private sector's solution to L.A.'s grocery gap. Food access in the inner city, they announced, would finally be addressed.[59]

How much changed in the decade after the civil unrest? Was there greater food security? Had the supermarkets kept their promise? A person strolling through the farmers' markets that transform streets and parking lots into fields of locally grown, colorfully appealing fruit and vegetables or sampling international cuisine in restaurants and eateries that reflect the city's diversity might have assumed that L.A.'s food systems had changed for the better. There was a boom in farmers' markets, community gardens, and new, healthy, school food programs. But in low-income communities, residents were still hard-pressed to find a food store with even a modest selection of affordable produce, let alone fresh local crops. Fast food remained the standard prepared meal available to many.

Despite the stronger economy of the late 1990s, millions in the Los Angeles area still had a hard time affording their daily meals. In 2001, 584,000 went hungry at some point during the year.[60] Meanwhile, supermarkets continued to be all too hard to find. In 1992, there were thirty-two chain supermarkets and twenty-three independent supermarkets in the low-income parts of Los Angeles surveyed by Rebuild L.A. In 2002, there were thirty-one chain markets and twenty-six independents.[61] Little had changed to ensure that all residents had access to fresh food. While there were more farmers' markets in greater L.A. than in any other part of the nation, few were based in low-income neighborhoods. The one type of food source that flourished in low-income communities was fast-food restaurants. An activist group, the Community Coalition, surveyed a two-square-mile area of South Central L.A. and found fifty-two fast-food locations and just one sit-down restaurant.

The positive changes could be traced to the steady growth of a movement comprising community and advocacy organizations. From operators of food pantries who fought hunger when the federal government weakened social safety nets, to community gardeners who cultivated food and hope in plots throughout urban areas, to parents who mobilized to convince the Los Angeles school board to eliminate soda drinks from school vending machines, groups had begun to tackle the issues that *Seeds of Change* had identified.

In 1996 this loose network of food activists convinced the Los Angeles City Council to create a Los Angeles Food Security and Hunger Partnership (LAFSHP) to examine food-related problems and possible policy solutions. Political in-fighting within the LAFSHP undermined the coalition, and by 1999 it had ceased operations. The community groups involved kept their collaboration alive, however. In 2001, a broad range of groups led by the Center for Food and Justice, the Los Angeles Coalition to End Hunger and Homelessness, and the California Food Policy Advocates met for a "Taste of Justice" conference, in which they strategized on ways to improve access to supermarkets and farmers' markets, boost community gardens, and improve school food, and reconsidered the role of a food-policy council for Los Angeles.[62] The conference in turn spurred the development of a food and justice network of organizations and community food advocates. The lesson for the food organizers was the importance of continuing to build and extend their movement, to ensure that policies were not only initiated but sustained.

Picture this: It's lunchtime for five hundred low-income students at 59th Street School in South Central Los Angeles, one of 430 elementary schools in the much-beleaguered Los Angeles Unified School District. Only about 25 percent of the students decide to select the usual hot meal of corn dogs, pizza, or pepperoni calzoni. Incredibly, the other 75 percent of the students line up for the latest innovation in school cafeteria food: a farmers' market fruit and salad bar. A subsequent study of the salad-bar program at this and two other public schools, by a UCLA Public Health School team, indicates that the average daily intake of fruits and vegetables increased by more than 40 percent due to the existence of the salad bars. Over in the Santa Monica school district, where the Farmers' Market Salad Bar Program was established three years earlier, students at all twelve of the elementary and middle schools (the two high schools would establish their salad bars the following year) were able to choose a farmers' market salad bar for their meal. The Santa Monica district, led by a food-services director who, though initially a skeptic, had become a passionate supporter of this "farm-to-school" concept, would in turn become the leader in institutionalizing a revolution in the school lunch program. Not only was the food healthy, but, to paraphrase the ad, it "tasted great." When famed Berkeley restaurateur Alice Waters (owner of Chez Panisse) visited one of the salad bars in Santa Monica and had a salad-bar lunch, she pronounced the produce as fresh and tasty as any of her twenty-five-dollar salads.[63]

The Los Angeles region, with its flourishing farmers' markets and growing sustainable-food and justice movement, inspired similar farm-to-school initiatives throughout California and around the country. In many ways, this dynamic new food movement symbolized what was best and most challenging for Progressive L.A. activism. Home of the first fast-food drive-through outlet, Los Angeles had also become the home of a school lunch touted by the doyenne of nouvelle cuisine.

THE WHOLE SCHOOL: EDUCATIONAL CHALLENGES

School issues, obviously, were not limited just to what was being served in the cafeteria or sold in vending machines. In 2001, Bret Harte Preparatory

Intermediate School, Cahuenga Elementary, Jefferson High, and other public schools in Los Angeles held classes under conditions that a legal brief filed against the state of California characterized as "[shocking] the conscience."[64] These schools had too few certified teachers, too few advanced-placement classes, and too few functioning restrooms. There were too many leaking ceilings and too many vermin. There were not enough classrooms to house growing school-age populations, and school supplies were inadequate. Some students could not take textbooks home after classes because their schools did not have enough books for each student. Others had to stand or sit on tables due to a lack of chairs.

That many students were still able to learn under such difficult circumstances is in part testimony to the resilience of students, families, and educators and to their ability to overcome such barriers. But time and change were against them. In a city and region where the population was increasingly young, poor, and immigrant, public education in Los Angeles at the turn of the century was at the center of competing political agendas.

During the 2001–2 school year, the Los Angeles Unified School District, the second largest in the country, encompassed the City of Los Angeles and parts of more than twenty surrounding cities. It served 736,600 K-12 students (more students than the separate populations of four U.S. states).[65] Enrollment rose 15 percent in less than ten years, up from 640,000 students in 1993–94.[66] The district had 36,700 teachers, 41,000 nonteacher regular employees, and a $5.9 billion annual budget.[67]

LAUSD was a microcosm of the area's demographic complexity. Its student body offered a snapshot of the next generation of Angelenos: the region's upper crust was largely excluded, since the district, like most large public school districts, taught disproportionate numbers of minority and low-income students. In 2001, 71.4 percent of LAUSD students were Latino (up from 60 percent in 1990), 12.4 percent were Black, 9.6 percent White, and 6 percent Asian and Filipino. Forty-four percent of students in the LAUSD were classified as English learners, 93.5 percent of these as Spanish speakers. The district's children spoke over eighty languages at home. Seventy-four percent of students were poor enough to qualify for free or reduced-price school meals.[68]

During this period of growth in student enrollment, the district failed to keep pace, resulting in overcrowding and a last-minute rush to build and expand schools. By 2001, some schools housed nearly twice the number of students they had been designed to teach. Almost twenty thousand students were bused out of their neighborhoods solely due to overcrowding. LAUSD estimated it needed eighty-three thousand new seats to make it possible for all students to attend a neighborhood school on a multitrack calendar.[69]

The space crunch could be blamed on a combination of poor planning, limited local resources due to the 1978 statewide initiative Proposition 13, voter rejection of local school bonds in the 1980s, delays in tapping into available state funding, and the difficulties of siting and constructing new schools in crowded urban neighborhoods. The district exacerbated the problem of a shortage of vacant land by insisting on building enormous schools rather than experimenting with smaller campuses. The troubling saga of the Belmont Learning Center—built over old oil fields to replace a crowded high school in a low-income neighborhood, left vacant for years for fear that seeping methane would endanger students' health, then revived in 2002 after tens of millions of dollars had been lost in delays, tests, and construction overruns—was emblematic of LAUSD's seeming inability to do anything so fundamental as to provide facilities for its students. As of late 2001, the district's plans to build additions to forty schools while constructing seventy-eight new primary, elementary, middle, and high schools had not advanced much. With just four of these projects completed and only five under construction, it appeared unlikely the district would catch up to student growth, let alone meet its ambitious five-year timetable for reducing overcrowding.[70]

In the face of the challenges of growing up poor and the distractions of overcrowded, often crumbling schools, how were students in the LAUSD faring academically? Under most measurements of educational success, from graduation rates to test results to college attendance, the district, despite some progress made from the early 1990s to 2001, was not providing all students with a sound education. It is difficult to pinpoint precise graduation rates, due to the numbers of students who switch school districts, but it is estimated that about 60 to 65 percent of students in LAUSD completed and graduated from high school in the mid- to late 1990s. On the other hand, statistics compiled by the State Department of Education reveal that the dropout rate in the district fell sharply from the early 1990s to 2000, from 12 percent to 5.5 percent. Despite this significant improvement, the district's dropout rate in 1999–2000 was still almost twice the state average, and there were significant disparities among ethnic groups, with Hispanics and Blacks more likely to leave school than Asians or Whites.[71]

By the late 1990s, California, in the name of school accountability, began requiring standardized testing of students in lower grades. There were a host of controversies surrounding high-stakes testing, including fears that schools would adopt narrow, teach-to-the-test instructional approaches, and

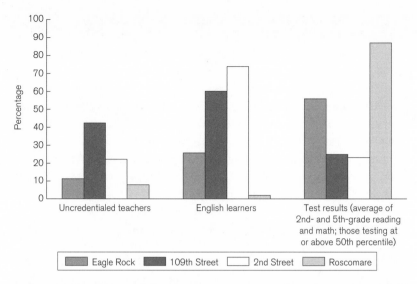

FIGURE 8   Comparison of learning environments in four elementary schools: four Los Angeles zip codes. (Sources: Los Angeles Unified School District, 2001–2, *School Accountability Report Cards for 2nd Street Elementary, 109th Street Elementary, Eagle Rock Elementary, and Roscomare Elementary* [Los Angeles, 2002].)

that students would be held back for their schools' failure. In fact, the early results of testing created more negative news for LAUSD. Only 29 percent of LAUSD students tested scored 50 percent or above on the Stanford 9 reading test. Thirty-six percent reached this goal on the mathematics portion of the test.

It was no surprise that test results confirmed a wide gulf of educational inequality within the district, let alone in comparison with suburban school districts. A comparison of elementary schools chosen at random within each of the four neighborhoods profiled in chapter 3 (Eagle Rock Elementary in northeast L.A., zip code 90041; 109th Street Elementary in the 90059 zip code in South Central; 2nd Street Elementary in the 90033 zip code in East L.A.; and Roscomare Elementary in Bel Air on the Westside) shows that the richer the neighborhood, the more supportive the learning environment, at least in terms of quantifiable conditions such as percentage of teachers with credentials. Not surprisingly, testing results mirrored these demarcations.[72]

On the brighter side, the year-to-year improvement in test scores was higher in schools in low-income areas.[73] But the rate of change on matters ranging from test achievement to school construction was still so glacial that many students, parents, and community members took matters into their own hands and pressured the district to improve conditions and opportunities. Parent and student groups opposed state initiatives that curtailed bilingual K-12 education. Immigrant students won a change to the law that had forced noncitizens to pay out-of-state tuition at California public universities. And the Industrial Areas Foundation brought together a coalition of community groups and unions to organize parents to demand better school performance.

Among the many grassroots campaigns around education, one that was particularly innovative in empowering a multiracial coalition of students and challenging the critical issues of overcrowding and crumbling infrastructure was South Central Youth Empowerment through Action (SCYEA), a project of the Community Coalition that focused on both the immediate physical conditions of schools and the broader learning environment.

At Fremont High School, for example, SCYEA surveyed over a thousand students. They found that 40 percent of students were assigned classes they had already taken and passed, over 50 percent of students lacked textbooks and materials for one or more classes, 50 percent of the students were in classes with over forty total students, and 80 percent of students had *never* talked to a school guidance counselor about preparing for college. Faced with evidence of neglect, SCYEA students (and parents) organized a Fremont 911! demonstration in front of LAUSD headquarters.[74] Their fact-finding and activism helped to convince a citizen committee charged with overseeing school construction funds from state Proposition BB (Better Buildings) to allocate an additional $199 million for repairing existing schools. In a related effort, the Community Coalition sponsored neighborhood meetings to devise ways that local residents could be involved in decisions on siting, designing, and constructing new schools. One consideration was how to avoid situations where the district would use eminent domain to seize and destroy affordable housing to build a school.[75]

The SCYEA didn't stop at school doors. They noticed that neighborhoods surrounding schools were clustered with concentrations of billboards advertising tobacco and alcohol products. Students in the coalition led a struggle to replace the addiction-promoting advertising on many of these billboards with antitobacco messages they designed themselves. Looking to their own future as graduates, the students also convinced the LAUSD school board to take a position against Proposition 209 to eliminate affirmative action in California colleges. The SCYEA campaigns, similar to a number of other community and education-related initiatives focused on LAUSD, indicated that while school reforms begin in the classroom, they ultimately need to extend to the whole school, from the classroom and cafeteria to the communities they are part of.

PROMOTORAS FOR EVERYONE: COMMUNITY HEALTH AND WELLNESS

Diabetes is on the rise in Los Angeles and nationwide. By 2000, it was already the seventh leading cause of death in L.A. County, where 7 percent of adult L.A. County residents—around 475,000 people—had been diagnosed with the disease. Another 2 to 3 percent of adults in the county probably had the disease without knowing it. The incidence among L.A. County Latinos forty years or older was double that of Asians and Whites in the same age group, and African Americans were half again as likely as Whites and Asians to have the disease. Diabetes, like many illnesses, is caused partly by genetic factors and partly by behavioral and environmental circumstances, with obesity increasingly being recognized as a key factor. The more common type 2 diabetes, typically an adult disease, was even starting to show up among adolescents due to a surge in overweight children. The disease requires regular medical treatment: a problem in a place like Los Angeles, where many residents lack health insurance. As a result, while only 20 percent of diabetes sufferers *with* health insurance were not under a doctor's care for the illness, 51 percent of people with diabetes but *without* health insurance were not getting treated.[76]

The problem of diabetes illustrates how individual health and wellness in the Los Angeles region transcends the medical world of doctors and diagnoses and involves the totality of conditions and quality of life in L.A. The number of families and children living without health insurance in L.A. reflects the region's profound economic inequality. Rising obesity and diabetes attest to lack of parks, to difficulties in accessing fresh food in some neighborhoods, and to transportation planning and urban design policies that limit walking and biking. Violence has been a leading cause of death and disability among some ethnic groups in L.A., exposing the unequal burden of crime, while asthma, lead poisoning, and other ailments have been associated with environmental factors common among the poor.

Between 1991 and 2000, average life expectancy in L.A. County increased by 2.6 years. Thanks to medical advances and a decline in smoking rates, deaths from coronary heart disease, stroke, and lung cancer each fell by 25 to 35 percent. Homicides, suicides, and accidental deaths also declined. The 48 percent jump in fatalities from diabetes represented a notable countertrend.[77]

Despite the overall good news about life expectancy, a 1999 survey of Los Angeles County residents found that 21 percent of respondents reported their health to be poor or fair. The survey revealed a significant geographic divide, with residents of the county's south service planning area twice as likely to report poor or fair health (28 percent) as residents of the west planning area (14 percent).[78]

Another way to quantify health is to trace leading causes of death and disability. The three leading causes of death in L.A. County in 2000 were coronary heart disease (14,378), stroke (4,178), and lung cancer (3,772). Health experts have increasingly focused attention on "disability-adjusted life years" as a broader indicator of disease in a community. Disability-adjusted life years are a total of years lost to premature mortality and of years spent living with a disability. The three leading health problems in L.A. County, according to these criteria, were heart disease, alcohol, and violence. The leading causes of disability and lost years of life varied by ethnic group, however, pointing to the need to tailor treatment and public health campaigns to the community served. In Los Angeles County, African Americans were most affected by violence, heart disease, and diabetes; Asians by alcohol, depression, and osteoarthritis; Latinos by alcohol, violence, and depression; and Whites by heart disease, emphysema, and alcohol.[79]

Most important, access to high-quality health care is vital for preventing, detecting, and treating medical problems and encouraging healthy behavior. As an example, early detection of HIV, combined with treatment by "drug cocktails" of new medicines, brought a measure of hope to AIDS patients and those infected with HIV. Deaths from AIDS in Los Angeles dropped tenfold from 1995 to 2001: one of the most significant health victories during that period.[80] Between 1990 and 1998, most infant health indicators in L.A. County also improved. The percentage of pregnant women receiving early prenatal care rose from 71 to 84 percent. Infant mortality dropped from 8 to 5.9 percent, though the percentage of babies with low birth weight increased from 6.1 to 6.6 percent. In all three of these areas, L.A. County ranked above the national average.[81]

But lack of access to health insurance and medical services threatened to undermine these and other health gains and to exacerbate health disparities. The City of Los Angeles had the third highest rate of uninsured families of all U.S. metropolitan areas (behind only El Paso and Jersey City): 31 percent uninsured compared to a national average of 19 percent.[82] Of low-income L.A. County residents, 1.9 million qualified for Medi-Cal, California's version of Medicaid, and therefore had some government assistance in paying for treatment.[83] But millions of working poor Angelenos lacked health insurance or government health assistance.

Though there were over 100 general-care hospitals and over 150 licensed primary-care clinics in L.A. County in 1998, those unable to pay for health care were turned away from many facilities.[84] In Los Angeles, a large fraction of people without insurance found their way to County-USC Hospital, near downtown, which treated patients who could not pay or could pay only a little for medical care. The hospital took in everyone from gunshot victims to flu patients: seven hundred thousand every year, three-fourths lacking health insurance. Visitors got treatment if they were willing to endure waits that could stretch to nine hours or more. But the effect of channeling millions of uninsured patients to a few safety-net hospitals has further strained public-health infrastructure. Facing a large shortfall in hospital funds, by late 2002 the County Board of Supervisors had voted to reduce the number of beds at County-USC and to close Rancho Los Amigos, one of the nation's most highly ranked rehabilitation hospitals. After both of these actions were blocked by the Federal District Court in 2003, the county appealed to the Ninth Circuit Court of Appeals.[85]

Recognizing the difficulties that low-income residents faced in staying healthy, Progressive L.A. activists have focused on the health-care gap as part of a broader community agenda. One successful grassroots strategy for improving health care in low-income neighborhoods was the community-health-care-promoters model that several L.A.-area nonprofit organizations adopted. In 1995, for example, the Esperanza Community Housing Corporation started training community members, primarily women, as *promotoras*—bilingual community health leaders. The promotoras served a low-income, immigrant neighborhood where over half the residents lacked health insurance or access to health care. One hundred and thirty-five promotoras were trained by 2001. They advocated for immunization, coordinated a healthy-homes project to improve environmental conditions in neighborhood housing, and engaged in other health education efforts. Esperanza's eventual goal was to place promotoras on the boards of clinics and other health facilities in the community, as part of a grassroots effort to provide services in a manner that met the needs of residents.[86] Eventually, it was hoped, promotoras would not only educate and help to empower their own communities, but also help to change the health-care debate from a medical model, in which costs determined treatment, to a community model, in which health was also seen as a function of community well-being.

L.A. CONFIDENTIAL:
CRIMINAL JUSTICE AND PUBLIC SAFETY

In 1998, when Rafael Perez, a veteran of the Los Angeles Police Department's (LAPD) Rampart Division, was caught stealing and selling cocaine from the evidence room, many assumed that a rogue officer had been rooted out. However, Perez's effort to reduce his sentence by providing incriminating evidence against colleagues revealed a pattern of criminal behavior and an underlying culture within the LAPD that tolerated and even promoted brutality, as well as the suppression of civil liberties of immigrants, youth, and suspected gang members.

In 1979, in an effort to address the street-gang problem in L.A., the LAPD formed an antigang unit known as CRASH (Community Resources against Street Hoodlums) and focused its efforts on a select number of divisions, including Rampart, an area just west of downtown, populated by large numbers of recent immigrants. Perez told how he and other members of his unit framed, planted evidence on, turned over to the INS, and even beat and shot suspects in the name of gang suppression. These officers had been rewarded by LAPD brass and local politicians. In the aftermath of the Rampart scandal, with over three thousand convictions potentially tainted by false police testimony, the city faced a projected cost of $200 million from lawsuits brought by victims of rogue officers. The entire LAPD was ultimately placed under a federal consent decree aimed at rooting out abusive and illicit practices.[87]

Urban crime issues are usually reduced to a simple equation: the more law enforcement reduces crime, the more livable a city is. In Los Angeles this assumption had been complicated by a recurring pattern of police misconduct and inadequate reform and the use of tactics often perceived as antilabor, anti-immigrant, and antiminority. Through nearly its entire history, the LAPD has been divorced from civilian oversight, responding instead to a series of imperious, long-serving chiefs. The department has seen itself as an elite, paramilitary force, a pioneer in crowd control, SWAT tactics, and, since 1965, the prevention and containment of urban riots—a self-image that made the LAPD's failure to respond effectively to the 1992 civil unrest all the more of an indictment of its leadership.

Consistent with its policing philosophy, the LAPD was relatively small in numbers, while Los Angeles' population grew around it. And while L.A.'s changing demographics transformed the city, the police remained largely White. As the LAPD lacked the moderating influence of civilian control or a strong "walk the local beat" tradition, its interaction with many communities took on features of an occupation. Many neighborhoods "experienced" the police on a feast-or-famine basis. They lacked sufficient daily officer presence in the community to ensure safe streets, then at infrequent intervals saw police conduct mass sweeps for gang members, drug activity, and the like. The scale of the interventions all but ensured that innocent people would be swept up in it.

Los Angeles' minority communities had experienced the heavy hand of the police for decades; the videotape of Rodney King brought it to light for the rest of the world to see. In 1991, after the beating of King but before the trial, acquittal, and civil unrest, a commission led by attorney and civic leader Warren Christopher (soon to become President Clinton's secretary of state) released a report outlining an agenda for reform of the LAPD. The Christopher Commission called for a greater emphasis on community policing to repair trust between the police and the public. It also advocated improved training, and tracking of problem officers to cut down on abusive incidents. The commission had concluded that a relatively small number of "repeat offenders" were responsible for many of the department's problems.[88]

The leadership of the city and the police department failed to seize this opportunity to pursue meaningful police reform. Mayor Richard Riordan, elected in 1993, had campaigned on a pledge to hire more cops, not challenge their practices. During Riordan's two terms, the Christopher Commission's recommendations on improving training and changing the culture of the department were not pursued as high priorities. During the decade following the civil unrest, policing, crime, and public safety in Los Angeles were shaped more by state and nationwide criminal-justice trends than by local initiatives.

As the 1990s progressed, crime rates fell sharply in L.A., as they did across the country. From 1990 to 1993, between 300,000 and 350,000 serious crimes, including 1,000 murders, were committed each year in the City of L.A. By the late 1990s, the serious-crime rate had dropped to 150,000, while the murder rate fell to 400. After this trough, crime inched back up (to 175,000 serious crimes and 587 homicides in 2001).[89] Through good times and bad, residents of lower-income neighborhoods faced more dangerous streets. Crime rates within the city were around 50 to 80 percent higher in East and South L.A. than on the Westside, in West Valley, and in the northeast. The LAPD's Central Community Police Station reported crime-incident rates four to five times as high as the city average.

Still, despite these disparities, the dominant trend remained a significant drop in crime. Criminologists attributed the decline to a mix of factors. The end of the early-1990s recession and a lower unemployment rate cut into the desperation that could lead to criminal activity. A settling of turf battles over drug distribution, combined with gang truce efforts, slowed the drugs, guns, and gangs bloodshed that had been fueled by the 1980s influx of crack cocaine. More effective law enforcement strategies also played a role.

One constant over the 1980s and 1990s, as crime rates rose, fell, and rose again, was the huge rise in the prison population that made the United States' rate of incarceration among the highest in the world. This increase was driven by a political climate that downplayed prevention and rehabili-tation in favor of imprisonment. When the lock-them-up approach was applied to drug infractions, prison populations soared. In 1980, 63.5 percent of male prisoners statewide were imprisoned for crimes against persons, and only 7.4 percent for drug offenses. By 2000, just 46.7 percent of male prisoners were being held for offenses against persons, and 26.1 percent were doing time for drug-related offenses.[90]

California's new "three strikes" law, enacted in 1994, followed by Proposition 21 (which focused on juvenile crime), adopted in 2001, intensi-fied the state's rush to incarcerate. Between 1994 and May 2001, more than fifty thousand inmates were sentenced as second or third strikers.[91] Though the law was sold to the public, in the wake of a prominent child-abduction and murder case, as a way to lock away repeat violent offenders, more than half of those caught in its net for third strikes were convicted for nonviolent crimes. Some received twenty-five years to life in prison for such petty offenses as theft of cookies, golf clubs, or $150 worth of videotapes.[92] The three-strikes approach also tightened the criminal justice system's grip on L.A.'s Black community. In Los Angeles County, where African Americans make up 10 percent of the population, 47 percent of male second strikers were Black, 35 percent Latino, and 15 percent White. Proposition 21 allowed teens as young as fourteen to be charged as adults for certain crimes, dis-cretion resting with prosecutors rather than judges.[93]

As a result of the growing pressures for a punitive criminal justice sys-tem, the numbers of inmates in California prisons jumped from 24,569 in 1980, to 97,309 in 1990, and to 160,655 in 2000.[94] The social consequences were immense. Many families had relatives in prison or on parole. And the rising costs of incarceration (7 percent of the state's general funding in 2001) diverted resources from social programs. Despite a prison building boom fueled by voters' fears and the political power of the state prison-guard union, state prisons became severely overcrowded, the occupancy rate rising from 99.3 percent of intended capacity in 1980 to 192 percent in 2000.[95]

The drive to incarcerate and criminalize youth, in particular, was countered by progressive efforts such as the gang truce and intervention work and broader attempts to reform policing practices and training. First established in 1992, days prior to the civil unrest, the truce between affiliates of the two largest gangs in Los Angeles, the Bloods and the Crips, was initiated by veteran gang members who wanted to decrease violence and increase opportunity in their communities. Modeled after the 1949 Egypt-Israel peace accord authored by U.S. ambassador Ralph Bunche (who grew up in the Los Angeles neighborhood where the gang truce was initiated), the truce brought together longtime rivals who participated in joint celebrations, economic ventures, volunteer activities, and political activism. As one participant reflected, "Instead of shooting each other, we decided to fight together for black power." In the first few months of the truce, the areas where it was in effect experienced precipitous drops in homicide and attempted murder rates. As an example, homicide rates plummeted 88.2 percent, from seventeen in 1991 to two by June 1992.[96] Beyond the decreasing rate of violence, there was a palpable change in livability in communities impacted by the truce, as participants became engaged in activities such as bone-marrow drives and poetry festivals.

Truce efforts spread beyond South Los Angeles and its predominantly African American gangs to include Latino gangs as far away as the San Fernando Valley. Individual efforts to initiate and maintain the truce soon developed into community-based organizations such as Amer-I-Can, Hands across Watts, Homies Unidos, Unity One, Barrios Unidos (which had been organized much earlier), and Communities in Schools. These groups worked to provide alternatives to gang life in the form of cultural, recreational, life-skills, and job-training programs. Leaders of many of these organizations directly sought public support. Two city programs, L.A. Bridges and Hope in Youth, were formed and contracted with organizations doing gang intervention work. Those engaged in the work complained that the programs were underresourced and that the constant threats to reduce funding forced truce leaders to focus on protecting funding and away from actual work with gang members.

Law enforcement was not always supportive of gang truce work and at times was openly hostile to it, arguing that it was merely an excuse for gang members to unify against police. This hostility and suspicion were directly demonstrated in the consistent harassment of truce leaders. One such incident involved the arrest by Rampart Division CRASH officers of Alex Sanchez, a respected leader of Homies Unidos, the truce organization active in the area covered by the infamous Rampart Division. Sanchez was picked up by LAPD officers but was not charged with a crime, instead being turned over to the INS, in direct violation of Special Order 40, a city police department rule that bars officers from stopping individuals solely for suspicion of violation of federal immigration laws. Through the activism and organizing of his colleagues and others, Sanchez successfully fought deportation and has returned to work with Homies Unidos.

In addition to efforts to proactively address the gang problem with civic-minded alternatives, activists also sought to reform the LAPD, whose Rampart Division had behaved at times much like a gang. Building upon the work of longtime anti–police abuse organizations, such as the Coalition against Police Abuse and the ACLU, the Coalition for Police Accountability, a collection of over forty civil rights and community groups, formed in 1999 in the wake of the Rampart scandal. The coalition sought to "improve the policies and practices of the LAPD and to restore the legitimacy of the people's faith and trust" in the police department.[97] Through a series of public protests and press conferences, the group pushed for a number of reforms, including increased civilian control of the LAPD and implementation of the federal consent decree focused on tracking of problem officers, increased response to civilian complaints, and tracking of data on potential racial profiling.

Despite Rampart, and despite an unreconstructed LAPD, the activism and organizing inspired by the gang truce work and police reform efforts have had positive community impacts. These efforts have further underlined the enormous importance of preventing and reducing violence in the neighborhoods, in the face of a police department that continues to protect and serve some while treating others as suspects rather than as constituents and collaborators.

Despite its reputation as an unlivable city—smog capital, freeway haven, fast-food headquarters, and home to a baton-wielding, quick-on-the-draw police force—Los Angeles has also generated some of the nation's most innovative and dynamic social movements, for which the struggle for a more livable city remains a passionate goal. As such movements become part of a changing city and a more diverse and complex region, the outcome of that struggle, including its political and policy dimensions, remains central to defining what the Next L.A. will be.

PART III

Politics and Policy

Identifying an Agenda for the Next L.A.

Introduction

In its March 8, 2001, issue, the alternative publication *L.A. Weekly* devoted its cover story to the emerging new progressive politics in Los Angeles. The article, entitled "A Vision for the City," included a roundtable discussion hosted by the *Weekly*'s editor, Harold Meyerson (coauthor of chapter 5 in this book), that included several of the leading labor, community, environmental, and social justice movement activists in the region. The roundtable was organized in part to discuss the Progressive Los Angeles Network (PLAN) Assembly, to take place two days later, where an initial progressive policy platform—in effect, an agenda for Progressive L.A.—would be unveiled. The platform had been developed by several hundred activists, community leaders, and academics and policy analysts over the previous year. The platform was seen as a living document, responsive to the dynamics of political activism, social and cultural change, and the economic and environmental upheaval that increasingly defined Los Angeles.

This section describes the background of the political and policy dynamics in contemporary Los Angeles, including the role of the region's progressive social movements and the various attempts to construct a policy agenda for the city. Chapter 5, "Shifting Coalitions," traces political dynamics in Los Angeles from the dominance of the post–World War II civic elites to the twenty-year mayoral reign of Tom Bradley and the subsequent battles during Richard Riordan's ascendance in the 1990s. Chapter 6, "Setting an Agenda," explores two contemporary experiences in agenda setting, the L.A. 2000 Partnership, which was established in 1985, and Rebuild L.A., the consortium of business and community figures formed in the wake of the L.A. civil unrest of 1992. The chapter then compares those efforts with the development of the progressive agenda through the work of PLAN and its broad network of activists. The concluding chapter, "A Vision for the City," explores the tensions of geographic secession, ethnic conflict, and progressive politics in the region. It also looks at the potential for the three governing themes of Progressive L.A.—social and economic justice, livability, and democratic participation and community empowerment—to reshape Los Angeles in the years to come.

5   Shifting Coalitions

L.A.'s Changing Political Landscape

THE STATE OF THE CITIES

When George W. Bush arrived in Los Angeles on April 29, 2002, the tenth anniversary of the civil unrest, it seemed reasonable to assume he would make a pronouncement about a policy for America's cities. His father's tepid response to the April 1992 events had reflected his lack of interest in urban issues. George W. Bush similarly dampened expectations that his appearance at a Black church in South L.A. represented anything more than a short interlude in his fund-raising and politicking. He talked about "hope" and "faith" but offered no specific policy proposals.[1]

Following the April 1992 civil unrest, hundreds of journalists and urban-policy experts, as well as presidential candidate Bill Clinton, had descended on the city. The timing for pulling together a major urban policy seemed right. The Cold War had ended. When the Berlin Wall had fallen and the Soviet Union had collapsed, there had been much public discussion about the prospects for a "peace dividend" to reorder national priorities and address long-unmet domestic needs. Moreover, the civil unrest had occurred in the midst of presidential and congressional elections, and America's urban crisis had become—briefly—a hot topic. But it wasn't long before the plight of America's cities—including the focus on Los Angeles—returned to political obscurity.

This cyclical interest in an urban policy is not a recent phenomenon, nor has it been simply confined to Los Angeles. Since the end of World War II, business leaders, government officials, community activists, labor leaders, scholars, and others have proposed bold plans to revitalize the nation's urban

---

This chapter was coauthored by Harold Meyerson.

areas. A long litany of federal programs—urban renewal, Model Cities, public housing, welfare, community development block grants, and many others—have come and gone. Each time there have been those who declared that
the nation had waged a "war on poverty" and that poverty had triumphed.

But the reality has been much more complex. Federal funds to revitalize
cities have been a drop in the bucket compared with federal subsidies to
encourage people and businesses to leave cities and move to the suburbs.
Federal transportation policies have primarily promoted highways that
opened up outlying areas to development of suburban housing tracts, shopping malls, office parks, and industrial centers. Federal housing policies have
made it easy for middle-class families to get mortgages to buy homes in the
suburbs but have made it almost impossible to do so in the cities. Even the
Department of Defense contributed to the postwar exodus to the suburbs by
funding defense contractors with facilities in suburbs and by moving military installations out of cities and into suburbs and rural areas. Through
much of the twentieth century, federal policies ended up primarily promoting the exodus of good jobs and middle-class families from cities and widening the economic gap between cities and suburbs. In doing so, they also
exacerbated the fiscal crisis of urban areas, thereby undermining efforts to
address the problems of poverty and provide basic services such as schools,
parks, and public safety.

Los Angeles has been at the forefront of such trends. More than any
other urban area, L.A. has reflected the federal government's tilt toward
suburbanization, highways, auto dependency, and an addiction to military
spending. Los Angeles' business and civic elites forged local growth coalitions and policies that in turn promoted a combination of suburban sprawl
and downtown redevelopment while locking out the poor and many working people from the benefits of both. As a consequence, the economic and
racial disparities that led to the wave of urban riots in American cities during the 1960s emerged first in L.A., most dramatically with the Watts riots
of 1965.

In this chapter, we look at the changes that have occurred in Los Angeles
politics in the post–World War II era, highlighting the shifting electoral
coalitions and governing regimes that emerged. Throughout this period,
grassroots challenges to urban renewal, displacement, racial discrimination
in jobs and housing, police misconduct, and environmental pollution triggered movements for reform. These social movements catapulted local liberal and progressive politicians into positions of influence—people such as
Ed Roybal, Henry Waxman, Tom Bradley, Jackie Goldberg, Tom Hayden,
Gloria Molina, Maxine Waters, Mark Ridley-Thomas, Mike Woo, Sheila

Kuehl, Gil Cedillo, and Antonio Villaraigosa. These movements and their political allies initially had to contend with a reasonably well-organized business elite that sought to shape the city's policy agenda, which has included suburban development, downtown renewal, and token incorporation of minorities (first Jews, then Blacks, Asians, and Latinos) into the business and political power structure. But progressive forces were nevertheless able to make significant gains, particularly by gaining access to public office and patronage.

By the end of the Tom Bradley era, in 1993, Los Angeles no longer had a well-oiled and coherent corporate power structure. It would have been difficult to name more than a handful of business executives who could genuinely be called civic leaders, with the kind of moral authority and political clout that went beyond their own business or industry. L.A. became increasingly linked to the global economy, and decisions about its economic future were made in corporate boardrooms in Europe, Australia, Asia, Canada, and other U.S. cities. Most local business and political leaders had no long-range vision or agenda for the city. Instead, they focused on making local deals. For example, they pushed to construct a subway—which they claimed was necessary for L.A. to become a "world-class" city—and then maneuvered to channel construction contracts to politically connected firms that in turn incurred immense cost overruns. They wielded their political influence to build hotels, office buildings, luxury housing, and megacomplexes like the Staples Center (where the L.A. Lakers play) and the Disney concert hall.

It had in fact become clear by the early 1990s that few business and political leaders had given much thought to addressing the city's widening economic and cultural divide. But while the "business of government" continued with a daily program of deal making and vote swapping, it was not clear who was looking out for those who were left out and left behind, for those who were struggling to pay rent, who were stuck in traffic, who suffered from the region's polluted air, or who lived in neighborhoods victimized by crime and inadequate schools.

The response to those political failures came in April 1992. While some of the civil unrest was confined geographically to South Central L.A., morally and politically the events rippled much further out, ricocheting across the entire city and the whole metropolitan area. The civil unrest became a testament to the vacuum of moral and political leadership in Los Angeles. As a result, throughout the decade and into the beginning of the twenty-first century, Los Angeles witnessed an ongoing struggle to fill that vacuum. Who could define a new vision for Los Angeles in the new century? Who could inject that vision into the public debate and forge a coalition to translate that vision into public policy? Could progressive forces—community groups, immigrants, unions, faith-based institutions, environmentalists, women's rights and gay rights crusaders, and many others who constituted the diverse social movements that had taken root in Los Angeles—sort out their differences, mobilize their constituencies, and contend for political power?

A FRAGMENTED LOS ANGELES

By the 1950s, Los Angeles had grown from a small town into a burgeoning metropolis, though the city, despite its size, still remained tightly controlled. A small, coherent, almost entirely WASP civic elite attempted to promote and control the city against the backdrop of explosive suburban growth. During this time, the increasing preoccupation of the elite was to provide a physical and civic center (by creating cultural institutions, importing the Dodgers, and so on) for a city frequently said to lack one. At the same time, the very nature of L.A.'s growth tended to decentralize the city in ways that ultimately undermined the efforts to strengthen the center.

The decentering process had many roots, beginning with real estate. For a quarter-century, beginning in 1945, a small group of savings and loan executives and tract home developers spatially transformed the L.A. region. In 1950, L.A. County was still a major agricultural county, one of the most productive in the United States. By 1970, it had virtually no agricultural activity. Tract homes were built in units of five thousand and ten thousand during these years. Three prominent bankers and developers—Ben Weingart, Mark Taper, and Lou Boyer—developed the city of Lakewood, north of Long Beach, chiefly for the huge number of white- and blue-collar workers in Long Beach's giant aerospace factories. Their "Lakewood Plan" enabled the tract to become incorporated as an autonomous city (and in the process erected some de facto racial restrictions) without having a heavy tax burden placed on either the new residents or the developers. The new city of Lakewood contracted for its basic services with the County of L.A., rather than pay for starting its own police, fire, and street-maintenance departments or by annexing to the city of Long Beach. In short order, the Lakewood Plan became a model for the incorporation of new municipalities across the county. In only a few decades, Los Angeles County became home to eighty-eight separate cities, of which Los Angeles, the nation's second largest, was merely the most prominent.[2]

Even prior to the Lakewood Plan, Los Angeles had accommodated major corporations by allowing them to form their own cities for tax purposes.

Movie studios, aerospace, and oil companies carved out their own little municipalities across the county. Thus, major concentrations of employment were spread across the San Fernando Valley and down the coast from Santa Monica to Long Beach. With tract housing spreading out in a similar pattern—most prominently promoted by the home-building firm Kaufman and Broad—a new model of urbanism was born. The workforce did not commute into a central location, as they did into Manhattan or Chicago's Loop. A street railway system, the legendary "Red Car," spread across the county, but in 1947 it was purchased by a consortium including General Motors, which over the next fifteen years dismantled it. With the growth of the suburban tract also came a new development in American consuming: the suburban shopping center.

Right after the war, the elite's major concern was the growing influence of New Deal liberals and leftists, spurred on by a spurt of union organizing and the increasing numbers of Jews and Blacks in L.A. In 1946, one of the L.A. elite's key figures, *L.A. Times* political editor Kyle Palmer, recruited a young lawyer, Richard Nixon, to run against Congressman Jerry Voorhis, a onetime Upton Sinclair Socialist turned Democrat. His opponents accused Voorhis—a solid progressive, but no radical—of being a tool of the CIO-PAC, the political wing of L.A.'s industrial unions. Nixon's victory launched his political career and prefigured a fifteen-year period of nearly unbroken triumphs for Los Angeles' right-wing establishment. Labor unions remained numerically strong during this period, but their political energy was sapped by internecine Communist/anti-Communist wars during the late 1940s and then subsided into relative quiescence from the 1950s through the 1970s.

The inner circle of the city's unelected power structure—a kind of shadow government—was a small, elite clique called the Committee of 25, formed in the early 1950s. They ran the city's major business establishments and law firms. They controlled its foundations, its hospitals, its cultural institutions, and its universities. (The boards of USC and CalTech were their exclusive domain.) They sat on each other's boards and gave to each other's favorite charities. They had lunch downtown at the exclusive California Club and Jonathan Club, both off-limits to Jews, Blacks, and Latinos. (The Jewish moguls of the film industry might as well have been in another world as far as the city's WASP business elite were concerned.) They were all men and, for the most part, Republican. They hated unions, supported the Cold War, opposed subsidized housing, disliked Jews, and had little use for racial minorities. Their voice was the *Los Angeles Times*. Asa Call (CEO of Pacific Mutual Life Insurance), Norman Chandler (publisher of the *Times*), James "Lin" Beebe (partner in the downtown law firm of O'Melveny and Myers), and John McCone (a prominent executive of ship-building and engineering firms and later director of the CIA) were some of the key figures in this tight power elite. They picked people to run for local and state public offices, spearheaded "blue-ribbon" committees on the city's future, and channeled philanthropic funds into cultural organizations that served the upper class and social service agencies that provided Band-aids for the poor.[3]

In the 1950s, the chief thorn in their side was L.A. Mayor Fletcher Bowron, a liberal Republican in the Earl Warren mold. Most offensive to them were Bowron's ambitious plans for public housing. His deputy hous-ing director, Frank Wilkinson, had long been a target for FBI and LAPD sur-veillance because he supervised what was at his insistence an integrated public housing project in Watts. The police agencies and the press went after Wilkinson as a way to damage Bowron, who was defeated in his 1953 reelec-tion bid by Congressman Norris Poulson—a candidate whose entire cam-paign was conceived and funded by the Committee of 25. For the next twenty years, no progressive initiatives would come out of city hall.

From the late 1950s through the mid-1960s, L.A. saw the Dodgers move from Brooklyn into a downtown-adjacent stadium, and the construction of the Music Center adjacent to the civic center and the County Museum of Art on the Wilshire corridor. The Music Center was largely the handiwork of Dorothy Chandler, doyenne of the family that owned the *Times* and more local real estate than anyone else. She also supported her son Otis in his largely successful efforts to transform the paper from a parochial, right-wing propaganda sheet into a nationally respected publication.

The Chandlers and their allies were successful in promoting downtown L.A. as a cultural and financial center. But this "success" came at a serious price. Downtown business interests both lived off the wealth generated by L.A.'s car-culture sprawl and were threatened by it. As early as the 1920s, the first nondowntown department store, Bullock's Wilshire, featured the world's first drive-up auto entrance. Immediately after the war, numerous department stores along the Wilshire corridor (precursors to the suburban malls) started taking shoppers out of downtown. In response, the downtown elite—the *Times* most particularly—began a campaign both to "clean up" downtown (routing a politically protected bar-and-prostitution district) and to erect a cultural center there.

At the peak of its power, the role of L.A.'s civic elite had been magnified due to L.A.'s weak mayor and district election system for City Council. It was so full of checks and balances that it was nearly impossible to get things done without the support of the business community. This situation was no accident. Early in the twentieth century, business leaders "reformed" the city's government structure to restrict the ability of unions, immigrants, political parties, and other potentially unfriendly forces to wield much influence. They gave the mayor few powers. In fact, in 1965, political scientist Edward Banfield wrote that L.A.'s mayor is "almost too weak to cut ribbons."[4] District elections, in turn, established a kind of minifiefdom for the fifteen members of the City Council, since each council member was largely responsible for deciding which development projects would get approved and who would get the contracts to do them. The fiefdom approach also meant that there was little incentive to forge a governing majority in the council around a broader policy agenda, particularly one that could address deep-rooted social and economic problems. Equally important, during the postwar era, many of the most important decisions affecting Los Angeles were made by semiautonomous special district agencies—such as the Community Redevelopment Agency, the Metropolitan Water District, and the Metropolitan Transportation Authority—to which lobbyists and contractors had greater access than ordinary voters did. By the end of the 1960s, in the wake of the Watts riots, a political vacuum had begun to emerge. It was fueled by the anger and protests in the streets, the absence of political accountability, and the lack of a coherent policy agenda to address the stresses of suburbanization and the problems of the inner city.

A FEEL-GOOD ERA:
THE BRADLEY YEARS

In America, city politics are often the politics of ethnic succession. In 1949, community activist Ed Roybal, from the 9th district, centered in Boyle Heights—an area heavy in Latino and Jewish populations—became the first Latino elected to the Los Angeles City Council since 1881. Roybal vacated his seat in 1962 and ran successfully for Congress, but it took until 1985 for another Latino to win a City Council race. In 1953, when twenty-two-year-old Roz Weiner (later Wyman) was elected to the council from the 5th district, she became the first Jewish member of the City Council in the twentieth century. She and Roybal became the liberal wing of the predominantly conservative council. For example, Weiner supported Roybal's proposal to create a Fair Employment Practices Commission in the city, a measure that failed to win council approval. After Weiner broke the religious barrier, it took another twelve years for the number of Jews on the council to increase from one to two, when Ed Edelman in 1965 defeated Wyman and

Marvin Braude was elected to another seat. Prior to that, Gil Lindsay, appointed to fill Roybal's seat in 1962, became the first African American on the City Council, while Tom Bradley and Billy Mills became in 1963 the first African Americans to be elected to the council (from the 10th and 8th districts, respectively). Since 1963, there have consistently been three African Americans on the fifteen-member City Council.[5]

These elections reflected the emergence of a Jewish-Black coalition in the 1950s and 1960s that ultimately changed L.A. politics. The great postwar migration of Jews to L.A. had been matched by an even greater postwar migration of African Americans. A number of Black, Jewish, and Black-*and*-Jewish liberal organizations were formed, reducing the influence of the old WASP elite and, in 1973, helping to bring Tom Bradley to city hall. More than a decade before Chicago, more than a decade and a half before New York, L.A. had created the model for the Black-led urban liberal coalitions that were to play a major role in American politics until the mid-1990s.

Politically, both the Jewish and Black communities had mainstream as well as liberal reform wings. They contested for power, with different candidates and different views on policy. The 10th City Council district, predominantly Black and Jewish, was the center of the reform faction among both groups and, equally important, the meeting ground for liberal activists from both groups. The rise of influential Jewish leaders and, later, Black leaders in reform politics, and the eventual emergence of a Black-Jewish alliance, paralleled the rise of another, at times overlapping, force in L.A. politics.[6] Beginning in the late 1950s, a Democratic Club movement, initially inspired by the candidacies of Adlai Stevenson, the Illinois governor who ran for president in 1952 and 1956, attracted young liberal activists—disproportionately Jewish and Black—across town. Some of the activists in this movement had been initially involved in Upton Sinclair's EPIC movement and 1934 campaign for governor.[7] Some were involved in labor and civil liberties struggles in L.A. and elsewhere. As with everything else in L.A., many had been born outside the region, moved to L.A., and found a niche in various political and community forms of activism.[8]

These alliances grew during the 1960s, playing a key role in civil rights activism and opposition to the Vietnam War. A major breakthrough in the electoral area was Bradley's 1963 election to the L.A. City Council, thanks in part to the emerging Black-Jewish coalition. Bradley's 10th district included large populations of both groups, and both groups mixed in Bradley's New Frontier Democratic Club. A few years before, Bradley had met Maury Weiner, a progressive Jewish activist recently transplanted from New York, when they had both worked on one of Ed Roybal's campaigns. By 1963,

Weiner had become Bradley's chief lieutenant, a position he was to hold until well into Bradley's first term as mayor. At the time of his council race, Bradley faced opposition from more centrist forces in the Black community, aligned with then Assemblyman Mervyn Dymally, who disparaged the notion of coalition with White progressives. Nonetheless, Bradley prevailed.[9]

With Black and White liberal political mobilization and cooperation accelerating throughout the 1960s, Bradley first challenged incumbent Sam Yorty for mayor in 1969. Bradley's campaign recruited an unheard-of fifteen thousand volunteers—a tribute to the liberal, civil rights, and union networks forged by Bradley's supporters and to the excitement of participating in a historic election that would elevate an African American to the mayoralty of a major city.[10] Yorty defeated Bradley by successfully retailoring the rhetoric of Alabama governor George Wallace for an L.A. electorate. He accused Bradley of being a tool of Communists and the Black Panthers. Bradley was both Red-baited and Black-baited. The heated and close race engaged voters, who went to the polls in record numbers. (In fact, the turnout in the 1969 race has not been surpassed in a city election since—not just in percentages, but in raw numbers, despite the fact that L.A. today has almost a million more people.)

In 1973, Bradley tried again—this time waging a more mainstream, media-savvy campaign that stressed his twenty years on the police force. The 1973 election marked a numerical high point for participation by Black L.A., which constituted 26 percent of the electorate that year—a figure that has been shrinking ever since. In his second race, Bradley was funded chiefly by a small group of Westside Jewish liberals who had also provided much of the funding for liberal and antiwar presidential candidates Eugene McCarthy and George McGovern. His finance chair was Max Palevsky, whose administrative assistant was a young lawyer named Gray Davis (later California governor). Four years earlier, Yorty had siphoned off just enough votes from enough Jews and Latinos to survive. In 1973, Bradley ran better in both the Jewish and Latino communities and brought this new coalition into power.[11]

Tom Bradley's early years in office could be considered L.A.'s "feel-good era." Bradley nearly carried the White vote in the 1973 election (he carried it decisively in all his subsequent reelections). Never in America had this many White people voted for a Black candidate. More than just a mayor, Bradley—a figure of great dignity and almost sphinxlike reserve—became a symbol of L.A.'s racial enlightenment, an image he reinforced by fostering cross-racial alliances (although he also declined to get involved in an early-1970s fight for compulsory busing to integrate L.A.'s schools). Throughout the 1970s, Bradley made Los Angeles feel good about its mayor and about itself.

Pursuing policies of affirmative action, Bradley substantially integrated the city's workforce. His appointments to city commissions broke the conservative, WASP stranglehold on the city's levers of power. For example, while the Black proportion of the overall municipal workforce increased from 21.9 percent in 1973 to 26.7 percent by 1990, the proportion of Blacks among top officials, administrators, and professionals increased from 6.3 percent to 22.7 percent. The proportion of Blacks on key city commissions also increased, from 15 percent to 20 percent; among Latinos, from 9 percent to 16 percent; among Asian Americans, from 7 percent to 13 percent; and among women, from 32 percent to 47 percent. In a break from his predecessors, his key city hall advisors and commission appointees included Blacks, Latinos, Asians, Jews, and women.[12] And unlike Yorty, who had actively shunned a range of federal Great Society programs targeted at helping cities, Bradley made L.A. a center of the social welfare and public employment programs of the 1970s, drawing on the federal antipoverty and urban renewal programs to carry out his agenda.

Like most postwar Democratic mayors, however, Bradley struck up an alliance with business interests to promote and to revive the city's downtown.[13] Quickly, the remnants of the old elite realized they could do business with Bradley. With the assistance of the city's Community Redevelopment Agency (CRA), whose chair was a Bradley-appointed labor leader with strong ties to construction unions, downtown L.A. became home during the 1970s and 1980s to a generation of gleaming high-rise office towers. Downtown had a skyline at last.

Perhaps the peak of the Bradley "feel-good" period was 1984, when Los Angeles hosted the summer Olympic games. The region's business leaders came together under the leadership of Peter Ueberroth, a travel company executive, to build the infrastructure and sports facilities needed. He persuaded major global companies like Coca-Cola, IBM, and Fuji Photo to sponsor the games and pay huge fees for the privilege of doing so. The L.A. Olympics were the first privately financed games ever. They made an unheard-of profit of $215 million. *Time* magazine was so impressed it named Ueberroth its man of the year.[14]

Bradley presided over the Olympics with great pride. But this would be, in some ways, his last hurrah. By the mid-1980s, the Bradley coalition had begun to falter. The passage of the statewide Proposition 13 in 1978, the drastic tax-cutting measure that had already limited the ability of cities to raise funds, and the election of Ronald Reagan in 1980 and his subsequent reduction of federal funds for urban social and community development programs, put the squeeze on the cities. In Los Angeles, Bradley was obliged to dramatically reduce the funds for community improvement efforts. At the same time, Bradley also began to neglect his original political base in the city's poor neighborhoods. According to the *L.A. Weekly,* for example, from 1988 to 1992 South Central received fewer "per person in poverty" economic development, job training, and human services funds than the more affluent West L.A.[15] Bradley, however, did manage to secure federal and other local funds to begin a much-criticized subway project—a source of lucrative contracts for political allies on the Metropolitan Transportation Agency board. But, overall, as the money dried up, Bradley became increasingly reliant on private banks, developers, and investors, as well as the support of the Central City Association and the Chamber of Commerce, to promote the redevelopment of the central business district. By the end of its twenty-year reign, the great promise of the Bradley coalition had dissipated, with progressives left to contend with a top-down policy agenda amid a growing economic and social divide.

SHIFTING COALITIONS

Bradley's 1969 and 1973 campaigns had brought together the city's political outsiders—primarily Jews, Blacks, and Latinos—some of whom had joined forces in the civil rights and antiwar trenches before forging an alliance to take over city hall. But as the Bradley administration made its peace with the downtown growth coalition of corporations, developers, construction unions, and the *L.A. Times,* the separate elements of Bradley's electoral coalition also began to pursue their own agendas and establish their own political operations.

The first major shift occurred within the Black-Jewish coalition. Two Westside-based young Jewish lawyers proved particularly adept in reaching across town—and, eventually, across the country—for allies beyond and sometimes in conflict with the Bradley coalition. Henry Waxman and Howard Berman came of age as leaders of the California Young Democrats and as strong and early opponents of the Vietnam War. In the late 1960s and early 1970s, they won insurgent campaigns for State Assembly seats, with Waxman going to Congress in 1974. They also successfully facilitated the campaigns of a series of protégés—like themselves, liberal and Jewish—for seats through the Westside and much of the San Fernando Valley. But their reach did not stop there. Berman, who aspired to become Assembly speaker, cultivated allies and helped to fund and recruit legislative candidates in the

Black and Latino communities as well, while Waxman, eager to advance up the congressional ladder, did the same for congressional candidates.

The form of their machine was at least as notable as its reach. Working with Howard Berman's brother Michael, who became an influential political consultant, Waxman and Berman developed a political operation for an age of demobilization. As early as 1968, the year of Waxman's successful, low-dollar insurgent campaign for a Westside Assembly seat, Michael had developed targeted political mailings several years before anyone had come up with computerized voting lists. As the number of liberal foot soldiers began its steady downward slide after the late 1960s, Waxman and Berman developed a way to win elections without many volunteers. With a campaign treasury raised from their large and loyal core of funders in the Westside Jewish community, Michael Berman perfected the art of targeted mail and phone-banks and put his skills at the service of their allies. In essence, what the two Bermans and Waxman created was a substitute party, which did almost everything a real party would do: raise money, print and mail campaign literature, select candidates, even draw the district boundaries for reapportionment.[16]

The paradox was that while Waxman in particular became one of the most principled and effective congressional liberals of the past quarter-century, he helped to perfect a political system that placed little premium on mobilizing new or sometime voters, and great premium on mobilizing money. Initially, Michael Berman's slate mailings—which unwary voters assumed came from the Democratic Party (itself so broke that it put virtually nothing into the mail)—were open free of charge to like-minded liberal candidates, but he soon began charging campaigns for the privilege of appearing on the slate. Corporate-funded initiatives quickly became the meal ticket for Berman slate mailers, and progressive local initiative campaigns frequently couldn't afford the price of inclusion. In 1984, Jobs with Peace, a progressive grassroots organization, tried to pay its way to get its municipal military-to-peacetime conversion initiative onto a Berman slate but was outbid by defense contractors. By the late 1980s, Waxman had distanced himself from the operation; by the mid-'90s, Michael Berman had retired. By which time, however, the for-profit slate, produced by consultants with few if any ideological criteria, had become a staple of L.A. politics—and increasingly of local politics everywhere, as the power of political parties in the postpatronage age continued to wane. Since the 1980s, campaign-season politics in L.A. has come to consist chiefly of candidates' raising money that buys them a place on a range of consultants' slate mailings. At the same time, phony slate mailings have frequently been used as a device to confuse and misrepresent issues as well as the positions of elected officials, as in the case of the hotel industry's initiative in the 2002 election to undercut Santa Monica's groundbreaking living wage ordinance.

Even at its high point, the Berman-Waxman machine was an alliance of politicians, donors, and campaign technicians. There was no organizational base to their coalition, even though, on certain issues, affiliated Berman-Waxman politicians were able to play influential roles. Waxman in particular had one of the most wide-reaching agendas of any member of Congress (no one has done more to expand federal medical coverage, for instance) and, with other allies, introduced important health and quality-of-life initiatives. At one point in the mid-'90s, Waxman led the federal-level fight against tobacco companies while the state-level ban on smoking in public places was being pushed by Westside Assemblyman Terry Friedman and the citywide ban was advanced by Westside Councilman Marvin Braude: all three from overlapping districts.

The Westside also put its mark on national politics as a source of major funding for liberal candidates and causes. By the late 1960s, a core of Westside liberals—Max Palevsky, Stanley Sheinbaum, Norman Lear, Harold Willens—had emerged as a major force in national liberal politics, funding the campaigns of presidential candidates Eugene McCarthy and George McGovern and kindred figures. They felt quite at home within the Bradley coalition as well, and played an indispensable role in funding his first two mayoral campaigns. Thereafter, however, their interest focused more on the national, or even global, level than it did on the local. They and their fellow liberals routinely funded progressive presidential aspirants and congressional and senatorial candidates from around the nation. In time, each cultivated his own particular causes—Sheinbaum funding Middle East peace ventures, Lear the People for the American Way, Willens the nuclear freeze, Palevsky his own magazine. But, with the exception of Sheinbaum, they showed less and less interest in their own city. Thus, another potential civic elite largely withdrew from the political life of the city.

Meanwhile, Black community leaders and politicians were building their own political operation and moving into political offices. Just one out of seventy-seven significant elected officeholders in Los Angeles County was Black in 1960; by 1967, nine of those positions were held by Blacks.[17] The number of Blacks in the State Assembly and Senate grew steadily from the 1960s through the 1980s. These trends were the result of the overall growth of the Black population, Bradley's barrier-breaking election (which showed that Whites would support a Black candidate), the increasing concentration of the Black population in particular neighborhoods, the redistricting of City

Council and state legislative districts to make them safer for Black candidates, and an increase in the number of Black professionals who (along with Westside liberals) contributed to campaigns.

Until Bradley was elected mayor in 1973, the organization orchestrated by state legislators Jesse Unruh and Mervyn Dymally was the key political organization in the Black community. While it operated outside the civil rights organizational arena, it fed on some of the activism inspired by the freedom movement, but was less a crusade than a political machine focused on patronage. Almost every Black voter in L.A. supported Bradley in his early campaigns and took enough pride in his accomplishment to continue to support him in subsequent races, even though he paid less attention to their neighborhood concerns, such as affordable housing, jobs, and public safety.

Bradley sought to consolidate his power by encouraging allies—Black and White—to run for public office and by helping to recruit campaign aides and raise money. Bradley's candidates typically prevailed, but in some cases the Dymally organization's candidates won. These two factions differed little on policy matters; they were both generally supportive of the liberal agenda. The biggest difference was over "approach and style," as well as personal loyalty, as political analyst Raphael Sonenshein puts it.[18]

The career of Maxine Waters reflects these political and personal dynamics.[19] Born in St. Louis in 1938, Waters moved to L.A. in 1961, worked in a garment factory, raised two children, and earned a sociology degree from Cal State Los Angeles. After the Watts riots in 1965, she became an assistant Head Start teacher and was active in community organizations, while also becoming a political operative and key player within the Bradley coalition. She was chief deputy to David Cunningham, a Bradley ally who succeeded him as the member of the council from the 10th district. She managed the campaigns of Bradley allies Robert Farrell, who was running for the council, and Kenneth Washington, for the State Senate. In 1976, she ran for an open State Assembly seat in the 48th district, then comprising low-income and working-class Black areas and (in the neighboring city of South Gate) White working-class voters. She drew on her network of Bradley supporters for money and campaign workers and decisively beat a candidate supported by the rival Dymally organization.

Waters served in the Assembly for fourteen years, where she was a key ally of Speaker Willie Brown and a vocal and effective advocate for liberal and progressive causes, including limits on police strip searches, support for tenants' rights, and divestiture of state pension funds from South Africa. She soon broke ranks with the Bradley organization and developed her own independent political base. She and Bradley often supported rival candidates for council and legislative offices. When Augustus Hawkins—who had been elected to the legislature in 1934 on the EPIC wave and later became the first Black congressperson from California—retired in 1990, Waters ran for his seat and won.

In Congress, Waters continued to be a progressive crusader. She received almost perfect scores on her voting record from groups such as the ACLU, Americans for Democratic Action, the League of Conservation Voters, and the AFL-CIO. She chaired the Congressional Black Caucus and sponsored legislation to strengthen the antiredlining Community Reinvestment Act. In 1988 she was a key backer of Reverend Jesse Jackson's presidential campaign, but she also later effectively mobilized Black voting support for more moderate Democratic candidates, including Bill Clinton and Al Gore. She was one of six members of Congress who voted against U.S. involvement in the Gulf War in 1991. Even as a congresswoman, she has been a strong presence in L.A. politics.

Throughout her legislative career, she has combined behind-the-scenes deal making with protest politics, due to her passion for justice and the fact that she has had a safe seat. After the Rodney King beating, for example, she led rallies demanding the resignation of Police Chief Darryl Gates. In the wake of the 1992 civil unrest, Waters became much more visible on the national stage as a spokesperson for Black grievances and justice issues, but she also used her influence to help real estate developers and other business supporters to win city hall approvals and federal grants. However, her opposition to some coalition-building efforts ended up alienating a number of local progressives and separated her from the multiracial political movements that had reemerged in the mid- and late 1990s.

Just as Waters broke from the Bradley organization to forge an independent political base, other Black progressives kept their distance from Waters. One of them was Mark Ridley-Thomas, who had become a movement activist in the 1980s and had served for a decade as executive director of the Southern Christian Leadership Conference of Los Angeles, the local affiliate of the organization founded by Martin Luther King, Jr. Through SCLC, Ridley-Thomas forged contacts with community activists and became involved in grassroots campaigns against police brutality and for civil rights. In 1991 he was elected to the 8th City Council district. Soon after taking office, he created an "Empowerment Congress" in his district to bring together residents, businesses, religious institutions, and neighborhood groups to help to set his council policy agenda. The Empowerment Congress was subsequently cited as a model for local participation in government, such as neighborhood councils. Like Waters, Ridley-Thomas became a strong voice for neighborhood development, environmental justice, and affordable housing within his district, and sought to reach out beyond his district to forge progressive and liberal alliances among Whites, Latinos, and Asians. For much of the 1990s, he and Jackie Goldberg formed an alliance as the key progressives on the council, until both, due to term limits, successfully moved on to the State Assembly.[20]

While both Waters and Ridley-Thomas maintained safe seats due to their strong base in the African American community, changing demographics in their districts presented a new kind of challenge—and potential opportunity. Since her election to Congress in 1990, Waters has never had a serious challenger, but the changing demographics of her district indicate some of the political realities, based on race and ethnicity, that have been emerging in Los Angeles. According to the 2000 census, Waters's district is now 54 percent Latino. With Latinos increasingly living in neighborhoods once dominated by African Americans (just as Blacks moved into neighborhoods once dominated by Jews), there is potential for both cooperation and conflict over redistricting, jobs, housing, schools, and other issues.

Although Latinos were becoming the largest demographic group in L.A., it took longer for Latino candidates to get elected to the City Council. As the politically weakest and most disenfranchised group in Los Angeles (a function both of immigration status and long-standing economic and political biases), Latinos had seen their community broken up—spatially and politically—for decades. The Eastside, long the center of Latino L.A., had six freeways (three east-west, three north-south) running through it by the 1970s, far more than any other area in Southern California. (By contrast, the only area in Los Angeles that had been able to keep out a freeway altogether during the freeway-boom years had been the affluent Westside.) Similarly, after Edward Roybal went from the City Council to Congress in 1962, reapportionment of federal, state, county, and city districts so managed to fragment the Latino community that for years Roybal was its only elected representative at any level of government.

Still, there had always been some level of community organizing within this most fragmented of communities, and it accelerated with the rise of the United Farm Workers in the 1960s and the Vietnam War and civil rights protests that shook East L.A. high schools in the late 1960s and early 1970s.[21] By the early 1970s, Eastside residents were able to elect two state assemblymen—Richard Alatorre and Art Torres—who came to dominate local Latino politics for two decades.

As accomplished Sacramento insiders allied, after 1980, with California

Assembly Speaker Willie Brown, Alatorre and Torres made sure that the 1980 state and federal reapportionment created a number of Latino legislative districts. (The creation of more Latino City Council and county supervisorial districts didn't take place until the huge migration of the 1980s made it all but impossible to keep Latinos off those bodies—though creating a Latino seat on the County Board of Supervisors still required a court order.) Soon, Alatorre and Torres were anointing other Latino candidates and providing them with the funding to win their elections. The funds came from a range of contractors and developers who got their contracts by virtue of their ties with this new political machine; the most prominent such organization was TELACU (the East Los Angeles Community Union), a onetime community-development corporation. But while the Torres-Alatorre operation generated contracts, not that many jobs were actually created. It had no mass-member political institutions working for it or that it could reward. It had no incentive to register or mobilize large numbers of voters. The legislative districts where its candidates ran were safely Democratic; appointment was tantamount to election.[22]

Meanwhile, with Republicans controlling the governor's office from 1982 through 1998, most Democratic money for voter registration and mobilization was controlled by Assembly Speaker Willie Brown, who always invested resources in the handful of suburban swing districts—usually heavily White—that were assumed to be the most contested. Hardly any money was available for the safe Democratic districts of East L.A. or South Central. Thus, while Latino L.A. was growing, and then exploding with the advent of the great migration that began in the early 1980s, mainstream politicians invested little time or money in mobilizing its voters until well into the 1990s.

While Torres and Alatorre cultivated their power base, they did little to reach out to other liberal forces. Another key Latino political figure, an L.A. councilwoman and then county supervisor, Gloria Molina, became a defector from their ranks and set up her own political organization, which backed candidates opposed to Torres and Alatorre's in Latino districts. Molina cultivated relationships with liberals and feminists across town through the early 1990s, although she subsequently let many of those relationships lapse.

By the early 1990s, Alatorre had achieved the apogee of his career as a backroom player: he became the dominant force on the board of the Metropolitan Transportation Authority, from which he directed hundreds of millions of dollars in contracts toward allies. At the same time, he was barely able to win reelection in his own council district over a challenger he outspent better than ten to one. As a generator of contracts, the machine had never been stronger; as a generator of votes, it had never been weaker. Unlike Black L.A., Latino L.A. was growing—but like Black L.A., it was critically undermobilized and frequently cut off from potential allies around town.[23]

A CONSERVATIVE BACKLASH

While Bradley was mayor, many of the institutions that had helped to establish his political base began to crumble. The auto, steel, and tire industries, which had provided unionized middle-income jobs to thousands of Angelenos, all closed down. These industrial unions had played an important role in the liberal wing of the Democratic Party, mobilizing money, troops, and coalitions. As the industrial unions declined in membership and clout, the dominant political force within organized labor increasingly became the building-trades unions, whose major concern was a steady stream of construction jobs, and thus its support for unfettered growth.[24] The political organizations, the Democratic Clubs and large industrial unions, in which the Bradley forces were rooted, all saw their numbers and clout greatly diminish. With the Mexican economy in a shambles and with Central America immersed in civil wars, a huge migration from the south began to transform L.A. Entire industries—from garments to gardening— sprang up or expanded, and wages in many sectors, such as construction and building maintenance, were slashed to take advantage of this seemingly bottomless pool of cheap labor. The new immigrants, however, had no point of entry into local politics, and many of them had no citizenship status, in any case. The Reagan revolution in federal urban policy greatly reduced inner-city employment programs, just as the number of decent-paying blue-collar jobs were also in decline. A sizable gang culture grew among the city's Black and Latino youth.

Meanwhile, three distinct but sometimes overlapping revolts broke out that challenged Bradley's coalition of liberal activists interested in social justice and of business interests concerned with revitalizing the downtown economy.

The first revolt was the gradual withdrawal of support, primarily among White middle-class voters, for the public schools and other government services that came to be disproportionately patronized by the nonvoting, non-White population. As in many American cities in the 1970s, Los Angeles school officials were pressured into adopting busing as a tool to address the racial segregation in the public schools. At the start of the 1970s, a court ruling ordered cross-city busing of K-12 students to integrate L.A. schools. It was an important cause for some Los Angeles progressives, but it soon became clear that they had underestimated the opposition to the proposal throughout the city. In fact, busing provided the opening wedge for a distinct San Fernando Valley conservatism. In 1973, Bobbi Fiedler, a right-wing activist, won election to the school board on an antibusing platform and acquired allies in subsequent elections. A vocal opponent of school busing, Alan Robbins, ran against Bradley in 1977; he lost, but his campaign helped to keep the issue alive. The next year, a liberal member of the school board, Howard Miller, lost his seat as the result of a recall movement by busing opponents. Miller was replaced by busing foe Roberta Weintraub, who joined Fiedler on the generally probusing board.[25]

A much-scaled-back busing program was implemented, later to be jettisoned as the district grew so heavily non-White as to make integration impossible (at least in terms of integrating White students with students of color). The racial makeup of the schools reflected the residential segregation of the city's neighborhoods. The conflict over school busing led to a gradual exodus of many White middle-class families (and, to a lesser extent, of Black, Hispanic, and Asian middle-class families) from the public schools. It was the largely White electorate that turned its back on a public school system that, from its vantage point, was increasingly attended by other people's children, not its own.

Also in the 1970s, two right-wing political activists led a crusade against property taxes and, as a result, against government spending. Longtime right-wing gadfly Howard Jarvis, an operative with the L.A. Apartment Owners Association, and his colleague Paul Gann, an antitax activist, authored an initiative that tapped into the growing anxiety of homeowners, particularly seniors on fixed incomes, whose property taxes were soaring amid the inflation of California housing prices. Their solution, which state voters overwhelmingly enacted in that year's June primary, was Proposition 13, which rolled back and froze property taxes on all residential and commercial property.[26] With that, local governments and school districts lost their chief source of funding, and it fell to state government to provide annual stipends to counties and school districts to keep them running. While some of its appeal was no doubt a generalized skepticism about politicians and government, some was no doubt due to the reality that escalating housing prices had dramatically pushed up property taxes for many working-class and middle-class homeowners, whose incomes had not increased at the same rate. Certainly its founders, Jarvis and Gann, viewed the measure as a vehicle to mobilize a right-populist majority opposed to further public spending and in favor of steadily dismantling the public sector. Many of those who voted for Proposition 13 could not have anticipated the consequences in terms of the severe decline in public services that came in its wake.

Proposition 13 had profound effects on California, most of them disastrous. School spending declined precipitously: per-pupil spending in California, which ranked fifth during the mid-1960s, fell to forty-second by the late 1990s. Already by the mid-1980s, the construction of new schools in Los Angeles had just about ceased—though a huge immigrant influx was already beginning to overwhelm the capacity of the district to absorb them. This led to a particularly vicious political circle: a bond measure for new schools, which now required a two-thirds vote to pass, would be placed on the local ballot. Increasingly, the parents of the children who would benefit were immigrants who could not vote; increasingly, the voters who did get to the polls were Whites whose children were not in district schools. Not surprisingly, the bond measure would fail, and the problems of the schools would only grow worse.[27]

The third revolt focused on resistance to unfettered real estate development. While the Bradley administration and its downtown business allies were adding new skyscrapers to the central business district, other real estate developers were pushing many so-called downtown functions outward, to the Westside, Century City, the San Fernando Valley, and the mid–Wilshire corridor. These parts of L.A. (along with booming office centers in Glendale, Pasadena, Burbank, and even Ventura) competed with the old downtown for business tenants. Some homeowner groups in these areas began to complain that L.A. was becoming overdeveloped and, over time, began to resist some aspects of the city's business-led growth machine. As the freeways and streets grew steadily more congested and less navigable, many middle-class homeowners began to organize to influence zoning and land-use decisions made at city hall.[28]

Despite the Westside's history of strong support for Bradley himself, many residents began to see the real estate growth machine as inimical to the quality of life in their neighborhoods. In 1986, City Councilman Marvin Braude and fellow Westside Councilman Zev Yaroslavsky placed a measure on the city ballot—Proposition U—that greatly limited further high-rise construction all across L.A., except in designated areas such as downtown and Century City. With traffic increasingly grinding to a halt in neighborhoods that had never experienced congestion before, Proposition U passed handily. Slow-growth politics were to be the basis of Yaroslavsky's planned run against Bradley in 1989, which was shaping up as Bradley's first serious challenge. Hiring an environmental activist as his new chief of staff, however, Bradley abruptly threw his growth juggernaut into reverse, even canceling projects in Yaroslavsky's council district that the councilman had already approved. It was pork-barrel politics in reverse, with two politicos vying to see who could authorize the fewest new projects. This was not a game that Yaroslavsky could win, and ultimately, he pulled out of the race, though in fact he had already helped to end the period of unrestricted growth in Los Angeles.[29]

The growth of the San Fernando Valley created a counterforce to both the downtown business elite and the liberal constituencies among Jews, Blacks, and Latinos. With a population of more than a million, it alone was larger than every other city in California except Los Angeles itself. The Valley had a larger proportion of Whites and homeowners than other sections of Los Angeles, although the number of Blacks and Latinos grew substantially in the 1990s. The Valley had its own business community, primarily small- and middle-size firms, which formed a "powerful economic sector but one that was almost completely divorced of formal ties to other areas of the city," as one analyst put it.[30] These firms formed a number of business trade organizations, including the United Chamber of Commerce of San Fernando Valley, the San Fernando Valley Association of Realtors, the Valley Industry and Commerce Association, and the Economic Alliance of San Fernando Valley, each upset by what it perceived to be city hall's bloated bureaucracy, complex business licensing and permitting process, and high taxes. Perhaps most important, the Valley had its own daily newspaper, the *Daily News*, which could not compete with the *Times* for citywide circulation but focused its attention instead on becoming the voice of the Valley.

A conservative backlash was building. It laid the groundwork for the election of a business-oriented mayor, Richard Riordan, while helping to form the basis of a movement for secession, especially in the San Fernando Valley, which had first emerged in the 1970s, reappeared in subsequent decades, and gained significant momentum by the start of the new century.[31]

THE RIORDAN INTERLUDE

By the late 1980s, the Bradley coalition was slowly coming unstuck. Each key segment of the coalition—Blacks, liberal Jews, industrial unions, moderate business leaders—was going its own way and getting lost. As the 1993 mayoral election approached, it was also becoming increasingly apparent that there were virtually no remaining citywide institutions—no cross-racial alliances or political structures, no unions or even business elites—

much less institutions capable of renewing the Bradley forces' lease on city hall. The urban liberal coalition of the previous three decades seemed more and more to resemble a historic artifact.

When the events of April 29, 1992, erupted, it appeared that everyone, from the mayor to the *L.A. Times,* was taken completely by surprise by the ferocity of the streets. The first night of the civil unrest, Tom Bradley's aides had to sneak him out of the First AME Church, where he was delivering a talk, lest the outraged crowd outside attack him. Throughout the next day, false reports of violence spread throughout White L.A., leading some to think that various citadels of Westside civilization (such as the upscale Beverly Center shopping mall) were under attack, when in fact they were not. Residents of at least one Hollywood Hills canyon erected barricades and formed a heavily armed patrol to repel marauders, who never showed up. L.A. suffered a world-class traffic jam created by tens of thousands of Angelenos driving west and north away from the flash points of the civil unrest. On its second day, when the majority of those arrested were no longer Blacks, but Latino immigrants who had engaged in looting, all law enforcement and normal order vanished from the inner city. In the broadest sense, the urban liberal coalition that Tom Bradley had forged two decades earlier went up in smoke.[32]

When Bradley announced that he would not stand for reelection, it appeared his coalition would not outlast him for long. The Bradley coalition's candidate in the 1993 mayoral field, Mike Woo, was a councilman from the Hollywood area and the first citywide standard-bearer for the city's Asian population. Woo had also been the champion of immigrant workers and was the one council member (and only non-Black politician) to attend demonstrations demanding the dismissal of Police Chief Darryl Gates following the Rodney King beating. Woo's stance toward Gates thus mirrored Bradley's criticisms of Chief Bill Parker in the aftermath of the 1965 Watts riots.

But 1993 wasn't 1973. The immigrants whom Woo championed were not yet voting. While Woo's activities were appreciated by some in the Black community, he did not have strong ties to Black politicians or community leaders. Tension between some Black residents of South L.A. and Asian immigrant retail store owners, particularly those who owned liquor stores, may have alienated some Black voters from supporting Woo.[33] At the same time, the heavily White districts in the San Fernando Valley were lost to Woo (as they had been to Bradley), leaving the Westside districts that had been a Bradley stronghold. But these districts were lost as well, despite the fact that some of them had given two-thirds of their presidential vote to Bill

Clinton. Many Westsiders ended up supporting a Republican businessman whose chief issue (one that was able to resonate in a still frightened city) was to bolster the police force. As a result, with the economy in a downward spiral, the immigrant population not yet enfranchised, and the city reeling in the aftermath of the civil unrest of 1992, the overwhelmingly Democratic City of Los Angeles elected Republican Richard Riordan. Riordan's verbal clumsiness and lack of a political record were more than compensated for by the more than $6 million of his own money he poured into his campaign, enabling him to defeat Woo by a 54–46 margin in their runoff election.[34]

What was most striking about Woo's failure, though, was his inability to put forth a clear and direct agenda for the city. Like Mayor David Dinkins in New York City, who was defeated by Republican Rudy Giuliani that year in an equally heavily Democratic city, Woo was reduced to talking about the mosaic, the racial tapestry of the city, that his campaign had come to symbolize. There were no further planks in the liberal platform. With Woo's defeat, the Bradley regime was finally destroyed.

Riordan took office in July 1993, devoid of a specific mandate except to expand the police department—and that, by virtue of federal assistance and a rising economy, he was able to do. He waged a desultory fight to privatize city services, which he quickly abandoned. In the hours and days after the Northridge earthquake, he took command of the city bureaucracy coordinating L.A.'s recovery efforts, only to relinquish that command when the crisis passed.

By the time Riordan took office, L.A. no longer had a coherent corporate power structure. In terms of major private employers, L.A. had become a city of branch managers rather than a city of corporate headquarters. Local aerospace companies had closed their factories and merged into a handful of companies—none of them headquartered in L.A. Such long-standing L.A.-based companies as Hughes, North American, Douglas, and Lockheed were absorbed into firms based elsewhere. A similar process overtook L.A.-based oil giants, such as Union Oil and then ARCO. Locally headquartered banks and savings and loan associations—Security Pacific, Home Savings, American Savings, First Interstate—were purchased by banking consortiums headquartered in other cities and states. Even the entertainment studios were largely owned by companies headquartered elsewhere; only the Disney empire had a corporate headquarters located in L.A. Even the *L.A. Times* succumbed to merger mania when the Times-Mirror Company was purchased by the Tribune Company, based in Chicago. (By 2002 the city's largest private employer was Kaiser Permanente, based in Oakland.)[35]

The absence of a coherent corporate power structure, in turn, reinforced the growing political and policy vacuum. In its place, L.A. politics became more focused on deal making and ethnic rivalries. Local politicians relied on contributions from a wide variety of firms with a direct stake in local policymaking. These included contractors that did business with the Metropolitan Transportation Authority, the port, the airport, and other government agencies, as well as developers seeking zoning approvals and tax breaks.

Riordan was the perfect representative of this deal-making political culture. He didn't come to city hall as a businessman who'd run a major enterprise. He had been an attorney who had made a killing in leveraged buyouts, restructuring Mattel and sundry other corporations. He had no background, that is, in public leadership, and was comfortable chiefly working behind the scenes, not least because his public presence and speaking style were painfully awkward. His pro bono behind-the-scenes efforts before he ran for mayor had included funding the successful campaign to remove Rose Bird and other liberal justices from the California Supreme Court in 1986, serving as the attorney for the archdiocese, and starting up the LEARN program to reform L.A. schools. He'd become the leading contributor to Tom Bradley by the mid-'80s, as well as a major funder for certain moderate Republican candidates around the state. He had no record of involvement in Republican causes, however, beyond occasional check writing. His own political advisor, William Wardlaw, a partner in his law firm who had guided the anti-Bird campaign in 1986, was a leading Democrat, having managed Alan Cranston's 1980 U.S. Senate campaign and chaired Bill Clinton's 1992 presidential bid in California.[36]

Riordan's proclivity for working in private, and for taking unannounced out-of-state vacations, meshed perfectly with the needs of L.A.'s electronic news media in the 1990s, which shunned political and governmental coverage in favor of tabloid news. (One independent survey of L.A.'s seven major TV stations during the ten days preceding the 1997 mayoral race found that the stations' 11 P.M. newscasts had a combined total of twenty-two minutes of coverage of the race, with no coverage at all on the CBS and NBC affiliates.)[37]

It was only after his reelection in 1997 that Riordan's behind-the-scenes efforts began to pay dividends. Without a well-organized corporate elite with overlapping business and social ties, Riordan knew that if he wanted to get business support for his initiatives, he'd have to organize it himself. In fact, Riordan identified a new business leadership whom he hoped would be willing to assume some of the functions of a civic elite, having been emboldened and enriched by the booming market of the 1990s and by a number of acquisitions that had enriched them even more. Working with home-building and insurance magnate Eli Broad, his close friend, Riordan raised the funds to complete the Disney concert hall; put together an offer for a football franchise that Broad would partly own, an offer the NFL seriously considered but then rejected; and landed the Democratic Convention in the year 2000 for the new downtown Staples Arena.[38] Most of the members of this new elite, like Broad and supermarket owner Ron Burkle, were long-time Democratic power players, and some, like David Geffen, were pillars of the entertainment industry.

During his last two years in office, Riordan organized this group to play a role in local politics that in some ways resembled how the old elite had intervened in city politics and municipal governance. In 1999 and 2000 Riordan raised money from roughly thirty business leaders to fund his initiative to establish a charter-revision commission independent of the City Council. He also raised money from them to fund a slate of candidates whom his lieutenants had selected to run for the commission. In this he proved half successful: the commission initiative passed, but a rival slate backed by the newly energized labor movement was elected.

Like many big-city mayors, Riordan sought to displace the sitting school board with candidates and policies more to his liking. Unlike the mayors of Chicago, Detroit, and Cleveland, who used their political wiles to persuade their respective state legislatures to permit them to take over their school districts directly, and unlike Rudy Giuliani, who used his political moxie to dominate the New York district, Riordan, who was notably lacking in political wiles, instead enlisted his usual cohort of thirty rich guys to engineer a takeover of the L.A. schools. They funded a campaign for four candidates (three of them opposing incumbents). Riordan's choice of candidates was somewhat less divisive than the kind of slate that had routinely been assembled by earlier civic elites, as all four of Riordan's candidates were endorsed by the conservative *Daily News*, the centrist *L.A. Times*, and the leftist *L.A. Weekly*.[39] While Riordan's use of the elite to recruit and fund candidates mimicked earlier civic elite practices, what was new about the Riordan regime was that the man who had previously fronted for the elite was now the man actually pulling the strings behind the scenes.

But this new elite was fragile at best, depending on the glue of one man—the mayor—to hold it together. It did not emerge organically from the business community. It did not reflect a growing civic-mindedness of the city's major employers, investors, and business operators. And the civic booster coalition that Riordan pulled together did not outlast his mayoralty.

THE EMERGENCE OF THE
LABOR-LATINO-PROGRESSIVE COALITION

While Mayor Riordan was trying to pull together the city's economic elite, another Republican officeholder—Governor Pete Wilson—played a key role in mobilizing Los Angeles' sleeping giant of Latino mass politics. He did it unwittingly, through his support of Proposition 187—but it helped to trigger a political upheaval that subsequently began to reshape Los Angeles' political landscape.

It was Proposition 187—the initiative intended to deny the use of public facilities, including schools and hospitals, to undocumented immigrants— that brought many Latinos into the political process. Trailing his Democratic challenger, Kathleen Brown, in his 1994 reelection campaign, Republican Wilson seized on 187 as the wedge issue that would win him the vote of White Democrats in search of a scapegoat for the deep recession in the California economy. Wilson calculated correctly: enough Democratic voters switched allegiance that he dispatched Brown quite handily.[40] And he was disastrously wrong: so profound was the indignation of California Latinos that they began, soon after the 1994 contest, to naturalize, to register, and to vote—and vote Democratic—in record numbers.

The Latino backlash began during the course of the 187 campaign itself. On one L.A. high school campus after another, immigrant Latino students, accompanied by their nonimmigrant friends, walked out and began demonstrating in the streets, protesting their imminent expulsion should 187 pass. Two local Latino leaders engaged the students as a way to channel the walk-outs toward more explicit political goals. One was Gilbert Cedillo, head of the racially diverse county employees union, who had already built several community-labor coalitions. Cedillo enlisted the students in anti-187 phone banking and precinct walking in Latino communities. The other was Juan Jose Gutierrez, head of One-Stop Immigration, who enlisted the students in One-Stop's anti-187 activities. Together, Cedillo and Gutierrez organized a massive anti-187 demonstration in downtown L.A., attended by nearly one hundred thousand protestors.[41] The two organizers differed over the demonstration's symbols, with Gutierrez arguing that marchers should be allowed to brandish Mexican flags, and Cedillo contending that the flags would only guarantee electoral disaster. Gutierrez prevailed, and many of the students did carry flags as a sign of pride. But the focus on the demonstration's symbols ultimately came to be used by initiative supporters as part of an anti-Latino message, with overnight polling by Brown's gubernatorial campaign after the demonstration indicating that support for 187 had risen 8 percent. Despite this electoral defeat, the measure was subsequently struck down by the courts.

The flag controversy anticipated some of the ongoing debates in Latino L.A. over the politics of Latino mobilization, with some arguing for a nationalist, ethnic-pride strategy, others counterposing a coalition-oriented, class-based approach, and yet others combining elements of both. But more than any single political event, the passage of 187 created a single, unifying focus: the need to embark on unprecedented naturalization and registration drives. By 1995, L.A.-area citizenship classes were swamped with tens of thousands of applicants.[42]

Even before the sea change brought about by Proposition 187, Latino representation on elected bodies was increasing. When Richard Alatorre moved from the state legislature to the City Council, the mantle of the heavyweight Latino in the state legislature shifted to L.A. state senator Richard Polanco. Through his mastery of reapportionment, Polanco succeeded in creating more Latino congressional and legislative districts. He also developed a corps of fund-raisers and campaign technicians, whom he sent not only into the legislative districts, but to the small cities on L.A.'s Eastside—Bell, Huntington Park, South Gate, and many more—which immigration had made overwhelmingly Latino. By the mid-'90s, Latinos had replaced Whites in the governing bodies of the Eastside towns, and Latinos made up a full quarter of the Democrats' State Assembly delegation.[43]

In some of these races, voter registration and mobilization were unnecessary: these were districts ripe for the taking. In every one of these races, contested or not, Polanco's candidates appealed almost exclusively to Latino voters. A narrow nationalism was the lingua franca of Polanco's candidates. In Polanco's most notorious campaign, that nationalism was combined with a classic dirty trick. A Democratic primary to replace the term-limited incumbent was held in a San Fernando Valley State Senate district in June 1998; the contestants were a Jewish former assemblyman and a Latino city councilman. At the last minute, the Polanco forces sent a mailing to Latino voters in the district, alleging that the former assemblyman had once been involved in posting private guards at polling places to deter Latino voters. The mailing neglected to mention that the nature of the assemblyman's involvement had been to sue, on the Democrats' behalf, the Republican candidate who had hired the guards. Polanco's candidate narrowly prevailed— at the cost of considerable ill will among other Democratic constituencies.[44]

Polanco's "Latino strategy" relied on the sheer weight of numbers, on the demographic transformation of previously White districts. By 1996, when Loretta Sanchez upset far-right Republican congressman Bob Dornan in his northern Orange County district, and two years later, when Sanchez won an overwhelming reelection while a Latino Assembly candidate in the same Orange County terrain also prevailed, it looked as if Polanco's surmise would be vindicated. Sanchez was the fifth Latino member of Congress from greater L.A. No other American city had more than two.[45]

But while Latinos were entering the electorate and flocking to the polls, the content of their politics began in some situations to turn away from the narrower nationalism Polanco espoused toward a more radical version of Tom Bradley's multiracialism. One of the key figures in this shift was the new head of the Los Angeles County Federation of Labor, Miguel Contreras.

When Contreras took office in the summer of 1996, it had been nearly forty years since local labor had mobilized masses of its members at election time. But Contreras, like Polanco, knew which districts had changed through an influx of immigrants. He also commissioned polling of both union members and the new immigrants, and thus identified a series of issues of particular concern to both groups. The chief concern the polling uncovered wasn't any ethnically focused set of issues, but rather the concerns of low-wage earners. Reaching out both to the new immigrants and to union members, with a ballot measure campaign to raise the state minimum wage and to reject the party of Pete Wilson, the County Fed initiated ambitious naturalization, registration, and get-out-the-vote programs. Thousands of volunteers walked precincts in districts in such longtime Republican bastions as Long Beach, Glendale, and Pasadena. On election day, those districts ended up in the Democratic column, one of them for the first time since 1916, and labor produced the votes that enabled the Democrats to retake the State Assembly.[46]

In the municipal elections in the spring of 1997, an even greater number of County Fed–related volunteers turned out on behalf of a massive school-construction bond measure, Proposition BB. This was the kind of measure that a largely White electorate had been routinely rejecting for two decades. Now, however, that electorate was less White than it had ever been, and with a stunningly high turnout rate among Latino voters, BB passed handily.

Later that year, Contreras took on Polanco in a special election for a vacated Assembly seat that had major implications for the future of Latino politics in L.A. The district, adjacent to downtown, was probably the most immigrant-heavy in the state. The Polanco-sponsored candidate, universally viewed as the favorite, was Vicky Castro, an L.A. school board member who was known for her near-exclusive focus on Latino concerns in pedagogical matters. Her opponent was Gil Cedillo, the former head of the county workers union and an anti–Proposition 187 activist, who ran with

AFL-CIO backing. Castro campaigned on a platform of advancing Latino causes, such as bilingualism. Cedillo pitched his campaign to union members and newly registered immigrants, sounding themes of economic justice. In a stunning upset, not only did Cedillo win, but there were 25 percent more voters than was the norm in a special election, reflecting in part the importance of mobilization.

In 1998, the County Fed was part of the successful statewide June primary campaign to defeat Proposition 226, the Newt Gingrich–backed initiative that would have greatly curtailed union political-action programs by making it more difficult to use union dues for political purposes. In November, labor produced so high a turnout in historically low-turnout Latino and Black precincts that every statewide Democrat ran about 6 or 7 percent higher than all polling had predicted, in what turned out to be the greatest sweep that California Democrats had known in forty years. The County Fed mobilized over ten thousand volunteers in the June primary, and a like number in November. The days when L.A. elections consisted of fund-raising and mailing only, when the very notion of volunteers was dismissed as idle fancy, had come to an end.[47]

What was particularly important about these elections was that they shattered assumptions about Latino politics. Pundits routinely asserted that Latinos came from culturally traditional backgrounds and would therefore reject the culturally permissive Democrats. The most common predictions were that Latinos would certainly not be as liberal as Blacks and, thus, that the politics of America's cities would turn rightward when Latinos finally entered the electorate in larger numbers.

To be sure, polls have indicated that Latinos are indeed more conservative than Blacks on welfare and their antipathy to police practices. Some election results have shown that Latinos tend to conservatism on cultural questions; for example, they narrowly opposed the initiative legalizing marijuana for medicinal purposes on the 1996 California ballot, an initiative that voters narrowly enacted.

But once inside the schoolhouse or workplace door, Latino voters have at times turned left. On matters of economic opportunity and equity, on questions of education and mobility, they generally stood to the left of the general electorate. On the same ballot where a majority of Latinos rejected the medical marijuana initiative, they supported by an 86 to 14 percent margin raising the state minimum wage—a more lopsided margin than in any other group in the state. On L.A. school bond measure Proposition BB, they gave the proposal 84 percent support. On the initiative to cripple union political programs, Proposition 226, they voted no by a 75 to 25 percent margin. Indeed, Latinos opposed 226 even more than they opposed Proposition 227, which terminated bilingual education in California.

Perhaps the most telling example of organized labor's new political self-confidence was its endorsement and support for Hilda Solis in a 2000 Democratic primary race against incumbent congressman Marty Martinez in the 31st congressional district. The district, 59 percent Hispanic and 28 percent Asian, includes parts of East L.A., Alhambra, San Gabriel, Rosemead, El Monte, Baldwin Park, and Asuza. The daughter of a union shop steward, Solis earned an undergraduate degree from California Polytechnic State University and a master's from the University of Southern California. She won a seat on the Rio Hondo Community College board in 1984 and was elected to the State Assembly in 1992. In 1994, Solis became the first Latina elected to the State Senate, where she made a name for herself as a vocal and effective feminist, environmental advocate, and labor ally. In 1996 she jump-started an initiative campaign for a higher minimum wage with a fifty-thousand-dollar contribution from her own campaign coffers.

Four years later, she decided to take on Martinez, an eighteen-year veteran of Congress originally elected with the support of the Berman-Waxman machine. Martinez was a mainstream Democrat with a reasonably liberal voting record, but he was not a leader on any issue. In 1998 he angered union leaders and progressives when he offered to vote for the Clinton administration's fast-track trade-negotiating authority in return for White House support for a freeway extension in his district. He also alienated prochoice voters by voting for a ban on late-term abortions. Berman and Waxman stayed neutral in the contest between Solis and Martinez. Solis won the support of EMILY's List and the Sierra Club, but it was the all-out effort of the County Fed that had the biggest impact. Solis's 62 to 29 percent victory was one of the few instances in modern political history in which a progressive Democrat ousted a centrist congressional incumbent. As Contreras saw it, it also marked an extension of the Fed's political operation to the county's working- and middle-class suburbs.[48]

Commentators have widely noted the strong Latino affinity for Democratic candidates in California, particularly in distinction to Texas, and have ascribed this to the differences between immigrant-bashing Pete Wilson and immigrant-welcoming George W. Bush. That's part of the story, certainly, but it doesn't account for the huge outpouring in California on issues of schools, unions, and workplace equity. There is, in fact, another point of differentiation between California and Texas: in California, the newly energized, Latino-led union movement spearheaded the political mobilization of the Latino community. In Texas, which ranks forty-eighth among the states in its rate of unionization, there was really no such movement at all during the 1990s.

Nor was this the first time in U.S. history that a wave of immigrants saw its members mobilized and its politics shaped by a coalition of unions and community groups. Like L.A.'s Latino immigrants, the Polish, Czech, and Slovak coal miners and steelworkers of the industrial heartland had been there for decades before they entered the political process, and it was widely assumed that their cultural traditionalism had made them particularly unsuitable for parties or candidates committed to shaking up the existing order. Then, in 1935, the newly formed CIO sent hundreds of organizers into their communities to build a union around such economic equity issues as union rights, Social Security, and a minimum wage, and those immigrant workers became a key part of the New Deal coalition. The politics of historically Republican Pennsylvania, Indiana, Ohio, Illinois, and Michigan were turned around in the election of 1936 by a union-led program of political acculturation. Much the same thing showed signs of happening in L.A. in the latter half of the 1990s, potentially foreshadowing what could happen in other major cities with new immigrant populations.

PROGRESSIVE MOBILIZATION IN 2001

By the end of the twentieth century, L.A. faced a kind of economic—and political—conundrum. It had become home to more private wealth and great fortunes than it had ever known. Increasingly, the wealthy of the world went to live there; increasingly, the indigenous wealthy, entertainment lawyers, high-tech entrepreneurs, and the like thrived as the market ascended. Yet most of the resident rich had fortunes that weren't dependent in the slightest on the condition of the L.A. economy as such, and much of the major property interests in the L.A. economy were still controlled by overseas investors who had snatched them up in the late '80s. The kind of financial elite whose fortunes ebbed and flowed with those of the city, like the Chandlers, who had once owned the largest chunk of the San Fernando Valley, was nowhere to be found. Economic elites no longer played a coherent role in shaping the region's economy and its related political outcomes.

Into this economic and political vacuum emerged a newly revitalized Progressive L.A. Already by the 1980s and early 1990s, a number of progressive political figures had begun to seek office, working closely with and, for some, becoming the voice for many of the city's grassroots activist groups. One of those who stood out was Jackie Goldberg, a longtime community activist who was first elected to the school board in 1978 and subsequently served on the City Council and then in the state legislature.

Goldberg in many ways embodied the evolving sophistication and political sensibilities of Progressive L.A. A radical activist at Berkeley in the 1960s, a leader in the fight around school busing in the 1970s, and among the earliest political figures to come out as a lesbian, Goldberg became one of the most effective advocates inside the corridors of political power for a range of social movements, including the new immigrant-based labor movement.[49] Although considerably to the left of most of her City Council colleagues, she nevertheless—through a combination of charm, humor, persistence, persuasion, and vote trading—managed to push through much of her legislative agenda by cobbling together majorities.

Goldberg became best known among progressives as the person capable of helping to pull together the various (and sometimes conflicting) strands of the progressive community, as well as teaching progressives how to agree and how to disagree. She was the author and champion of the city's pioneering living wage ordinance and played a key role in directing more city funds to get landlords to fix up slum buildings. She also fought for and helped to apply the emerging new concept of "accountable development," which demanded public goals be met (such as a living wage) for developments receiving public subsidies, and became an effective champion of the rights of gays and lesbians, immigrants, and the poor.

As a politician and activist, Goldberg became a master of the inside/outside game. She utilized her close ties to grassroots groups to help to lobby City Council members while she worked them inside city hall. The two-year campaign to win the living wage law—which seemed a radical idea when first proposed—epitomized this kind of inside/outside strategy. Goldberg served as a key spokesperson and legislative guru, while the Living Wage Coalition (backed by key unions, community groups, and clergy) played the role of strategist, grassroots organizer, and the voice of L.A.'s working poor. Eventually, it passed unanimously.[50]

As a City Council member, Goldberg hired a staff of community organizers—led by the chief of staff, Sharon Delugach—to help to mobilize constituents in her economically and ethnically diverse, and politically contentious, district. Her staff helped her to keep in touch with the kind of civic housekeeping matters—empty lots, potholes, recreational needs—that bind voters to elected officials. Despite the glitz associated with her district (which included Hollywood), the actual neighborhood was among the most rundown areas of the city. She and her staff helped to organize residents and property owners to demand stronger police protection, graffiti removal, housing expansion, improved lighting, and revitalization of the business district.[51]

All of these factors came together in the late 1990s, when Goldberg led a campaign to require the Trizec-Hahn firm to incorporate a "community benefits" package in its retail, hotel, and theater development project in Hollywood. Its key provision was the commitment from the retail stores in the project to pay their employees a living wage with benefits. This deal became a model for a proposed citywide accountable development ordinance that was championed by unions and community groups under the banner of the Los Angeles Alliance for a New Economy (LAANE).[52]

One sign of Goldberg's effectiveness on the City Council was that all the major candidates seeking to fill her seat (she was forced to leave the council as a result of term limits and ran successfully for the State Assembly) pledged to follow her example. Eric Garcetti, the eventual winner, also decided to establish a community organizing staff in his district office and play the inside/outside game that Goldberg had perfected. Garcetti's effectiveness as the key sponsor of the Housing Trust Fund plan in 2001 and 2002 illustrated that role.[53]

At various times, progressives encouraged Goldberg to run for mayor, but she declined to do so, recognizing perhaps that despite her effectiveness as a bridge builder on the City Council, a Jewish left-wing lesbian would have enormous obstacles to overcome to win a citywide mayoral race. Moreover, many progressives and liberals believed that among the city's key progressive leaders, Assembly Speaker Antonio Villaraigosa had the strongest potential to forge a citywide coalition to win the mayoral race, once Mayor Riordan had left office, as a result of term limits, in 2001. Indeed, many activists hoped that the race to succeed Riordan would help to accelerate a fundamental realignment of citywide political forces. It could also help to identify the challenges facing progressive forces in L.A. and in other cities seeking to create the next urban progressive coalition and political shift in America's cities.

Villaraigosa represented the leading edge of that emerging progressive coalition. A onetime organizer for the L.A. teachers union and president of the local ACLU board, Villaraigosa was elected to the Assembly in 1994 from a district north of downtown that, like Tom Bradley's council district of old, featured a mix, in this case, of White and Latino voters. From his first campaign, Villaraigosa had sought, like Bradley, to build a multiracial base of support. He articulated much of the rhetoric and policy directions of Progressive L.A. He was first and foremost the candidate of the labor-Latino alliance, but he also identified with the new urban-oriented environmental-ism, the increasingly sophisticated housing movement, and many of the other constituent groups and issue-based movements that had come to rep-resent Progressive L.A. at the turn of the twenty-first century. The labor-Latino alliance, however, was key to the electoral strategy that Villaraigosa had begun to craft. His ties in this area were deep and extensive. It was not just that he was a labor organizer himself; he was also an old friend and ally of Contreras and María Elena Durazo, the leader of Local 11 of the Hotel Employees and Restaurant Employees Union.[54]

Villaraigosa, Durazo, and Gil Cedillo had all met during their early twen-ties in CASA, an organization devoted to organizing immigrant workers, documented and otherwise. CASA was the creation of the legendary Bert Corona, a veteran radical who was the contemporary and urban counterpart of Cesar Chávez. Indeed, many of the key figures in L.A.'s labor-Latino alliance learned their politics and organizing by working either with Corona or with Chávez.

For Villaraigosa, the challenge was how to craft an electoral strategy to get to 50 percent of the vote. When Bradley was first elected in 1973, Black voters constituted 26 percent of the electorate. Even with the rapid growth of the Latino electorate, and with all the hoopla and fervor that having a serious Latino mayoral candidate generated within the Latino community, that was a tough figure for Latinos to match.

Villaraigosa's most serious problem in crafting this new type of electoral coalition was that much of Black L.A. felt threatened by the rise of Latino L.A. Latinos were quickly becoming the largest population group in the few remaining districts that had sent Blacks to city hall, the state legislature, and Congress. They demanded to be hired at venerable South Central insti-tutions, like Martin Luther King County Hospital, that owed their exis-tence in part to post-1965 civil rights struggles. Some Blacks believed that Latino immigrants brought down wages and increased joblessness for inner-city Blacks. Anyone doubting the extent of this often unspoken ani-mosity could see this emerging divide in a district-by-district breakdown of the 1994 vote on Proposition 187, the measure targeting illegal immigrants. While the Latino districts on the Eastside of Los Angeles and the liberal Jewish districts on the Westside opposed the measure, the Black districts of South Central narrowly joined the more conservative White San Fernando Valley districts in supporting it. In sum, Villaraigosa would not be able to count on winning a significant share of the Black vote, despite his efforts to be inclusive.

As part of his electoral strategy, Villaraigosa also looked to the Westside, as Bradley had before. And there he encountered a problem, for his opponent was not going to be Sam Yorty, whom many of the residents of the Westside had despised. As in other urban areas, many of the voters who had supported Yorty and created the urban White backlash of the 1970s had long since left the city by the time the new century commenced. Throughout the 1970s, these voters had been behind the successful campaigns to thwart integrated school busing and to enact Howard Jarvis's Proposition 13, which all but eliminated property taxes as a source of new municipal revenue. With the collapse of aerospace in the early '90s, however, most of these Angelenos were unable to find jobs providing a comparable income, and moved to surrounding states where living expenses were lower. In much of the western San Fernando Valley, however, those onetime Yortyites who did remain consolidated their power in neighborhood homeowner associations, but their power was mainly limited to blocking any new developments. The last gasp of these groups in citywide politics was the secession movement of 2002, a number of whose leading proponents had played key roles in the Proposition 13 campaign twenty-four years before.

The outmigration of hundreds of thousands of these people from L.A. County moved local politics decisively leftward. It also meant, however, that Villaraigosa would be opposing a moderate centrist, not a right-wing populist. Indeed, in 2001, Villaraigosa's opponent turned out to be James Hahn, not a right-winger, but a mainstream Democrat with some modest liberal credentials. Hahn had been the city attorney for twelve years, and he also had a following in the Black community, thanks to his father, a longtime L.A. County supervisor and ally of the civil rights movement. At the same time, the impending secession measure to create a new city in the San Fernando Valley, thereby breaking up Los Angeles, further put an electoral squeeze on Villaraigosa: he could hardly support breaking up L.A. as he sought to become its mayor. But how could he gain even a significant minority of Valley voters if he clearly opposed this initiative? With a more lukewarm reception in the Westside, a likely conservative backlash in the Valley exacerbated by the secession drive, and the loss of the core constituency of African Americans, Villaraigosa was obliged to develop a campaign that was as much a movement-building and political-restructuring effort as an electoral vote-counting exercise.

Hahn, on the other hand, had to consolidate his support within the African American community while cultivating support from its polar opposite, the remaining conservative White voters in the western San Fernando Valley. These voters had no affinity for a downtown Democrat like Hahn, but they had even less for the liberal Latino Villaraigosa. With his support rooted in this unlikely alliance, whose members shared little but trepidation toward Villaraigosa and the new L.A. he had come to personify, Hahn felt free to wage a slash-and-burn campaign designed to place his opponent on the defensive. While the attacks, including an ad hominem insinuation about a drug-related issue, had the feel of a Yorty-like campaign, Hahn was to some extent insulated from the charge of racism, in part because of the makeup of his coalition and in part because of the almost legendary status his father held in Black L.A. Hahn's father, Supervisor Kenneth Hahn, had represented all of South Central as well as neighboring communities on the County Board of Supervisors from 1952 through 1992 and was the first local politician to appear with Martin Luther King, Jr. Kenneth Hahn's Black staffers became some of the first Black officeholders in L.A., and a critical part of the junior Hahn's political support group. Young James Hahn, as city attorney, had also been a thorn in Riordan's side on several occasions, and in 1997 had soundly defeated a Riordan protégé who had challenged Hahn's reelection bid. The question for Hahn was whether he would be able to draw votes citywide for mayor, as he had already done in his races for city attorney. A base in the Black community was not, in itself, sufficient.[55]

In the April primary, six major candidates vied to make it into the runoff. Villaraigosa received the most, with 30 percent of the vote (152,031), followed by Hahn with 25 percent (125,139), and Republican businessman Steve Soboroff (106,189). Soboroff won among White voters, with 30 percent of the total, compared with 23 percent for Villaraigosa and 19 percent for Hahn. Villaraigosa beat Hahn among Jewish voters (26 percent to 15 percent), among Latinos (62 percent to 7 percent), among Westsiders (27 percent to 25 percent), and among Democrats (39 percent to 28 percent). Hahn led among African Americans (71 percent to 12 percent).[56] The runoff between Villaraigosa and Hahn thus came to depend on who could attract most of Soboroff's and City Councilman Joel Wachs's White, San Fernando Valley, Westside, and independent supporters, and on whether Villaraigosa could dramatically increase Latino turnout.

During the campaign, Villaraigosa had sought to articulate a broader, more inclusive view of a changing Los Angeles. He began to rely (though a bit too little, and a bit too late) on a younger group of African American organizers and leaders, such as AGENDA's Anthony Thigpenn and the Community Coalition's Karen Bass, who emphasized a more diverse set of issues and constituency-building efforts in their own organizing work in South Central. He drew heavily on the Latino-labor alliance and reached out strongly to urban environmental constituencies, from the Sierra Club to neighborhood-based environmental justice groups.

But Hahn had the advantage, in South Central, of drawing on a powerful set of Black elected officials (such as Maxine Waters), church leaders, community brokers, and others who had cut their teeth in campaigns during the Bradley years, while also appearing as the more conservative of the two candidates on matters associated with the Valley. Like Hahn, Villaraigosa opposed secession, but it was Villaraigosa who had come to personify the diverse and changing Los Angeles that was the ultimate, if unstated, cause of the secession drive. Despite a renewed politics of mobilization, engagement, and coalition building associated with the Villaraigosa campaign, the turnout in the June 2001 election remained at the historic low levels (around 25 percent of the electorate) that characterized municipal elections in Los Angeles and elsewhere. The 2001 election became less a watershed than a holding action.

The dynamics of the race were also influenced by how each candidate sought to position himself. As a Sacramento-based public figure, Villaraigosa was still an unknown quantity to most Angelenos. So while Villaraigosa used his resources to increase his name recognition, Hahn—who inherited a politically visible name and then kept it in the public eye as a local elected official—hoarded his resources until the last few weeks of the campaign, when he began airing a notorious attack ad against Villaraigosa. The ad recounted one whopper of a Villaraigosa mistake—writing a letter that requested a pardon for a convicted drug dealer—but it was the Willie Horton visuals that really did the trick. Surrounding a grainy image of Villaraigosa with sundry drug paraphernalia, it managed to make the former Speaker look like one of the heavies from the movie *Traffic*. Hahn and Villaraigosa had been trading leads in several opinion polls before the ad aired; once it started running, Hahn surged into a lead he was not thereafter to lose.[57]

Yet it was striking how close Villaraigosa did come. The challenge he faced was to put together a progressive electoral majority in Los Angeles without substantial support from the African American community, whose allegiance Hahn claimed for reasons that were chiefly historic—or perhaps genetic. Ultimately, Hahn, the mainstream Democrat, may have organized one last victory for the old Los Angeles. In a city that was becoming increasingly young and Latino, Hahn put together enough older White and Black voters to prevail at the polls.[58]

No candidate since Tom Bradley in 1969 had inspired the kind of dedication that Villaraigosa did among his followers. And when Hahn went on the attack, Villaraigosa seemed every bit as defenseless as Bradley had been in 1969. Villaraigosa's campaign had conducted a series of focus groups with swing voters from the Valley and turned up a particularly fearful asymmetry: Those voters were predisposed to credit a Hahn attack on Villaraigosa, but their latent mistrust of Villaraigosa was only exacerbated when he mixed it up with Hahn. Like Bradley in 1969, Villaraigosa refrained from going on the offensive. And like Bradley in 1969, he lost—in his case, by 7 percentage points.

Despite the outcome of the 2001 contest, it appeared that some trends were moving in a progressive direction. The electorate that went to the polls in June 2001 was 22 percent Latino (up from a scant 10 percent when Riordan was elected in 1993), and Villaraigosa pulled down 82 percent of this fastest-growing constituency. According to the *L.A. Times* exit poll, moreover, fully 49 percent of city voters identified themselves as liberal, while just 22 percent called themselves conservative. Villaraigosa also won the backing of 57 percent of voters under forty-five. Within the various constituencies of Democratic Los Angeles, the dividing line between Hahn and Villaraigosa supporters was often generational. The African American officials who rallied South Central for Hahn tended to be in their sixties and seventies, while many of Villaraigosa's endorsers were roughly his age (forty-eight) or younger. Hahn's labor supporters included the building trades and public-sector unions that had forged relationships with him while he was city attorney.[59]

Despite the outcome of the mayoral race, the 2001 elections helped to shift the public debate in L.A. to the left. By then, almost all politicians in L.A. were embracing the idea of a "living wage" as a standard. During the janitors' strike the year before, for example, while Goldberg got arrested and Villaraigosa walked picket lines, Mayor Riordan encouraged the owners of major office buildings to settle the strike and pay the janitors a living wage. Thanks to the work of the Housing L.A. coalition—which resembled the coalition that forged the living wage victory four years earlier—candidate (and then mayor) Hahn and most City Council members embraced the plan for a $100 million annual housing trust fund.

Villaraigosa's mayoral campaign bore electoral fruit later when he, and his close ally Martin Ludlow, were elected to the City Council in 2003. Backed by the County Fed and the same broad coalition of progressive forces that worked in his mayoral race, Villaraigosa unseated incumbent Nick Pacheco, a mainstream Democrat who had Mayor Hahn's backing, to win the right to represent the predominantly Latino 14th council district, which includes Boyle Heights, Eagle Rock, El Sereno, Highland Park, Mount Washington, Glassell Park, and other areas. The political forces that elected Villaraigosa also catapulted Ludlow into the City Council to represent the 10th district in South L.A., vacated by Nate Holden, an unpredictable politician with few progressive credentials. Ludlow was a veteran political and union organizer, having worked for SEIU (Service Employees International Union) and as political director of the County Fed, as well as having served as chief of staff for Villaraigosa when he served in the state legislature. Villaraigosa and Ludlow joined Eric Garcetti and Ed Reyes as the council's progressive wing, with strong ties to grassroots groups and with the potential to build bridges with the five or six council liberals. By the end of 2003, the progressive bloc on the council had already made its mark—for example, by sponsoring legislation to hold developers more accountable for affordable housing and decent jobs. Another sign of the progressive movement's growing clout was Mayor Hahn's decision to appoint Madeline Janis-Aparicio, director of LAANE and the city's leading living wage advocate, to the powerful Community Redevelopment Agency.

The question remains whether the 2001 election and its aftermath will become a new political line of demarcation, helping to establish a new vision of the Next Los Angeles, or instead usher in a period of political uncertainty and divisiveness. The answer is still uncertain, as the next phase in L.A.'s complex political history starts to be defined.

EPILOGUE:
TWO FUTURES FOR THE NEXT LOS ANGELES

Los Angeles at the start of the twenty-first century is clearly a city of destiny. But it's not so clear what, exactly, that destiny is.

In one possibility, the centrifugal forces so omnipresent in Los Angeles will pull the city apart before the new civic order can take hold. The smart money always seems to lean toward this option, of course: Los Angeles is everyone's dystopia, home to Nathanael West's riot as well as the real riots that shook South Central. Los Angeles becomes a land of gated communities and closed-off streets, of a million private secessions every day, the town the movies love to destroy, the city that has always been easier to leave than to fix and transform.

Another scenario identifies Los Angeles as the city that accommodates to and is transformed by the third wave of American immigration. It also becomes the city whose new residents join forces with others to create a new political order.

In many ways, contemporary Los Angeles resembles New York City at the turn of the previous century. At that time, New York was a cauldron of seething problems—poverty, slums, child labor, epidemics, sweatshops, and ethnic conflict. Out of that turmoil, activists forged coalitions of immigrants, labor, public health, and environmental advocates, middle-class suffragists, and upper-class philanthropists. Tenement and public health reformers worked alongside radical Socialists. While they spoke many languages, the movement found its voice through organizers, clergy, and sympathetic politicians. Their victories anticipated some of the intellectual and policy innovations of the New Deal period.

Contemporary Los Angeles is now discovering its own mix of challenges and political opportunities. Movements have been formed or renewed and have begun to find their own voice, learning to say "living wage," "livable communities," "affordable housing," and "social justice" in English, Korean, Spanish, and Vietnamese, among other languages. The challenges remain formidable: widening economic divides, sprawl, lack of open space, housing crises, a pervasive fast-food culture. Organizing—and the creation of political change—also faces formidable barriers: geographic dispersal, racial and ethnic tensions, hostile political traditions. Nevertheless, movements are taking root. Whether these movements will establish political staying power remains to be seen. But, despite reversals and continuing barriers, change is in the air.

6 Setting an Agenda

Policy Development and Social Movements

When two dozen or so community activists, policy analysts, and academics in the spring of 1999 began to discuss the need for a broad-based policy agenda for Los Angeles, they were faced with a classic conundrum for progressives. How can an agenda be designed through grassroots participation when the notion of *policy* itself is so often a top-down process requiring technical expertise? Policy development in Los Angeles and other regions had, in fact, long been the domain of the power brokers and their hired experts. The most influential and powerful lawyers, bankers, financiers, real estate developers, newspaper publishers, and manufacturers used their informal and formal ties to set the public agenda on key issues. Elected officials and politicians, in turn, often simply carried out the agendas established by these power brokers.

In Los Angeles, power was wielded principally by those who wanted anti-union, open-shop policies that also relied on a low-wage, often immigrant, labor force. It came to be associated with the role of real estate development and rampant speculation, the construction of big resource projects such as water facilities and freeways, and the development and promotion of large-scale cultural and civic projects such as the Music Center.

This informal, behind-the-scenes exercise of power in Los Angeles did not go unchallenged. At the turn of the twentieth century, when Los Angeles Mayor Fred Eaton announced the need to develop a new charter for Los Angeles, a number of groups advocating greater democratic participation, including Socialists and Progressives, strongly criticized the initial efforts to remake the city government. They were able to secure a role on the commission established to address how Los Angeles was to be governed.

During the 1920s and 1930s, advocates of public power fended off behind-the-scenes challenges to privatize Los Angeles' public utilities. Similarly, in the 1940s, a coalition of housing advocates successfully resisted the efforts to undermine plans to develop affordable public housing in the city. It was the housing issue that led to one of Los Angeles' classic exercises of elite backroom power—the selection of an obscure congressman named Norris Poulson to challenge incumbent Fletcher Bowron, who had up to then defied the power brokers on that issue.

This raw exercise of power was partly dependent on a cohesive set of players and interests—a civic elite—with a stake in regional matters. The inner circle of this civic elite—the city's unelected power structure or shadow government—was a small group called the Committee of 25, discussed in chapter 5. The group had formed in the early 1950s, seeking to replace or supplement earlier informal elite associations or organized groups such as the State and Local Government Committee of the Chamber of Commerce.

However, already by the 1960s, this relatively tight-knit group of power brokers was beginning to lose cohesion as a local and regional force. The law firms were opening national and international offices. The *L.A. Times* increasingly sought to define itself as a national paper and significantly shifted resources from local and state to national and international coverage. And the big banks and insurance companies were merging with other entities outside the region and even outside the state. These changes were occurring while the forces of globalization, already apparent by the 1960s, had begun to transform the notion of the "region" and the exercise of regional power. The informal exercise of power, such as it existed at the regional scale, was being redefined.

During this period, efforts had been made to reestablish some level of informal agenda setting, primarily through the activities of the Committee of 25. In some ways, the committee resembled earlier efforts at power brokering and agenda setting, with one member calling it "an informal instrument of government." The group met monthly, invited key figures involved in developing or carrying out policies (such as the city's chief administrative officer, the police chief, or the superintendent of the Los Angeles Unified School District), and then sought to identify an appropriate agenda and approach to particular problems. But the Committee of 25 turned out to be a transitional force, with indications that the exercise of power was becoming increasingly unwieldy and more diffuse.[1]

This diffusion of power was partly a reflection of the expanding national and international roles of some of the key players and the corporations and institutions they belonged to. Events were forcing a response rather than power brokers shaping events. This was a far cry from earlier informal gatherings at places like the downtown California Club, where decisions were made more easily and marching orders were given to key figures, such as the *Times*'s city hall correspondent, Carleton Williams. An event like the Watts riots of 1965 demonstrated how unprepared this civic elite had become to address the issues facing Los Angeles. By the 1969 mayoral election, new political dynamics had emerged, represented by the new progressive coalition of African Americans and Jews who backed Tom Bradley, as well as the revanchist, racist forces backing Mayor Sam Yorty. This was a very different kind of political situation than the Poulson-Bowron election sixteen years earlier, when a candidate was obliged to respond to the beck and call of the downtown power brokers like the Committee of 25.

The transformation of the Los Angeles region in the 1970s and 1980s shifted the political terrain in relation to power brokering and policy making. Those changes, discussed in previous chapters, included the deindustrialization of the region and a shift from heavy manufacturing to light manufacturing and service employment; the continuing patterns of sprawl extending to the fast-growth areas of the Inland Empire in Riverside and San Bernardino Counties and parts of Ventura and Orange Counties; and the rapid demographic shifts in the city, county, and region, including the huge influx of Latin American and Asian immigrants. Los Angeles in the process developed a two-tier economy that led to an increase in the numbers of the working poor as well as the underemployed. The number of people who were food insecure and without adequate housing or transportation grew significantly. Globalization trends, with Los Angeles' shift from a headquarters city to a "world city" with associated multinational branches and foreign investors, played a role in the city's changing political dynamics. A regional power vacuum, with its continuing diffusion of power, had emerged.

L.A. 2000

By the time Tom Bradley was elected in 1973, the Committee of 25 had largely been eclipsed as a significant political force shaping policy. Nor was there any longer a commanding center of power in the city or the region. Bradley's progressive coalition continued to influence certain areas of policy, such as minority hiring and a handful of environmental programs. These changes were not part of a comprehensive policy agenda, but instead were ad hoc responses to specific constituencies.[2]

The lack of either a strategic policy framework or an informal center of power to help to shape policy agendas led to Bradley's 1985 initiative to "shape a vision" for Los Angeles for the twenty-first century. He formed a blue-ribbon committee to fill the policy vacuum and named eighty-five key business and political leaders, academics, and experts from various policy arenas to become part of "L.A. 2000," the new committee. Bradley urged the group to "do more than just talk . . . [but] turn vision, commitment and sound planning into a road map that will take us exactly where we want to go."[3]

L.A. 2000 was a hybrid: part traditional blue-ribbon commission and part academic/policy wonk–oriented work group. It included only a few community-based advocates of particular issues such as housing or the environment. L.A. 2000 had a few dominant themes, such as regional governance, globalization, and growth management, that influenced the direction of its deliberations and helped to frame its final report. But the process and the recommendations were limited by the group's hybrid nature, its expertise orientation, and its affinity for broad concepts such as a jobs-housing balance, as opposed to focused policy initiatives and changes in policy orientation.[4]

The L.A. 2000 Partnership divided into six groups: Livable Communities, Environmental Quality, Individual Fulfillment, Enriching Diversity, the Crossroads City, and Government and Finance. The Livable Communities group focused primarily on regional growth issues. It addressed the need to establish a jobs-housing balance, a regional growth management plan (as well as a comprehensive plan for the City of Los Angeles), and a community and neighborhood or district planning process. The group identified the need to create ten thousand affordable housing units and made a handful of policy recommendations, such as the development of an Affordable Housing Production Trust Fund. Transportation recommendations included rail and highway construction, partly in light of its regional orientation. The needs for more and improved bus service and for increasing the role of bicycles as a transportation and commuter option were ignored. Nor was a pedestrian-friendly environment (that could link the idea of a "walkable city" with the theme of "livable communities") considered.

The Environmental Quality group focused on individual responsibility and behavior change ("the enemy is all of us") rather than public action. It also called for a regional approach, especially in developing an environmental management plan to overcome existing divisions between various jurisdictions and special districts. With respect to policy, the group combined conventional as well as alternative approaches, as in the area of water supply, where the traditional agendas of the water industry (to complete the State Water Project) were joined with more environmentally oriented goals of conservation, reclamation, and protecting groundwater sources. However, in this, as in other areas, the group's recommendations were too broad to be helpful in focusing attention on what policy changes were most important and how such changes could be brought about.

The third area, Individual Fulfillment, covered such issues as education, health and human services, and literacy. Similar to its call for the Regional Growth Management Plan, the task force proposed establishing a "Class of the Year 2000" Commission to track, evaluate, and make recommendations to improve school-based performance for each class level. The group could not agree on some issues, such as methods of financing health care systems, and it simply affirmed the need for action without making any specific policy recommendations.

The fourth area, Enriching Diversity, concentrated on L.A.'s income gap, including the growing number of low-wage workers. It emphasized the need for economic development and supported existing programs like enterprise zones and job apprenticeships. The group also identified the surplus land adjacent to the Century Freeway, including the much-coveted Alameda (transportation) corridor, as ripe for development and attracting new enterprises.

The Crossroads City task force (the fifth area) assumed the inevitability—and value—of globalization in establishing Los Angeles as a globally networked or crossroads city. It called for expanding the region's infrastructure, including the port, LAX, and the rail system, to enhance L.A.'s role in global trade.

The sixth area, Government and Finance, affirmed the need for regional governance. This task force anticipated the subsequent focus on "smart growth" policies aimed at redirecting growth toward more dense development and preventing sprawl. It called for the formation of a Growth Management Agency that could address regional impacts from transportation and housing policies, although it did not address the political obstacles to getting cities to cooperate on a regional basis.

Despite identifying some critical themes, what's striking about the L.A. 2000 document—linked in part to the group's process—is the shortage of specific policies to accomplish goals, change priorities, and redirect resources. For example, the Affordable Housing Production Trust Fund recommendation was limited to its call for developers and groups such as the Ford Foundation–backed Local Initiative Support Corporation to take the lead role in facilitating new affordable housing construction. Absent from the recommendation was an explicit public role—either in identifying funding mechanisms or establishing affordable housing mandates.

The "blue-ribbon commission" approach, with its dependence on elite civic leaders, further limited the capacity of L.A. 2000 to mobilize grassroots constituencies on behalf of its recommendations and broader goals. The call for regional governance, for example, failed to address such barriers as the lack of any democratic accountability in existing (or future) regional bodies. The L.A. area already had a major elected regional entity, the five-member L.A. County Board of Supervisors. With its "Five Little Kings" culture, its often misguided allocation of resources (divide by five), its "incumbency for life" political realities, and the size of each supervisorial district (the largest in the country), the supervisors should have been the focus of serious reform recommendations from the L.A. 2000 Partnership. But by ignoring the issue of democratic participation and political restructuring, the committee's discussion of regional governance avoided a key barrier to any substantive change in how regional decisions are made. Even where the L.A. 2000 Partnership took a controversial (and much needed) position, such as revising Proposition 13's requirement for two-thirds voter approval to a simple majority for any tax increase, the absence of any strategy for constituency building and mobilization undercut its recommendation. It also assured that such a recommendation would not be given much credence by policymakers.

The committee's participants had hoped that the L.A. 2000 report would stimulate, according to its chair, Jane Pisano, "the beginning of a dialogue that will lead us to the kind of city we want to be."[5] The report did generate modest media interest at the time of its release. But it lacked the political will and constituency base to translate its ideas into policy. Mayor Bradley invested none of his political capital in promoting L.A. 2000's proposals, and no business or civic leaders pushed its agenda after the report was released. L.A. 2000 (and its subsequent but short-lived descendant, the L.A. 2000 Partnership) became an abstract exercise in civic elite agenda-setting, with little to show other than a report to be issued and filed.

REBUILD L.A.

While the L.A. 2000 document identified the problem of the widening income divide, it underestimated, along with nearly all policymakers, the explosive nature of that divide. When the civil unrest occurred in late April 1992, political and economic figures, from Tom Bradley to other political leaders and corporate heads, were stunned by its ferocity. Within days,

Bradley sought to reconstruct a civic establishment to demonstrate the necessity of urgent—and visible—action. Unlike the L.A. 2000 appeal for new policies and regional governance, the group that Bradley called together saw its mandate as "unleashing the power of the private sector" to "rebuild L.A." Its reference point was the 1984 Olympics in Los Angeles, with its emphasis on private planning and funding. Under the leadership of Olympics wunderkind Peter Ueberroth, and with a board of eighty of L.A.'s top business and political figures, this new group, Rebuild L.A., set out to demonstrate that the private sector could achieve what government had not.[6] And once again, similar to L.A. 2000, only a handful of community activists, in conjunction with a much larger group of business and political leaders, participated in the formation of Rebuild L.A.

Rebuild L.A. quickly identified an informal agenda—job creation for riot-scarred areas—but it did so without involving any of the grassroots community groups that had already been mobilizing around those issues. The Rebuild L.A. leadership consisted, with the mayor's blessing, of several "loaned" business executives, such as Ueberroth and former Xerox executive Bernard Kinsey, Rebuild L.A.'s initial second-in-command. The group functioned in its first several months via press release and behind-the-scenes meetings with various industry groups and individual companies that were solicited to reinvest in inner-city neighborhoods.

In the first several months after the civil unrest, when media attention was most prominent, Rebuild L.A. was less an agenda than a series of pronouncements. Ueberroth was highly visible in this period, pressing his case for how private-sector initiatives could meet the challenge of new jobs for inner-city residents—a goal that subsumed all other community issues. By June 1992, Ueberroth was already proclaiming that Rebuild L.A. would facilitate the creation of fifty-seven thousand permanent, new inner-city jobs within five years. A few months later, at an October 1992 board meeting, Ueberroth expanded on those claims, stating that more than five hundred companies from the United States, Europe, and Japan were developing plans to invest more than $1 billion in inner-city areas. "Frankly," the one-time travel-business owner told the *New York Times*, "America doesn't solve problems unless it's done by the private sector."[7]

Given its initial focus on job creation to the exclusion of other community issues, such as housing, health care, or food security, Rebuild L.A. staked its claim that the private sector could produce new jobs on the assumption that reinvestment in the inner city was becoming increasingly attractive. But this claim proved to be more press release than reality. The promises of the supermarket industry were particularly striking in this respect. More than for any other business, Ueberroth and his Rebuild L.A. compatriots touted the enormous job-creation potential of new super-markets in the inner city. Indeed, within a few weeks after the civil unrest, Roger Strangeland, the chief executive officer of Vons, then the largest supermarket chain in the region, had already begun to meet with Ueberroth and his staff. Together, they sought to craft a major public announcement about Vons's intent to build new markets in riot-torn areas and to create hundreds, if not thousands, of new, relatively high-paying entry-level jobs.

As discussed in chapter 4 (page 113), Vons, along with several other major supermarket chains, had significantly abandoned inner-city commu-nities during the 1960s, 1970s, and 1980s. It had closed stores in those areas and invested in new stores almost exclusively in suburban locations. Of Vons's 329 stores in 1992, only a handful remained in areas either adjacent to or at the edge of the most economically depressed inner-city communi-ties. This had resulted in a significant decline in the access to fresh and rea-sonably priced food for local residents, as well as the loss of union jobs. (Vons's markets, for example, were covered by a contract with the United Food and Commercial Workers Union, and wages were considerably higher than at those stores without union contracts.)[8] However, a number of stud-ies in the late 1980s and early 1990s indicated a huge market potential in the form of underserved populations and lack of competition in the highly dense inner-city neighborhoods of Los Angeles—a situation found in inner-city areas around the country. But barriers to inner-city reinvestment, such as the difficulty in assembling land parcels and biases about doing business in the inner city, outweighed this modest interest among supermarket industry executives regarding inner-city reinvestment. Perhaps the largest factors influencing these discussions were the dwindling opportunities for *suburban* expansion and the restructuring and consolidation of the industry, spurred by the threat of competition from the big stores such as Wal-Mart.[9]

Strangeland worked with Ueberroth and the Rebuild L.A. team to make an immediate and dramatic announcement about Vons's intent to return to the inner city. At a July 23, 1992, press conference, less than three months after the civil unrest, Strangeland declared that Vons would build at least twelve inner-city stores as quickly as possible. This would entail an invest-ment of $100 million, creating between one thousand and two thousand permanent jobs with an annual payroll of more than $30 million. Vons would undertake the investment, not because "we are do-gooders or phil-anthropists," Strangeland declared at the press conference, but due to the company's business judgment about inner-city reinvestment opportunities for supermarkets, the core Rebuild L.A. argument. The Vons announcement, Ueberroth asserted, "provided a Good Housekeeping seal of approval to all those corporations throughout America who wonder: 'Should we really invest in the inner city?'" "They've stepped up," Ueberroth said of Vons. "They're the bell cow."[10]

The Vons announcement was quickly followed by announcements from three other major market chains—Ralphs, Smart and Final, and Food 4 Less—that they intended to build stores in inner-city areas. As a consequence, Rebuild L.A., in its first year, continually drew on the claim that at least thirty-one stores were going to be built in the inner city and that several thousand new jobs would be created. The supermarket claims became, in turn, the cornerstone of the early Rebuild L.A. strategy: define an opportunity, make some public claims, generate interest and enthusiasm, and then stake the process on those claims. It was an argument that was circular (claims about possible inner-city investment by private firms lead to interest in the idea, which leads to more claims), and separate from any public policy agenda or community engagement. Rebuild L.A. sought to demonstrate that the private sector could solve problems. It wanted to reverse the image of the private sector's abandonment of the inner city. "As a responsible corporate citizen and a leading area retailer," Vons's Strangeland remarked at his July 23 press conference, "we recognize the need to be at least a part of the solution—not a compounder of the problem."[11]

But claims of new stores and other reinvestments soon began to fade, while press coverage also became less extensive and more skeptical. At the October 1992 board meeting, Ueberroth announced that five hundred companies were ready to invest in inner-city L.A. But when pressed by Rebuild board members, he was able to name only seventy companies, and many of those appeared problematic.[12] In 1994, however, Vons was able to fend off some of the growing criticisms when it opened a new store in Compton, the first supermarket completed since Vons's 1992 press announcement. However, just six years later the Compton Vons market closed, as the chain once again abandoned an inner-city strategy to reorient itself toward middle-income and upscale customers.[13]

The criticism of overstated supermarket claims also influenced the direction of Rebuild L.A. Just one year after its formation, community activists and some media outlets began to challenge the identity and purpose of Rebuild L.A. Both Ueberroth and Strangeland left their positions. By 1995, Rebuild L.A. had changed its name to RLA and narrowed its mission to encouraging a few industry sectors located in the inner city to stay and expand. The new leadership lowered expectations and dropped the notion that only the private sector could turn things around. They understood that establishing a new supermarket required both community engagement and government support. By the tenth anniversary of the 1992 civil unrest, an Urban and Environmental Policy Institute study identified no net gain of supermarket chain stores operating in the entire area designated by Rebuild L.A. as needing new investment. The study—and the actions of the super-market industry—put to rest Peter Ueberroth's original premise that only the private sector could accomplish what government could not.[14]

The supermarket industry's retrenchment had several causes. Concentration in the industry had increased significantly during the mid- and late 1990s. National and even international mergers reduced the number of large operating chains (for example, within this time period, Ralphs, Boys Markets, Food 4 Less, and several other non-L.A. regional chains such as Kroger and Fred Meyer had combined into a single supranational entity). These mergers eliminated a number of the proposed markets while lessening competition. At the same time the square footage for new supermarkets increased, mimicking the cost-cutting warehouse stores like Wal-Mart.[15]

There were, nevertheless, success stories. In Newark, New Jersey, for example, a joint venture agreement between Pathmark Stores and the New Communities Corporation, a Community Development Corporation, pro-duced a shopping center centered on a Pathmark that turned out to be the *most profitable* of all Pathmark branches around the country. The location of the store was in one of the more devastated areas of Newark that had been scarred by the 1967 riots. Similarly, in L.A., Ralphs and Food 4 Less built new markets in two South Central neighborhoods, which were established with direct community participation and facilitated by public policies concerning store siting and permitting. But despite these few inner-city successes, the problem of access to fresh, affordable, healthy food, and higher-paying entry-level jobs, still remained. McDonald's and other fast-food outlets, with their low-paying jobs and poor food choices, became far more prevalent in South Central Los Angeles than full-service food markets.[16]

By 2001, the supermarket gap, parallel to the income gap, housing gap, transportation gap, food-access gap, and every other kind of gap, had continued to widen, even as Los Angeles, like other regions, experienced significant economic growth during the mid- and late 1990s. Another core problem that worsened was the working poor's lack of opportunity for job advancement. Rebuild L.A. was vulnerable to the criticism that its jobs strategy amounted to a "job gap"; that is, jobs with poverty wages and little opportunity for improvement. During Rebuild L.A.'s first year, a boisterous demonstration in October 1992 by Justice for Janitors put a human face on this job-gap issue (see chapter 3, pages 87–90, for more on Justice for Janitors).

The immediate occasion for the protest was a comment Ueberroth had made at a news conference announcing the launching of a job-training program sponsored by Toyota. Stung by criticism that such a program was primarily designed to produce minimum-wage jobs, Ueberroth responded that "minimum wage jobs brought dignity to those who labor in them." But the argument about *dignity* and its link to a living wage was precisely the rallying cry of the Justice for Janitors campaign. The December 1992 demonstration of several hundred janitors at the Rebuild L.A. headquarters focused attention on the increase in the numbers of working poor as well as the hazardous working conditions in many jobs.[17] And while the Justice for Janitors demonstration received only fleeting attention at the time, it effectively symbolized the limits of Rebuild L.A.'s claims about private-sector action.

The Rebuild L.A. experience paralleled the rhetoric but limited capacity of other top-down blue-ribbon committees and "riot commissions." "Political leaders ask for simple explanations which make it easier to act as leaders," two analysts wrote about such commissions. And with a public "anxious and searching for ways to understand the complex events," they can be "reassured and 'quieted' by single answers which . . . suggest that the problem in question can be easily solved."[18] Rebuild L.A. reflected the limits of such elite organizations, trapped by their own biases and unable to deal with problems because of inadequate resources and lack of organic connections to grassroots constituencies and the communities whose problems they presumably seek to address.

RECLAIMING THE PAST AND CREATING A PROGRESSIVE VISION FOR THE FUTURE

During the mid-1970s, a few progressive donors and funders began to meet with activists to create a new kind of community-oriented and community-led foundation in Los Angeles. Called the Liberty Hill Foundation after the 1923 episode at Liberty Hill (see chapter 1, page 17), the foundation was strikingly different from other L.A. philanthropies. A rotating community funding board of leading social, economic, and environmental justice organizers made the funding decisions. Grantees, many of them grassroots organizers on the cutting edge of social change activism, constituted a kind of who's who of Progressive L.A. The foundation had limited funds when it began—some groups received as little as six hundred dollars to help to jump-start their work. But it served a crucial function—providing seed funding for groups often too controversial for mainstream foundations.[19] During the 1970s and 1980s, these community organizing groups proliferated, at times even assuming functions that the government, particularly during the Reagan years, had largely abandoned, such as providing basic human services for the homeless or the hungry.

In the years following the 1992 civil unrest, several of those community groups became considerably larger and expanded their organizing among constituencies and around multiple issues. For example, the Community Coalition initially organized around the fight against the crack epidemic and the proliferation of liquor stores in South Central Los Angeles.[20] Liquor stores, some of which masqueraded as food marts, were a prime target during the civil disorders for providing easy access to liquor and for encouraging substance abuse and crime. The group also targeted other commercial operations, such as motels, that were magnets for crime and therefore contributed to making neighborhoods increasingly unlivable. The Community Coalition's efforts quickly expanded in the wake of the civil unrest, beginning to develop a wide range of community-building and issue-oriented organizing strategies. Education, community development, youth empowerment, food access, and other concerns became part of the Community Coalition's expanded agenda.

The rise of this new progressive constellation of community and issue-based advocacy groups paralleled important changes taking place in the Los Angeles labor movement as well. During the 1990s, as the labor movement in Los Angeles focused on the growing job and income gaps and the enormous demographic changes in Los Angeles, unions like the Service Employees International Union and the Hotel Employees and Restaurant Employees Union became centers for new organizing. Similarly, the environmental movement in Los Angeles was going through changes, influenced most directly by the rise of the environmental justice movement.

The growth of these movements created a critical mass of activism and support for a new progressive politics in Los Angeles. Missing, however, were the links between the different movements necessary to develop a broader, integrated perspective regarding the policy changes needed to make the region more livable and democratic. By the late 1990s, L.A.'s progressive movements had begun to achieve a level of political sophistication not seen since the 1930s and 1940s. High-profile campaigns provided striking victories around particular issues. These included such issues as the living wage initiative, the Housing Trust Fund battle, and urban park campaigns. The political sophistication and campaign successes around each specific initiative further underlined the importance of linking and uniting movements and developing the capacity among those movements to establish an overall *policy* framework and agenda for change.

How to develop those linkages and that capacity seemed particularly challenging, given the single-issue or group-specific focus of the community, environmental, and labor movements, and the oblique and unrepresentative nature of the policy process itself. The first challenge—identifying some sort of unity or at least a common language for progressive social movements—became the focus of the Progressive L.A. conference in October 1998. The conference, organized to explore the past, present, and future of progressive movements in Los Angeles, hoped in part to focus on what *L.A. Weekly* editor Harold Meyerson, in his speech at the conference, characterized as the need to reconstruct a "civic left" in the region and nationally. The discussion of the past was partly a tribute to past organizing, while also acknowledging the difficulty and complexity of constructing a regional progressive politics. The event was partly a celebration of the history of progressive movements and of historical memory. Historical accounts included such episodes as the 1942–43 Sleepy Lagoon trial and the interracial organizing that developed around it, the public housing battles in the late 1940s and early 1950s, the immigration battles in the 1960s and 1970s, and the emergence of the Bradley coalition. The conference was also designed to identify and celebrate a new generation of activism and political possibility.

The sessions that explored the contemporary movements and the development of future strategies and movements underlined the growth of the new progressive movements and their disparate nature, as well as the importance of extending agendas beyond specific issues or community concerns. Each of the speakers referred to the need to create and sustain a culture of organizing and political engagement and also identified the crosscutting issues and strategies that could reinvigorate the civic left.

A "Future of Progressive L.A." panel, which included activists and public officials, also discussed opportunities for a new progressive politics. At the same time, this session revealed some of the tensions and limits of a movement-building process. A dispute erupted over one particular issue (funding for a rail versus a bus system). Progressive movements have long had a tendency to self-destruct over differences about particular issues, and this could have been one of those moments. But panel member and then L.A. City Council member Jackie Goldberg helped to defuse the situation, commenting that movements "need to know how to disagree as well as what we want to build." The comment also put in perspective the need to develop a broader common language and policy platform, beyond specific disputes.

Despite the difficulties identified in the task, the October 1998 conference suggested that a new type of political and civic engagement was possible. The conference also catalyzed a new process for movement building and agenda setting. One goal was to create an overall progressive policy agenda for Los Angeles in the new century. Unlike the Rebuild L.A. and L.A. 2000 experiences, which sought to define an agenda without a community base or focus on mobilization, this agenda-setting initiative, which came together under the newly formed Progressive Los Angeles Network (PLAN), was driven by an activist and community-based constituency. Policy analysts, community organizers, environmental advocates, and labor activists sought to find a common language that identified specific policy initiatives within a broader social change framework. The underlying themes and principles for this agenda-setting effort—livability, democratic participation and empowerment, and social and economic justice—became the basis for that common language. The City of Los Angeles (and ultimately the Southern California region) provided the focus, the 2001 mayoral election the immediate occasion.

Beyond the immediate agenda-setting process was a larger goal of political reconstruction and social change. Ten years after the civil unrest and more than a century after Job Harriman and his Progressive L.A. supporters came close to instituting a new progressive agenda for Los Angeles, the challenges seemed great, but the opportunities seemed even greater.

7 A Vision for the City

Progressive L.A. in the Twenty-First Century

BREAKING UP LOS ANGELES

When James Hahn assumed office as mayor of Los Angeles, in July 2001, he was immediately confronted with the possibility that the city would be broken up into at least two, and possibly four, municipalities. Efforts were already under way to enable the San Fernando Valley, a sprawling land mass that had been annexed to the city in 1915 due to the availability of imported water, to become its own city. Similar secession attempts were beginning in San Pedro, an area that had become a part of Los Angeles at the turn of the twentieth century through a contentious battle to locate a harbor within the city limits. And there was even talk that Hollywood, first subdivided for residential development in the 1910s and made famous a decade later with the rise of the film studios, would seek to break away from Los Angeles to form its own municipality. If these secession efforts succeeded, L.A. would no longer be the grand metropolis envisioned by its former mayors as a world city. Instead, the city would shrink nearly as much as it had previously grown.

There were great ironies in these secession initiatives. At the beginning of the twentieth century, the undeveloped and dry farming areas of the San Fernando Valley were seized by syndicates of bankers, utilities, newspapers, railroad interests, and real estate developers for subdivision, annexation, and profit taking. Once it was annexed to Los Angeles, with a secure water supply, they continued to subdivide the Valley, which ultimately became the poster child for urban sprawl and traffic congestion.

The drive for secession was fueled by the realities of metropolitan fragmentation, a jobs-housing disconnect, and the feeling of separateness, of being a part of a place that had no center. The alienation and fears of some

Valley residents were magnified by the 1992 civil unrest; gun sales sky-rocketed during those events, though the riots never came close to crossing the Maginot Line of the Santa Monica–San Gabriel Mountains. Yet it was a jury in Simi Valley, the overwhelmingly White suburb at the edge of the San Fernando Valley, with its high proportion of LAPD officers who commuted into the central city, that reached the verdict about the Rodney King beating, which in turn sparked the civil unrest.

The San Pedro (or harbor) area had its own historical trajectory regarding the drive for secession. The early-twentieth-century harbor fight was a battle between competing corporate forces—the Southern Pacific and the Huntington interests—vying to control the region's major distribution routes and related opportunities for land speculation. San Pedro later evolved into a multiethnic, working-class community. At the same time, the Port of L.A. became a semiautonomous center of power, an engine of economic growth and jobs. The port's managers had also made plans to expand the port and develop a truck and rail route along the Alameda corridor, which would dramatically escalate the environmental and traffic hazards for harbor residents, as well as for some of the poorest communities in the region.[1]

The third major battleground for secession was Hollywood. To the rest of the world, Hollywood is a cultural icon. But to the people who live, work, and own property there, it is a place with many typical urban problems—housing, traffic congestion, crime, and poverty among them. Hollywood's secession drive was led by a few businesspeople and lacked widespread support. Secession supporters sought to promote the value of the name to establish a municipal identity, but were undercut in part when the famous Hollywood sign, situated in the Hollywood Hills, was ruled to be outside the proposed city limits. Furthermore, while a handful of the film studios and film production services and contractors still remained in Hollywood, a significant segment of the entertainment industry had relocated elsewhere. Six of the major studios, for example, had offices in the Burbank and North Hollywood areas, bordering the Los Angeles River and adjacent to one of the "soft bottom" sections of the river—in other words, a part that had not been channelized.[2]

This choice of location was ironic, given the movie industry's portrayals of the L.A. River—and of Los Angeles itself—as "stories of danger and violence," according to filmmaker Wim Wenders.[3] In these films, the uninviting, concrete-filled landscape of the river is a metaphor for the entire city as a hostile antienvironment, a bleak, *Blade Runner*–type view of Los Angeles. But the movie studios were now removed from that danger and violence, and from the lingering decay of the Hollywood neighborhoods; they were situated now in a place that provided a more pleasing view of the L.A. River, without its concrete straitjacket.

Developers and politicians targeted the real Hollywood for redevelopment, proposing big hotels, office buildings, and theaters. The most prominent project was a massive hotel/office project, planned by the Trizac-Hahn Company, at the corner of Hollywood and Highland, in the center of Hollywood. City officials recommended giving the developer huge subsidies to create the project, which would include a new theater that would become the home of the annual Academy Awards ceremonies. The developers and its boosters argued that the project would become a magnet for tourists and would bring international media attention to a renewed Hollywood. But community activists wanted to know how such a megaproject would help or hurt the quality of life in their neighborhood. Their City Council member, Jackie Goldberg, and the activist group Los Angeles Alliance for a New Economy (LAANE) argued successfully that any city subsidies should be linked to a package of community benefits. As city hall and progressive groups began making developers like Trizak-Hahn more accountable to the community, support for Hollywood secession weakened.

For Progressive L.A., secession raised the question of whether there was, in fact, a feeling of belonging and a shared sense of destiny among Angelenos from different neighborhoods, racial groups, and economic classes. Was Los Angeles the crown jewel for the forces of development and sprawl, associated with the real estate developers, financial interests, construction and engineering firms, utilities, and newspaper promoters who had helped to subdivide the Valley, push for a massive freeway system, channelize the river to allow for development along the flood plain, and essentially abandon the neighborhoods in the southern and eastern parts of the city? Was Los Angeles the world city envisioned by several of its mayors, and by business interests that welcomed foreign capital; established the hotels, services, and tourist infrastructure designed for a global commercial center; and welcomed immigrant workers, even as they resisted minimum workplace protections and security?

But there was another Los Angeles, a Los Angeles of EPIC clubs and zoot suiters; of janitors fighting for justice and parents and students advocating for farmers' market salad bars; of labor organizers mobilizing to rebuild communities and community organizers crusading for a living wage. For Progressive L.A., Los Angeles was a place of many cultures, ethnicities, movements, and neighborhoods, as well as a place to envision a more decent place to live, play, and work. This other Los Angeles, linked to its robust and diverse social movements, came closest to that vision of a "land of magical improvisation," as Carey McWilliams said of this region more than fifty years ago.

TENSIONS AND CHALLENGES

As has been made clear earlier in this book, Los Angeles is a place that has deep tensions and faces many challenges. It is fraught with racial, ethnic, class, and geographic divisions, as was evident during the 2001 mayoral election. Candidate Antonio Villaraigosa, heralded as potentially the first Latino mayor of an increasingly Latino Los Angeles, ran as the candidate who could help to unify diverse Los Angeles. His White opponent, James Hahn, carefully crafted his fragile coalition of conservative White San Fernando Valley voters, the city's police union (which included many White suburbanites), and African American voters in South Los Angeles.

Hahn's geographically and racially split electoral coalition (factions of which differed from each other not only in political and cultural terms, but also on many of the key issues that the next mayor would have to address) helped him to win, but it also was the source of new political tensions. His decision, shortly after assuming office, not to renew L.A. Police Chief Bernard Park's contract alienated many Black voters. Parks, an African American, had strongly resisted the police reforms recommended by the Christopher Commission in the wake of the 1992 civil unrest (although he had helped to reduce or eliminate some of the racial profiling and police violence that were directed particularly toward African Americans). He was considered an ally of key Black political, church, and economic-development interests, especially among older, more entrenched leaders in the Black community. At the same time, Hahn had received strong support from the police union, which was hostile to Parks's management approach and pressured the new mayor to dump the chief. Black leaders such as Congresswoman Maxine Waters and former Lakers star Magic Johnson (who had become an entrepreneur) felt betrayed by Hahn's action. Parks was subsequently elected to the City Council and became a candidate for mayor in 2005.

Secession was problematic for Hahn, given his electoral alliances. Aside from African American support in South L.A., he had run strongest in areas such as the San Fernando Valley and San Pedro. San Pedro's prosecession forces drew on what a publisher there called the ordinary resident's "great disconnect [with] the City of Los Angeles."[4]

Hahn, a San Pedro resident who lived in a modest home just blocks from one of the huge oil refineries on the harbor, experienced that discontent firsthand once he became mayor. Even his neighbors—such as Andy Mardesich, a Croatian immigrant who frequently confronted the mayor at city hall—were at odds with him. Secession support could be found throughout San Pedro's working-class neighborhoods, with their significant Croatian, Italian, and Portuguese immigrant populations. Part of San Pedro's discontent focused in fact on the port, which was run by an appointed Harbor Commission that pushed for port expansion, a strategy that translated into more dredging in the harbor and increased diesel emissions. These policies, in turn, hurt the very neighborhoods behind the drive for secession.[5]

Hahn also inherited more than three decades of discontent in the San Fernando Valley. The right-wing populist revolt spawned in the Valley had led to the passage of Proposition 13 in 1978. This tax-cutting measure triggered a protracted fiscal crisis for local governments and school districts and led to their growing dependence on state funding. During the 1980s and 1990s, Valley residents rebelled against two agencies that they saw as symbols of the absence of local control over Valley affairs. The first was the Metropolitan Transportation Authority (MTA), with its plans to construct a regional subway system. This plan reflected Mayor Bradley's vision of the greater Los Angeles region that fed into downtown L.A., but, in reality, the mayor's vision was divorced from the Valley's disparate commercial and residential centers. Though some of the plans called for new subway routes to the Valley, voters there joined with those in most other areas of L.A. in supporting a 1994 initiative to forbid the dedication of county tax and bond funds for additional subway construction.

The second Valley revolt came against the Los Angeles Unified School District (LAUSD). The state of the public schools became a Valley issue before it became a citywide issue. Valley homeowner groups had long practiced their own kind of Valley identity politics—for example, demanding the very kinds of quotas for mayoral appointments of Valley residents that would have appalled them if they had been demanded by Blacks or Latinos. These Valley groups argued that the district wasn't serving their needs and that LAUSD should be split up. As concern over the schools became a citywide issue, some right-wing Valley politicians—no longer in office, since Valley voting patterns had moved to their left—shifted their emphasis from the schools to the city itself.

As mayor, Hahn inherited a new layer of government. In 1997, largely to forestall the threat of secession, Mayor Richard Riordan had initiated a process to change the city charter and give the mayor more power over the budget and departments, while weakening the influence of the City Council.

With funding from his civic elite backers, he put an initiative on the ballot to establish a charter commission and to recommend reforms. Riordan also selected a slate of candidates to serve on the commission who supported his plan. Voters passed the initiative but favored a rival slate of candidates backed by the County Federation of Labor. Two separate commissions—one elected and one appointed by the mayor—were then established, and each began deliberations that confused rather than engaged the public.

Once charter reform passed, Riordan and the two sets of commissioners were obliged to add two key elements to the charter that the mayor had not initially sought. Under pressure from Valley secessionists, the charter commissions included provisions to establish neighborhood councils with advisory powers on all but the most major developments, and to break the city planning board into separate, neighborhood-based boards. Plans were also developed to expand the number of City Council seats. In short, the new charter was designed to give neighborhoods a stronger voice in local government.

In a sense, the measure was a quintessentially L.A. nonsolution: setting up a new governmental body (with loosely defined and largely advisory powers) to fill the void created by the disappearance of citywide political coalitions and more responsive elected and appointed officials. To be sure, neighborhood councils were designed to make government more accessible. A larger City Council was an important reform, in light of the fact that each council district represented 240,000 people. But the main goal of the advocates for neighborhood councils was simply to reduce support for secession measures before they came before the voters.

This approach didn't work, particularly for the Valley secessionists. Breaking up the City of Los Angeles—and creating a new city in the Valley, with a population of nearly 1.5 million, which would instantly become the sixth-largest city in the country—was explained in terms of accountability, but it was essentially done in the interest of power. The key secession advocates were, in fact, a new cast of Valley-based power brokers—primarily the leaders of homeowner associations, developers, and some local businesses. They hoped secession would strengthen their power base in a new Valley city. Their rhetoric focused on accountability and city services, concerns that resonated with those Valley voters accustomed to antigovernment arguments. The Valley secessionists argued that breaking up the City of Los Angeles would make local government more accountable. They tried to persuade Valley voters that the new city would resemble the much smaller cities of Burbank and Glendale—having an accessible government and responsive city services—when in fact it was more likely to generate yet another type of geographic and racial divide.

An undercurrent of racial and ethnic tension was a long-established reality in the Valley. Valley voters had been the backbone of Sam Yorty's political base in the 1960s, responding to his racist appeals. They led the opposition to busing in the 1970s, supported Proposition 13 at the end of that decade, and provided support for the anti-immigrant Proposition 187 in 1994. A new Valley city, however, would not be majority White. By a slim margin (43 percent to 42 percent), Latinos outnumbered Whites in the Valley as a whole, but White registered voters significantly outnumbered Latinos who were registered to vote (68 percent to 23 percent). The secessionists assumed the Valley power structure was likely to be dominated by Anglo/homeowner interests in the West Valley, rather than the poorer Latino neighborhoods of the East Valley.[6] The largest source of Valley revenue was generated by the pornographic film industry, which had made the Valley its home but which largely stayed away from the secession fight. Developers, West Valley homeowner groups, and other scattered business interests, including the Valley-based *Daily News*, remained the key backers of the secession movement.[7]

The secession campaign heated up in 2002 after the Hollywood and San Fernando Valley advocates secured a place on the November ballot. The harbor secessionists, however, failed to do so once the port was placed outside the proposed city and it was ruled that a new harbor city would therefore not be financially viable.

To succeed, the Valley and Hollywood secession forces needed to win a majority vote in their proposed new cities as well as in the City of L.A. as a whole. At first, the opposition to secession appeared muted and fragmented. The early organizing was led by the public employees unions, including the police and firefighters' unions, who feared that the new cities would undercut union contracts and the living wage ordinance. Housing activists feared that a new Valley city would not adopt L.A.'s renter protection laws or its newly won Housing Trust Fund. Other constituency groups that had fought hard for environmental and other measures similarly worried that the business-oriented leadership of a Valley city would ignore their victories.

The city employees' unions pushed Hahn to mobilize business support against secession. By the late spring, Hahn finally had pulled together a political coalition and fund-raiser operation, among a diverse coalition of labor, community, and business groups, that made secession a top priority. (Black civic leaders, angry at Hahn for firing Police Chief Parks, initially

194 / *Politics and Policy*

held back support for his antisecession campaign but ultimately provided the strongest support for the antisecession position.) A wide range of political leaders and influential Angelenos, including Antonio Villaraigosa, Richard Riordan, and Magic Johnson, joined with Mayor Hahn to oppose secession. Hahn, who in the past had seemed reluctant to attend public events and neighborhood meetings, became a much more visible figure. The *L.A. Times*, which opposed secession on its editorial page, also showered more attention on Hahn during the antisecession campaign than it had previously. Furthermore, Hahn's firing of Bernard Parks (and subsequent selection of former New York Police Commissioner William Bratton as LAPD chief) eventually came to be seen as a bolder move in light of his more aggressive and visible antisecession efforts.

Most important, however, without the antigovernment populist mobilization that had characterized the Proposition 13 revolt, and without a clear agenda for funding and improving government services in the new city, the secessionist drive faltered. Even in the Valley itself, the prosecessionist message saw a drop in support. By November 2002 the secessionist effort had collapsed. In the Valley, voters supported secession by the tiniest of margins, mainly because support in the West Valley outweighed opposition in the East Valley. Citywide, however, secession was defeated by a more than three-to-two margin.[8]

Though secession was defeated, political tensions and challenges still remained. It was clear that, ten years after the 1992 civil unrest, the economic, racial, and ethnic divide continued to influence the region's politics. Social justice, livable communities, crime, and decent jobs remained at the forefront of the agenda of activists.

The issue of land use, typically an arcane topic that mainly engaged developers, lawyers, planners, and communities (either in support of or opposed to a proposed new project), reflected the kind of challenges facing Progressive L.A.'s activist community. Although Los Angeles is one of the nation's largest cities in terms of its physical size, the city has been so overdeveloped that there is not much land available for new development. This is exacerbated by the huge number of contaminated sites—called brownfields—scattered around the L.A. landscape, particularly in low-income areas that were once home to industrial factories that used and discharged various toxic chemicals. The most dramatic example of this problem involved the controversy over the Belmont Learning Center, discussed in chapter 4 (see page 117).

The competition for scarce land was further exacerbated by L.A.'s desperate need for new schools, affordable housing, and parks and playgrounds.

Advocates for these issues were able, in recent years, to push separate legislation or to pass bond measures to expand state funding for schools, housing, and parks. But they clashed over where to put new facilities in a city
with limited available space. Each of the bureaucratic agencies responsible
for these facilities in turn had separate planning initiatives to identify and
purchase sites. They operated generally ignorant of each other's activities.
Under pressure to build new schools, for example, LAUSD purchased and
demolished apartment buildings housing low-income tenants. Tenant and
housing activists protested, arguing that the basic need for decent housing
should not take a backseat to the important need for new schools. Similarly,
community activists who believed that a particular location would be appropriate for a new park—particularly in low-income areas with little public
open space—discovered that a developer was proposing to build housing on
the site. This competition for scarce land threatened to become a war among
community activists, locked into their important but narrow agendas, who
otherwise might be on the same side of most issues.

To break the logjam, several Progressive L.A. activists, who over the
years had worked together on election and organizing campaigns and who
had developed mutual trust and respect, began a series of informal conversations in late 2001. They agreed that without some kind of "big-picture"
overview about potential sites, the competition would only lead to a frac-
tious zero-sum battle. No agency in the city government, they discovered,
had a complete list of such sites, including vacant land or buildings, owned
by private companies, individuals, or public agencies, which might become
parks, playgrounds, housing, or schools; underutilized commercial buildings ripe for razing or for redevelopment into schools or housing; and "nui-
sance" buildings, such as decrepit motels, that could be purchased, razed, and
developed for more useful purposes. Moreover, no agency had a complete
inventory of brownfield sites and the potential cost of removing toxic hazards so that they could be turned into places beneficial to the community.

In mid-2002, Assembly member and former city councilwoman Jackie
Goldberg convened a series of meetings with housing, environmental, education, and community activists, along with key officials in the different city
and state agencies involved in planning and funding parks, schools, and
housing. Goldberg pushed city officials to map all the potential sites in L.A.
that could be used for these purposes, so that advocates would have access to
the same information and could work together to identify appropriate locations. She also asked for help in crafting legislation to facilitate "joint-use"
projects—changing the rules, so that new schools and parks or new schools
and housing could be designed and built on the same sites.

Conversations and meetings like these were taking place across the city. As a result, activists were able to explore the common ground between movements that could help to forge a new identity—and a set of policies—for Los Angeles. But perhaps even more than the challenge of bridging these issue areas was the need to overcome Los Angeles' penchant for growth and its continuing fragmentation, which undermined any connection to place at the neighborhood level.

This concept of a fragmented metropolis has long fueled the assertion that "there is no there there," that Los Angeles, to recall the picture postcard mentioned earlier in this book, has remained the place that no one can find. In contrast, the strongest defenders of Los Angeles as a place have become those seeking to create a new vision for the city, including recent immigrants, who have been helping to construct new neighborhoods and new cultural traditions, and its radicals, reformers, and visionaries, who are seeking to remake Los Angeles into a more just and livable city.

We have argued that Progressive L.A. provides that vision of change and possibility. Its diverse movements convey a very different sense of place than the Los Angeles associated with the city's real estate speculators, civic elites, diesel-belching freeway corridors, and concrete-encased rivers. The ideas, reforms, and agendas of Progressive L.A. also provide the most compelling response to secession, fragmentation, lack of accountability, geographic and economic division, and the other challenges that Los Angeles faces today.

More than thirty-five years ago, in the wake of the Watts riots, Elizabeth Hardwick blasted Los Angeles in a vitriolic essay in the *New York Review of Books* as "a strip of plastic and clapboard, decorated by skimpy palms . . . this long sunny nothingness, born yesterday. . . . This promise of Los Angeles, this beckoning openness, newness, freedom," Hardwick argued, was really nothing more than a "stopover from which there is no escape."[9] For much of its history, L.A.'s progressive community has sought to address the city's fragmentation and balkanization, and to demonstrate that Los Angeles represents something far different than the vacuous and barren place that critics such as Hardwick have portrayed. There have also been moments when activists have come together to overcome the divisiveness that seems so much a part of the region's culture and geography. These activists have viewed L.A. as a city of possibility, which long-term residents and newcomers alike can reshape with a common vision of justice, democracy, and livability. Los Angeles, in this sense, becomes a richer, more nuanced, and complex place. It can be seen as the city that anticipates what the rest of the country will experience. It may be doing so again.

A Policy Agenda for the Next L.A.

This appendix provides a sketch of a policy agenda based on the work of L.A.'s progressive social movements. The agenda was developed by the Progressive Los Angeles Network Task Forces, drawing on various community-based initiatives and campaigns. The agenda was designed as a kind of baseline document, with recommendations for policy change at the municipal level in advance of the 2001 mayoral election, although they were developed with a regional framework in mind as well. As a sketch, the agenda represents a work in progress, a guide to action as well as a blueprint for policy choices in the years to come.

THE PROGRESSIVE LOS ANGELES NETWORK AGENDA FOR ACTION: A SUMMARY OF THE WORK OF NINE POLICY TASK FORCES—APRIL 2001

Housing

Guarantee a $100 Million Housing Trust Fund

- Los Angeles faces a severe affordable housing crisis, due to the increasing number of residents lacking affordable places to live and the city's historical failure to commit resources to deal with the problem. Local housing advocates determined that the most important first step that L.A. can take is to endow a *Housing Trust Fund* with guaranteed city funding of $100 million per year. This money could be spent to encourage the construction of more affordable housing, to preserve and restore existing housing, and to directly assist low-income residents with housing costs, as well as on other housing programs.

- To ensure that L.A. can boost the Housing Trust Fund to $100 million annually and sustain a commitment to affordable housing, the city needs to identify dedicated revenue sources. The primary source should be a "linkage" or "mitigation" fee on new commercial developments. The city should also explore additional revenue sources to supplement the linkage fee. These might include a percentage of the hotel transient occupancy tax and a percentage of the growth in the citywide property tax revenues.

Create More Affordable Housing

Each year, Los Angeles falls farther and farther behind its residents' needs for affordable housing. L.A. needs to bridge this gap, or overcrowding, slum housing, and homelessness will continue to rise.

- The city should adopt a citywide *Inclusionary Zoning Policy*, requiring all new residential developments to include a certain percentage of affordable housing units: 20 percent, say, as a realistic target. Requiring mixed-price residential developments will ensure that private housing builders are part of the solution and that affordable housing units are spread throughout the city. As an added benefit, more diversity in housing choices in new developments will help to break down residential segregation that divides the city by income and sometimes by race. Developers should have the choice to opt out of the requirement, but only if they pay into the Housing Trust Fund an amount equal to the difference between their units and the "affordable" price.

- Current zoning and land-use regulations in L.A. tend to limit affordable housing options or segregate it to certain parts of the city, as some neighborhoods are reserved for large houses on large lots or for retail establishments. The city should encourage creative solutions to the affordable housing crisis by decreasing minimum lot size in some neighborhoods, rezoning more areas for multifamily use, and facilitating mixed-use buildings that include commercial uses on the ground floor and residences above.

- Los Angeles needs redevelopment to improve the economy and revitalize depressed parts of the city; but redevelopment projects shouldn't bulldoze neighborhoods and displace affordable housing. The city should avoid displacing housing as a best option; when some displacement cannot be avoided, it should strengthen the current *replacement housing program* that is supposed to relocate residents of displaced housing units. This means ensuring that the location and design of replacement housing are determined by displaced residents, and that replacement housing is affordable and mixed-income.

Create Safe Housing

One out of nine apartment buildings in Los Angeles is judged to be in substandard condition, *substandard* being a polite term for such egregious deficiencies as lack of complete kitchen facilities or plumbing facilities, rodent infestations, lead-paint contaminations, and structural damage. Many of these units are overcrowded as well.

- To deal with the scandal of slum housing in Los Angeles, the City of L.A. should step up enforcement of housing safety laws and do more to expose slumlords. The city needs to expand the number of trained housing inspectors so it can meet its triannual inspection goals.

- When any serious violations of housing codes are detected, the city should take quick legal action to mandate compliance with health and safety rules, limiting extensions and appeals that allow owners to delay making vital repairs. One way to improve the housing enforcement process would be for the city to create a special *Housing Court.* The city should also cut through the shell corporations and other legal fictions that hide ownership of some housing units, by requiring disclosure of ownership of all apartments and by creating a public database showing ownership. The combination of shame and easier regulatory oversight will hopefully lead to improvements in maintenance. Sunlight, as the saying goes, is the best disinfectant.

- To deal with the worst housing abuses, when exposure and enforcement fail to get owners to act, the city should create a *receivership program for delinquent buildings.* The basic idea would be to apply penalties to landlords who violate health and safety codes and are delinquent on their property taxes, and to provide nonprofit community groups with funding to help them to purchase buildings that are in violation. The community groups would then work with tenants to revitalize the building. The city should also pursue state legislation to allow cities to directly take over properties with long-standing tax delinquencies, empowering L.A. to get housing units directly out of the hands of absentee slumlords and into the care of the community and tenants.

Empower Tenants
The best defense against dangerous slum housing conditions is educated, empowered tenants. Tenants need more accessible information on lead detection, eviction laws, rent payments, and code violations that affect their lives.

- For example, the city's *Rent Escrow Account Program* permits tenants to withhold rent and pay into an escrow account when code violations accumulate. The program is underutilized as a tool for improving building conditions. To spread the word about this important program and other housing-related information, the city should increase its own outreach to tenants and provide funding for community organizations, tenant groups, and labor unions to educate renters about their rights and responsibilities under the law—and do so in the variety of languages required to reach the city's diverse populations. L.A. should also put important housing information on city web sites so that tenants have access to records of code violations, impending sales, and other relevant information.

- The city should form a *Division of Tenant Empowerment* within the Department of Housing to assist tenants in enforcing housing rules, such as participating in building inspections; as well as in forming and organizing cooperatives to own and manage their own buildings. The city should also adopt a local *Tenant-Landlord Relations Act,* covering buildings with twenty or more units, including those in federally subsidized and public housing. The act would allow residents to vote on whether they want a tenant group as their representative. If more than one-half of tenants in a building or complex vote for a tenant group in elections overseen by a neutral party, landlords will be required to negotiate with the tenant group on issues of management, maintenance, security, evictions, and other issues.

The Urban Environment

Formulate a Livable City Plan
Many of the significant problems facing Los Angeles—pollution, traffic, and so on—can be traced in part to a lack of a vision or planning on how to best use our land and resources.

- The City of Los Angeles should create a *Livable City Plan* to get broad community input on the kinds of changes needed to improve quality of life, then to set concrete goals and plans for making these visions a reality. The L.A. Livable City Plan should integrate environmental and economic concerns to promote smart growth that improves environmental quality, transportation options, and employment and housing opportunities. The city would first gather information on current indicators and seek public input on priority areas for improving quality of life. Then the city, with advice from outside experts, would set strategies and a timetable for making measurable improvements. Progress toward the goals would be evaluated through reports to the public and internal accountability procedures, which should include targets and incentive/disincentive programs for different city departments.

Ensure Right to Know and Access to Decision Makers

People have a democratic right to know about environmental conditions that impact their lives, and to fully participate in decisions that will affect their futures.

- The city should minimize the loopholes that some developers use to avoid having to produce full environmental impact studies, side-stepping community input and participation. The city should also expand and improve the ways it publicizes environmental information. This will require creative environmental outreach and education to reach residents in neighborhoods, schools, workplaces, and through grassroots associations and neighborhood council meetings. The city should also do more to post environmental information on the Internet, following the lead of nongovernmental organizations. The city should ensure that all environmental-related commissions, boards, and agencies establish mechanisms for democratic input and community and worker access to decision making. L.A. should also use its weight to make regional environmental agencies more open to the public.

Rehabilitate Contaminated Land

The City of Los Angeles needs more affordable housing, more parks, and more schools, as well as more living-wage employers, and it needs sites to place them all.

- Vacant or underused land exists, but much of this represents "brownfields" land, sites that are contaminated or degraded in such a way that it is hard to immediately put them to good use. The City of Los Angeles should double the number of brownfield sites cleaned and made available for development each year, based on the right of communities to review and help to decide how to use these sites. *L.A. should create a database of brownfield sites* and other vacant lands in the city, and prioritize cleanup based on the toxic load on neighborhoods, and local needs for housing, economic opportunities, and park land. Brownfield rehabilitation should start with community recommendations, not just developer proposals.

Increase Parks and Open Space

The passage of California State Propositions 12 and 40, which increased state funding for open space, and the outpouring of grassroots demands for more parks throughout Los Angeles give the city the opportunity to regreen itself with new parks, creating venues for recreation, community gardening, and reprieves from hectic urban life.

- The city should aggressively pursue new parks, with a short-term goal of doubling park space in park-poor neighborhoods. This will require leadership to ensure that a significant proportion of state funds are dedicated to urban parks. L.A. must also commit city funds to new parks. For example, L.A. should facilitate the development of a *nonprofit land trust* to convert surplus city-owned vacant land into parks.

- To complement a push for new parks, the city should preserve and restore nature and natural places in and around L.A. for their own sake—and the benefits they bring to residents. Besides performing ecological services, such as filtering air and water and providing wildlife habitat, nature fosters an appreciation for diversity and interconnectedness. The city's conservation efforts should focus on remaining areas of high ecological value, including canyon and hillside watersheds, wetlands, and wildlife habitats and corridors.

Pursue Cleaner Air

L.A.'s air has improved in recent years but remains a blight over the city. Smog and other airborne contaminants are more than an eyesore. They pose a dangerous health risk, especially for children, asthma sufferers, and the elderly.

- The City of L.A. needs to push regional air regulators to strengthen controls on all sources of air pollution. And the city has a moral obligation to lead the way to greater use of clean vehicles and fuel. Cars, trucks, and other motorized vehicles are responsible for two-thirds of the region's smog and a majority of the cancer risks from air pollution. The city has started to switch to *alternative fuel vehicles,* but should broaden and accelerate this program so that half of all city vehicles in all categories are alternative fuel vehicles within four years. To encourage residents to follow the public example, the city should strengthen regulatory and financial incentives for individuals and businesses to switch to alternative fuel vehicles and establish more alternative fueling stations throughout L.A.

- While Los Angeles is leading the shift towards a zero- and low-emission future, it needs to focus immediate attention on the most pressing health threat from vehicles: diesel exhaust from buses and trucks. *Diesel exhaust* is a carcinogen that poses a risk to residents of neighborhoods, mostly low-income, where bus use is heavy, as well as to school children riding on or walking near school buses. The city needs to exert maximum pressure to ensure that the Los Angeles Unified School District and the Metropolitan Transportation Authority (MTA) phase out all of their diesel buses. The city should also work with MTA and the South Coast Air Quality Management District (AQMD) to identify areas where diesel fueled vehicles are driven through or idle in predominantly residential areas and near schools, and develop alternative routes to minimize neighborhood health risks.

- Though less numerous than vehicles, stationary sources such as oil refineries, chrome-plating shops, and gas stations contribute to overall air contamination; their emissions can concentrate air toxins in adjacent and downwind neighborhoods. To identify and reduce these toxins, the city should work with AQMD to require *better public notice of emissions from stationary sources.* Those sources whose emissions increase the risk of cancer by more than one case per million persons exposed, or increase the risk of other significant health hazards, should be required to prepare enforceable toxics-reduction plans.

Improve Water Quality, Reduce Water Demand
Los Angeles should develop a public health and integrated watershed management approach to water.

- To strengthen water conservation, the city should establish a *"no net water gain"* approach to new developments and provide resources for expansion of water conservation programs. The city should also foster a *landscape ethic of use,* beginning with the city's own properties and park lands, that emphasizes the use of native and less water-consumptive plants, groundcover, and landscape design. The Department of Water and Power (DWP) should focus on water reuse and conservation programs as a major source of "new" water, while experimenting with conservation-based and equitable methods of pricing water.

- Water is also a health priority. Water agencies like the DWP and the Metropolitan Water District should be given an explicit *public health mission to ensure safe drinking water*. This can be done by developing a watershed and pollution prevention approach to reduce contaminants in ground and surface drinking-water sources. Finally, the city should enforce and strengthen protection for rivers, coasts, streams, and wetlands. Better control of storm runoff from sewers is needed to prevent pollution of rivers, coasts, and streams. The city should increase protection of coastal areas and encourage the Regional Water Quality Board to enforce its new *zero trash limit* for the L.A. River.

Reduce Toxins in Homes and Neighborhoods

Our neighborhoods should be safe places to live, work, learn, and play, not hazards to our health. Too many L.A. neighborhoods are currently contaminated. Not surprisingly, some of the worst toxic contamination is near the homes of L.A. residents who have been politically and economically disenfranchised. An environmental justice movement has sprung up to combat pollution in these communities. Their goals of reducing toxic hazards deserve more support from the city.

- To combat lead poisoning, the city should work with the county to conduct blood tests to detect lead in all at-risk one- to six-year-old children and develop a stepped-up program for testing for lead-based paint in dwellings. When lead is detected in homes, the city and county should make sure that low-income residents are aware that Federal Housing and Urban Development funds are available through the county for remediation of dwellings with lead-based paint.

- Pesticides are another widespread environmental and health hazard, with special risks to children. The City of Los Angeles should reduce annual pesticide use by 75 percent by weight within five years, with at least a 10 percent reduction the first year. It is especially critical for the city to bring its leadership to bear in ensuring that the L.A.

Unified School District completely phases out toxic pesticide use on school grounds. These health threats from toxics are just two of the most serious and easily identifiable hazards facing L.A. neighborhoods. To provide a full picture of environmental health risks, the city should develop a *Toxics "Hot Spots" Program* that tracks the intersection and impacts of multiple sources of pollution in the hardest hit communities.

Encourage Clean Production

For Los Angeles, one of the world's great manufacturing cities, home to small, medium, and large production facilities, promoting cleaner production methods is key to a greener, healthier future. In many industries, cleaner methods exist but may not be widely adopted unless government steps in to give manufacturers a nudge through regulation and incentives.

- The City of Los Angeles should develop a *Pollution Prevention and Toxics Use Reduction Policy* and program that addresses workplace and environmental exposures from toxic production methods and materials. This program should support research and development of alternative products and processes that will prevent pollution and reduce the use of toxics, in collaboration with the workers who will use the alternative products and processes. Incentives and disincentives such as rapid permitting, tax credits, and publicity of companies' environmental records, should be tied to the program to encourage business to adopt cleaner methods.

Promote Clean Energy

As California continues to experience fallout from the failure of electricity deregulation, one silver (or green) lining is the opportunity to revamp our energy policies in the direction of energy conservation and environmentally beneficial renewable energy options. L.A.'s publicly owned Department of Water and Power needs to step up to the plate to use the current spotlight on energy issues to hasten a shift toward a more sustainable energy future.

- More than 70 percent of Los Angeles' electricity is generated from coal and nuclear power. These sources pollute the environment and contribute to global warming. L.A. needs to move toward greater use of alternative power sources that produce electricity in an environmentally friendly manner, including wind and solar power. The city should increase use of power from renewable sources by 50 percent, measured as a percentage of all power used. On the demand side of energy conservation, homeowners, design and building professionals, and cities across the nation are exploring construction and design methods that emphasize health, energy efficiency, and the environment. Los Angeles has developed *Sustainable Building Guidelines,* covering implementation of energy and water efficiency measures, use of recycled materials, and reduction of toxics for the rehabilitation of housing. This program should be expanded by enacting a *Municipal Building Policy* to design, construct, and manage city-owned facilities and buildings in a sustainable fashion; and increase retrofits of municipal buildings to reduce energy and water consumption.

Transportation and Land Use

The City of Los Angeles and its regional partners should adopt transportation and land use policies that help residents to get where they want and need to go, while making our transportation system more equitable, protecting air quality and open space, and making communities more livable. Transportation policies and incentives that elevate driving above all other ways of getting around aren't just short-sighted: they are unfair, when so many people in Los Angeles can't afford cars.

Los Angeles needs more diverse, connected forms of transportation. The system would start in our neighborhoods, which should be made safer and be designed to encourage walking and biking. Improved bus service would link all neighborhoods with effective transit. Finally, a system of backbone rail corridors can provide fast, high-capacity service, catalyzing smart growth in the form of transit-oriented residential and commercial development.

Make Neighborhoods Safer and More Walkable

One of the main goals of transportation policy should be creating communities with safe streets where residents can, and will want to, walk and bike more. Making communities more walkable and bikeable increases physical activity, cuts vehicular traffic and pollution, and promotes a vibrant civic and commercial life in neighborhoods.

- To safeguard pedestrians, the city and county should press the state to increase spending dedicated to the safety of pedestrians and bicyclists in equal measure to the dangers to them. In the L.A. region, many neighborhoods need additional safety features, such as raised medians where pedestrians can seek refuge, flashing pedestrian sig-

nals, and barriers, planters, and speed bumps to slow down traffic.
MTA should dedicate 5 percent of its transportation funding to
pedestrian amenities.

- Safer streets will encourage more walking; so will improved street
design, aesthetics, and pedestrian-oriented features. With L.A.'s
population becoming more diverse, its "car culture" can give ground
to a sense that streets can be public space: places to stroll, meet
neighbors, and shop. The city, county, and regional bodies should
make sidewalks wider, cleaner, and better lit; build bus shelters at
every bus stop that currently has no shelter; and beautify streets
with trees and other landscaping and design improvements.

- Biking is a healthy and environmentally friendly way of getting
from place to place. The city, county, and MTA should increase funding for bicycle projects to $25 million per year, working toward a
target of increasing cycling's share of trips to 10 percent by 2025.
This funding can extend bike trails throughout the region. Cycling
should be accommodated on all new roadway projects through the
incorporation of bike lanes or other bike safety features, and integrated into all transit facilities by providing bike racks, shower facilities, and so on.

Improve Transit Service

- Transit should enable people to reach jobs, schools, food markets,
health care and human services, airports, and retail and entertainment centers. The reach and convenience of transit need to be extended through additional bus and train routes. While new lines
are being developed, the City of Los Angeles should work with
MTA to make it easier to understand and use existing transit, by
distributing maps showing the entire transit network and implementing universal fare cards to allow seamless transit between
various bus lines, subways, and light rail.

- The city, county, and regional bodies should design and fund more
transportation programs specifically tailored to meet the needs of
low-income workers, especially participants in welfare-to-work programs and other job and social programs. These programs should
increase public transit services to and from places of employment,
residences, child care centers, and health and human services offices
used by welfare-to-work participants and other low-income workers,

including greater use of flexible paratransit services, such as vans, for locations and times outside the regular public transit routes and schedules.

Expand Bus Service

Improving bus service is a critical first step toward improving transit in a fair, efficient, and environmentally sound way. People without cars and the working poor with limited access to cars need buses to get to their jobs and to attend to other basic needs of life. Without an effective bus system, the existing rail system will be less effective, roads and highways will become more congested, and pollution will get worse.

- The City of L.A. should ensure that MTA implement its civil rights consent decree, improve its on-time bus service by 5 percent per year, and guarantee free passes for riders when buses are more than thirty minutes late. MTA should also expand its plans to buy new, clean buses, develop twenty new rapid bus lines, and create more bus lanes. Moreover, the city should ensure that bus fares are lowered.

- Improved and extended rail service can reduce car use, especially daily commuter trips. It should also complement bus routes, especially over long, arterial routes, so that buses can provide more frequent service along shorter routes. The city, county, and regional bodies should extend Metrorail and Metrolink lines to meet existing transportation needs and to serve as nodes for denser, smarter growth.

Promote Smart Growth

Los Angeles, like many regions of the country, faces a choice on how to develop. It can continue to sprawl outward, with weakening economic prospects for residents of the center city and inner suburbs, longer commutes for residents of far-flung housing developments, and increased frustration and pollution all around. Or it can choose smart growth, by coordinating the ways residents use land, create jobs, and get from place to place.

- The city should overhaul its zoning code to promote smart growth, so people can drive less and live nearer to where they work, shop, study, and play. As first steps, the city should create *mixed-use demonstration projects* in all city Districts; adopt a main street preservation ordinance banning new "big box" retail stores, which undermine local retail and community activity; and steer future development to locations near existing and planned transit stops.

- L.A. should also revise zoning rules to replace off-street parking minimum requirements with maximum parking spaces allowed, and severely restrict the ground coverage of parking facilities. The city should advocate flexibility in the state Field Act to allow more joint use of land and facilities by parks, playgrounds, and schools.[1] On a broader scale, the city should consider regional growth boundaries and green belt planning initiatives like the one around Portland, Oregon.

- Smart growth will also require changing some of the financial incentives that reward sprawl. Los Angeles should expand *free and discount transit pass programs*, especially for seniors, students, and lower-income residents. To discourage excessive car use, the city should develop appropriate parking and driving fees. One of the most effective ways to promote alternative transportation is to reduce "free" parking, which is actually subsidized by those who use it and the general public through higher rents, higher prices for goods and services, higher overhead for employers who have to provide employee parking, and lower pay for their employees. The city and county should enforce and strengthen their "cash-out" programs. The city should also raise its 10 percent tax on parking in pay lots or garages to generate additional funds and to encourage drivers to use transit, and work with regional transportation bodies to explore how to implement an equitable tax on gas or driving.

Manage Air, Sea, and Ground Transport
The Los Angeles region is a major trade and trans-shipment center. The challenge for L.A. is to maintain its ports and airports as economic engines, while minimizing their impacts on neighborhoods and the environment.

- The city, county, and regional bodies should consider high-speed rail as an alternative to trucking and air-goods transport where practical, and address toxic pollution and noise impacts from trucking. The city, county, and regional bodies should develop a regional plan to accommodate air traffic growth and relieve pressures on LAX by considering expansion and better use of the eleven other commercial airports in Southern California. They should also ensure that environmental and planning concerns are seriously addressed from an environmental justice perspective before any steps are taken to expand LAX.

Food and Nutrition

We need to improve Los Angeles' food system—the way food for L.A.'s millions of residents is grown, distributed, and sold. This means boosting access to fresh food and fighting diet-related diseases in L.A. The city should ensure that all neighborhoods have access to local supermarkets, farmers' markets, and gardens; expand government nutrition programs; promote sustainable family farms; and improve school food.

Create a Food, Hunger, and Nutrition Plan of Action

- While the City and County of L.A. have recognized the need to plan for basic needs such as transportation and water, they do not have a comprehensive plan for food security. As a result, efforts on hunger and nutrition are often disjointed and community groups find it hard to get answers on food-related issues. The city and county should jointly establish a *Food Policy Council* to advise decision makers on food, hunger, and nutrition issues. The Food Policy Council should aid the city and county in preparing an *Annual Report on Food, Hunger, and Nutrition,* and implementing a plan of action to address findings in the annual report. The report would measure food-related indicators. The plan of action should identify measures to improve the status of each of the problem areas identified in the annual report, including city and county actions and advocacy on state and federal issues.

Improve Fresh Food Access

Lower-income residents have to pay more for groceries, often don't have access to healthy food like fresh produce, and consequently suffer higher rates of obesity and diet-related diseases.

- To ensure that people in low-income communities have access to healthy food, the city should attract at least four new full-service markets and four new farmers' markets to low-income neighborhoods over the next four years. Los Angeles should work with community organizations and prospective market operators to meet this goal, which will require creative policies, such as easing parking requirements or providing incentives to build modest-sized (twenty thousand square feet) but well-stocked stores.

- By giving support to small and locally owned restaurants and food vendors, the city can encourage a more diverse and healthy mix of prepared food options in low-income neighborhoods. L.A. should help small restaurants and street and truck vendors by helping them to access credit, by providing health and nutrition classes, and by making certified kitchens at public sites available during off hours for use by microenterprises and for cooking classes. Los Angeles should simultaneously end city subsidies to fast-food restaurants and explore changing zoning to discourage fast-food restaurants where residents are in favor of doing so.

- While helping communities to attract new food markets and eating establishments, the city should also increase transportation options to allow residents of underserved neighborhoods to travel to existing markets throughout Los Angeles. L.A. should encourage the Metropolitan Transportation Authority (MTA) to develop a range of food access transportation strategies. At a minimum, bus routes must include more stops near markets and near Department of Public Social Services offices, where residents access food stamps. The city and MTA should also encourage markets to offer shuttle service and delivery in transit-dependent communities.

Promote Urban Agriculture

- Los Angeles can help people to enjoy the bounty of their own gardens and that of local farms. The city should boost community gardens, farmers' markets, and community-supported agriculture. The city should help community organizations to establish at least ten new community gardens over the next four years, and immediately create and fund at least one city staff position responsible for organizing and instituting community gardens and new farmers' market sites.

- Farmers' markets offer consumers a steady source of locally grown food and bring a burst of vitality to neighborhoods where the markets are located, drawing shoppers with spillover benefits for nearby merchants, and serving as community gathering points. To support the priority goal of bringing four new farmers' markets to low-income communities, and to expand farmers' markets throughout all of L.A., the city should pursue strategies that make newly launched markets more economically viable. The city should sponsor and help to advertise farmers' markets, allow markets to utilize the city's insurance, and encourage expanded use of food stamps and WIC Farmers' Market Nutrition Program coupons at markets.

- Community-supported agriculture and direct marketing opportunities can link city residents and local farmers. Los Angeles should urge consumers and businesses to contract with local farmers, with the city leading the way. By strengthening the connections between farmers and the city, Los Angeles will have laid the foundations for the next generation of family, sustainable farms. The city should work with the county to double the number of farms in Los Angeles County by contributing to land trust programs and establishing sustainable-agriculture programs at community and polytechnic colleges in the area.

Shore Up the Food Safety Net

Los Angeles' ultimate goal should be a food-secure city and region, where all residents can access and afford food from shops, farmers' markets, and urban gardens. But with hunger threatening 2.1 million people in Los Angeles County today, public and private food programs still play a vital role in ensuring that everyone has enough healthy food to eat. Food pantries are sometimes forced to turn away families in need, highlighting the fact that private emergency food systems should not and cannot be a substitute for a strong public safety net designed to meet the food needs of all residents.

- Most government food programs are at the federal or state level, but the City of Los Angeles can conduct and support outreach to increase participation in food stamps, school breakfast, child-care food, and WIC programs. The city can also work to bring more residents into these programs by supporting legislative changes to restore immigrants' access to food stamps. The city should use federal nutrition programs (augmented where necessary with local funds) to offer nutritious meals and snacks to all children participating in city-sponsored, -funded, or -affiliated programs, such as recreation, child care, and after-school programs. Finally, the city can help food stamp recipients to gain access to an expanded range of food choices by encouraging more stores in L.A., especially stores, cooperatives, and buying clubs that sell healthy food, to accept food stamps; and by seeking waivers allowing the use of food stamps to purchase prepared food.

Make Schools Healthy Places to Learn

The Los Angeles Unified School District (LAUSD), serving the City of Los Angeles and many other municipalities and sections of Los Angeles County, is the second largest school system in the country. The quality of school meals—Is the food nutritious and fresh? Does it taste good and appeal to students? Is food service supportive of the schools' education mission?—is an important determinant of students' health and their ability to learn at their full potential.

- LAUSD meals should surpass federal requirements in terms of nutritional content: particularly factors, such as freshness and minimal processing, that have health benefits and taste advantages. LAUSD should procure food items from local farms where practicable. To appeal to students, the district should serve food selections that reflect student diversity and the range of ethnic cuisines prepared in students' homes and neighborhoods. The same health standards applied to food items served as part of school meal programs should apply to food and snacks sold on campus. These "competitive" foods are not strongly regulated by either the federal or state governments, thereby exposing students, through vending machines and the on-school stores that sell them, to the temptation of junk food and fast food throughout the school day. LAUSD should allow only healthy snacks to be sold on school grounds.

- If schools are going to improve their students' eating habits the presentation of food is nearly as important as food quality. School food should be served in eating environments that are pleasant and stimulating, with ample seating and sufficient time for students to eat and enjoy their meals. Schools also need full-service kitchens to serve fresh, diverse food. LAUSD should ensure that all new schools being built have full-service kitchens, and should upgrade inadequate school kitchens whenever schools are undergoing renovations.

- Improving school food and ensuring that all students are served healthy, high-quality meals will eliminate discrepancies between what schools teach kids about eating habits and nutrition, and the reality of what is currently available, be it unappetizing meals or easily accessible junk food. The LAUSD can go farther in integrating food and nutrition into the district's teaching mission. Establishing a *Garden in Every School Program*, and incorporating garden-grown produce in school meals, would ensure that every child experiences the gardening and harvesting of edible foods while learning about the seasons, growing cycles, and food preparation.

- The LAUSD should establish a two-tiered system of public input to seek the advice and expertise of the community in improving school food. At the district level, LAUSD should establish an advisory board, comprised of parents, students, teachers, and community members drawn from each subdistrict. The advisory board could help to shape district-wide healthy school food policies. This new board should complement opportunities for input at the school level. Each school should invite students, parents, teachers and community members to tour food preparation and service facilities and provide feedback and suggestions on site improvements, menu ideas, and so on.

Democracy and Participation

Local democracy in Los Angeles is dangerously anemic. Voter turnout in recent elections in the City of Los Angeles has hovered around one-third. What can Los Angeles do to encourage broader public participation and a more vital democratic culture? We should pursue a mix of local, state, and federal reforms to increase voter participation by making it easier to register and vote. Voting is the most obvious manifestation of participatory government, but democracy has deeper roots, measured by the public's ability to take part in decisions that affect their lives. The local level is where these roots should thrive. Increasing avenues for local participation will let people reclaim democracy from the ground up.

Increase Voter Registration

- Registration is the first key to increased electoral participation. Instead of posing a barrier to participation, policies should be designed to welcome new voters. Despite ever-lengthening campaigns and saturated political ads, many potential voters do not focus on elections until shortly before election day. Our electoral system currently requires registration at least fifteen days in advance of an election, denying many who are qualified the opportunity to vote. The City and County of L.A. should support changes to state-election laws to allow *same day–election day registration.*

Make It Easier to Vote

- According to a survey conducted by the Census Bureau, the number one reason registered voters do not vote is that they are too busy, with a conflicting work or school schedule. To boost voter turnout, the City and County of Los Angeles should explore logistical reforms that give people more time to vote and more ways to cast their vote. Improving voting options can benefit voters who traditionally face difficulties getting to the polls, including the disabled, the elderly, and homebound caretakers, as well as people who work long hours, lack access to reliable transportation, or are temporarily out of town.

- There is no reason why all voters have to cast their votes on one election day. Stretching out the period in which people can go to the polls can boost participation by giving residents more opportunities to find time in their busy schedules. The City and County of Los Angeles should allow early voting up to seven days before elections. Allowing expanded early voting would provide an opportunity to move from punch-card voting machines to newer touch-screen technology, helping to restore confidence after the November 2000 presidential election. To begin to assemble the $100 million it would take to switch L.A. County voting machines to touch-pad technology, the city and county should commit local funds to increase trials of the electronic voting system, while lobbying aggressively for state and federal funding to fully upgrade L.A.'s voting system.

- Election days are usually set on Tuesdays, but there's a strong case for moving elections to weekends, when more people have free time. As an alternative, the city and county could promote voter participation by instituting an *election-day holiday* for their own workers. This would have a direct impact on the ability of public employees to get to the polls, would encourage private employers to allow employees time off to vote, and would increase the likelihood that polls are adequately staffed on election day.

- California already allows voters to vote by absentee ballot, provided they request an absentee ballot in advance of each election. Some states, such as Washington, allow all voters who request it to permanently receive an absentee ballot for every election. In California, this option is available only for persons with certain physical disabilities. The City and County of Los Angeles should urge the state to expand permanent absentee voting to all who request it.

- Mail voting is conducting elections using only absentee, mail-in ballots, with no physical voting locations. Los Angeles should consider testing mail-only voting to see if it increases participation in this region. Allowing voting over the Internet is another potential avenue for increasing participation. But with a wide "digital divide"

in Internet access between rich and poor and by ethnicity, Los
Angeles should move ahead with Internet voting only as part
of integrated and corresponding efforts to increase voting through
other means (by mail and in person).

Make Government More Representative

Deepening democracy requires more than making it easier to vote. Los
Angeles should adjust the structure of city and county government to make
them more responsive to the public, especially constituencies who have not
been part of the city's traditional power structure—immigrants, workers,
tenants, and so on.

- Los Angeles has the largest council districts and supervisor districts in
  the United States (more people live in each L.A. County supervisor
  district than in each of the fifteen U.S. states with the lowest populations). The county should explore expanding the number of supervisors, so that each district can be reduced in size. The existing winner-
  take-all election system, combined with large districts, favors
  establishment candidates. *Proportional representation,* the voting system used by most of the world's established democracies, is based on
  the principle that groups of like-minded voters should win representation in proportion to its share of the popular vote. Proportional representation cannot be used to elect a citywide official or a representative
  from a single-member district, but the city should experiment with it
  in new elected structures. *Instant runoff voting* can capture some of
  the same benefits as proportional representation in existing single-
  member districts. Because voters are not experienced with instant
  runoff voting systems, it currently makes sense as an option in special
  elections, which are increasing as term limits take effect.

- When elected officials delegate power to appointed commissions,
  boards, or other bodies, they need to ensure that appointments
  reflect the views and diversity of the community. It is part reality
  and part damaging perception that the majority of commission and
  board appointments in Los Angeles are awarded to Westside professionals and business owners who are often strong financial supporters of those who appoint them. City and county decision makers
  should appoint labor- and environmentally-oriented representatives,
  as well as business representatives; tenants as well as landlords; and
  community representatives where the decisions of a commission or
  board affect the well-being of a particular community.

Expand Democracy through Inclusive Neighborhood Councils

- A new system of neighborhood councils being set up in the City of Los Angeles holds both promise and peril for city democracy. In theory, the neighborhood council system will improve residents' opportunities to dialogue with elected officials. The city charter in fact requires L.A. to establish procedures for an "early warning system," to give neighborhood councils notice of and opportunity to comment on issues before decisions are made by the City Council, City Council committees, and city boards and commissions. Unfortunately, the procedures by which many neighborhood councils were established undermined some of their potential for public involvement in local decision making. Outreach was insufficient to overcome the time and language barriers that many residents face in learning about, attending, and participating in neighborhood council planning meetings.

- To capture the original promise of neighborhood councils, the city should ensure that the Department of Neighborhood Empowerment and all councils have specific criteria regarding the representation of traditionally underrepresented groups. This might mean putting disproportionate resources into outreach to those groups, providing child care so residents can attend council meetings, and such. Where necessary, the city should deny certification and funding to neighborhood councils that cannot demonstrate that they are representative of the residents and workforce in those neighborhoods.

Worker Rights

Throughout much of the twentieth century, Los Angeles had a reputation as an anti-union city. While the city has dropped much of its bias against workers, and labor unions have had success in recent years in empowering employees in various economic sectors, there is still much the city can do to support the rights, dignity, and economic security of all workers.

Establish a Commission on Labor Rights

- The City of L.A. should establish a *Commission on Labor Rights* to play a key role in establishing local labor policy. The commission would serve as a venue for recommending policies and practices that will continue to strengthen worker rights. It would review local labor rights enforcement practices, provide advice on the impacts of proposed legislation, and develop outreach, information, and referral services for workers. The commission should also observe and review labor disputes and allegations of violations of worker rights.

Protect and Promote Workers' Right to Organize

- The city and county should promote *card check neutrality* among all businesses with any kind of financial relationship with the city or county. Employers who refuse to agree to card check neutrality should be barred from receiving local subsidies of any kind or using city- and county-owned or -administered areas. The city and county should also ensure that no public funds (such as subsidies) are used for union busting.

- Labor rights are based on workers' ability to speak freely: to talk to fellow workers about forming a union and to get their views across to employers, officials, and the public. When workers are on a picket line or otherwise exercising their First Amendment rights, law enforcement should protect these freedoms. The LAPD and the Los Angeles County Sheriff's Department should strengthen their labor details; educate all officers on labor rights; and require contractors, subsidy recipients, and employers operating on public areas to allow workers to exercise First Amendment rights equivalent to what would be allowed on public land.

- Under federal labor law, employers are not allowed to fire, punish, or discriminate against workers who support unions—or even threaten workers over union activities. The city and county should encourage state and federal labor agencies to increase enforcement actions against employers that violate worker rights, and should grant expedited mediation to city and county employees who allege they have been dismissed in retaliation for exercising their rights.

Expand Living Wage Policies

The City and County of Los Angeles need to do more to ensure that everyone who works for a living can support themselves and their family with what they earn. In other words, they should attempt to ensure that workers make a living wage. Both the city and county have living wage ordinances to begin to address this problem, applying to some businesses that contract with the city and county.

- To lift more working families out of poverty, the city and county should expand their living wage laws, while also expanding minimum-wage and prevailing-wage programs, and boosting enforcement of all wage laws.

- The city and county should expand living wage laws in a number of areas. These include: (a) cover all workers providing government-funded services; (b) cover all private-sector employees whose employer has benefited from government subsidies; (c) cover all private-sector employees within economic development or other kinds of zones where businesses have benefited from public investments or are in areas operated by public authorities; and (d) cover all employer tenants of government-subsidized developments or areas operated by public authorities. To complement living wage requirements, the city should explore the feasibility of a *local minimum wage*. The city and county should expand prevailing-wage requirements by permitting government functions to be held only at facilities that pay prevailing wages, and by outsourcing for services only with businesses that pay prevailing wages.

- To strengthen enforcement of wage and hour laws, the city and county should cooperate with state and federal officials to increase inspections and enforcement actions against violators; identify publicly businesses that violate wage and hour laws similar to the way the Department of Health makes restaurants post their health "grades" in their windows; and bar repeat violators from bidding on government contracts. The city should also expand its worker-retention ordinance to apply to subsidy recipients, and adopt a contractor-changing rule requiring all businesses—not just city contractors—to give advance notification of subcontracting or contractor changes to workers, the city, and unions.

Strengthen Protections for Low-Wage, Nonunion, and Undocumented Workers

- From the garment industry to the restaurant industry, from those looking for work on street corners as day laborers to working in private homes as domestic workers and gardeners, nonunion, low-wage workers—most of them immigrants—endure daily hard work and sacrifice. The city and county should expand and protect these workers' rights. The city and county should target education about labor rights to immigrant and nonunion workers. The city and county should also endorse a declaration supporting the AFL-CIO Executive Council Resolution, which calls for a *general amnesty for undocu-*

mented residents and an *end to employer sanctions.* The city should enforce existing policies that prohibit cooperation between the INS and local law enforcement in all circumstances by ensuring that law enforcement officials respect and fully implement their provisions.

- City officials and law enforcement must adopt internal policies and practices of nonharassment against day laborers and street vendors. Law enforcement officials should be required to receive special training at the police academy on how to respond to issues relating to day laborers and street vendors without violating individual rights. The city should allocate more resources to current official day-labor sites and should create new sites.

Protect and Promote Public-Sector Union Jobs

- In Los Angeles and across the country, corporations are trying to get city and state governments to hire private companies to perform services that traditionally have been done by the public sector: everything from solid waste management to data processing. But if public services are just another business, the quality of services and public accountability can deteriorate as profit becomes the prime motivation in service delivery. To maintain and improve government services, the city and county should work with public employees drawing upon front-line workers' knowledge, to improve the quality and efficiency of public services, rather than privatize. The city and county should also require governmental entities that are considering privatization to demonstrate the economic necessity of contracting any work currently done by public employees; and should ensure that public-sector union jobs and contracts are preserved in the context of radical reorganizations of government services (i.e., potential succession, hospital mergers, etc.). The city should expand the *Bureau of Street Services City Jobs Program* (which has successfully helped low-income residents and created new unionized public-sector jobs) to include more city departments and create more public union jobs.

Economic Development

To build a stronger and fairer economy, and a more livable city, the City of Los Angeles should foster quality jobs; consolidate city economic development functions into an effective, accountable department; and ensure that public money supports workers and the local economy. The city promotes job creation through a variety of programs, departments, and funds. All city job-creation efforts should prioritize the creation of high-quality jobs that pay living wages; provide medical, child care, job training, and other benefits; are unionized; employ local residents; will remain located in L.A.; meet community needs; and avoid negative environmental impacts.

- L.A.'s *Workforce Investment Act* (WIA), overseen by a Workforce Investment Board (WIB), is the primary program through which the city promotes job training and employment for low-income residents, welfare-to-work participants, youth, and others. The city should broaden participation in and oversight of the WIB by appointing WIB board members who support the goal of creating quality jobs and linking with community colleges and union apprenticeship programs. To make sure the WIB meets job seekers' long-term needs, the board should take an "assess-first" approach, which addresses the job-training needs of public-assistance recipients and those facing multiple barriers to employment, rather than a "work-first" approach, which throws participants into jobs without adequate support. The board should also set individual training accounts high enough that participants can obtain high-quality training and provide support services such as transportation and child care. The city should cover employers that use the Workforce Investment Board under the city living wage ordinance. Participating businesses should also be required to give priority to residents from low-income communities and residents referred through the one-stop training system.

Consolidate Economic Development Agencies

The City of Los Angeles undertakes economic development efforts through a host of agencies and programs, including dozens of financial grants and tax breaks for businesses, such as Industrial Development Bonds, Section 108 loans, Hiring Tax Credits, City Tax Free Zones, and so forth. The fragmented system fails to add up to a long-term vision for a stronger, fairer local economy.

- All city economic development functions should be consolidated into a single *Economic Development Department*, organized around five key functions: Industrial Development, Commercial Development, Finance, Workforce Development, and Policy and Research. Since the Community Redevelopment Agency is increasingly being used by the city as its de facto economic development agency—administering Economic Development Administration–funded projects, brownfields programs, and the Targeted Neighborhood Initiative— it makes sense to bring the CRA into the new department as well.

Hold Subsidy Recipients Accountable

- Los Angeles subsidizes businesses, in the name of economic development and job creation, through an array of programs. This public investment doesn't always pay off in terms of sustained economic benefits. Subsidies and tax breaks should be used wisely to build economic security and improve quality of life. The City of Los Angeles should collect better information on subsidized projects, and give the public a right to know about and participate in decisions on what companies and projects receive subsidies. The city should also require businesses that receive public subsidies to meet conditions and standards, including obligations to create a minimum number of new jobs; hire a minimum percentage of new hires from the local neighborhood and low-income areas of the city; exceed local, state, and federal environmental requirements; and not relocate out of L.A. for a minimum number of years. Recipients that fail to meet conditions should be required to pay back the city.

Procure and Invest Responsibly

- The City of Los Angeles isn't just a government entity and representative of the people of L.A. It's also one of the biggest economic actors in the region. Whether as contractor, bank depositor, or investor, the city can and should use its money to influence L.A.'s economy for the better. The city should favor local, responsible businesses in its Purchasing and Contracting Programs. The city should adopt an *Antisweatshop Procurement Policy* that buys garments only from companies that demonstrate they are complying with all labor, occupational safety, and environmental regulations; and that disclose the locations of production facilities. The city should also adopt a "bad boy" policy that bars companies that have been convicted of violating labor, environmental, and other laws from bidding on contracts or procurement for five years.

- The city invests around $3 billion in idle cash in a variety of bank accounts and other financial instruments. To ensure that this public money supports banks that serve all communities, in 1992 the L.A. City Council passed a *Linked Banking Ordinance*. Unfortunately, the city has been slow to develop regulations for this ordinance, to fund its implementation, and most importantly, to shift money based on rankings of banks. The city should fully implement and enforce this important regulation. The city should also target pension money in investments that are financially sound and benefit communities and workers. The city's primary obligation is to manage this money to ensure an adequate rate of return. But unlike Wall Street investments, where the highest rate of return is the only consideration, pension funds must also provide for the good and welfare of retirees. Their welfare cannot be walled off from the communities and the world in which they live. To invest pension funds responsibly, the city should set investment guidelines that take account of worker and community interests, including investing in local, economically targeted enterprises.

Notes

INTRODUCTION. A LAND OF EXTREMES

1. Carey McWilliams, *Southern California: An Island on the Land* (Santa Barbara, Calif.: Peregrine Smith, 1973), 21. Original publication was in 1946 (New York: Duell, Sloan and Pearce).

CHAPTER 1. A MOSAIC OF MOVEMENTS

1. Jeff Stansbury, "Workers and the Municipal State: Los Angeles in the Progressive Era, 1890–1915" (paper presented at the Institute for Labor and Employment Conference, University of California, Santa Cruz, 19 January 2002), www.ucop.edu/ile/conferences/grad_conf/pdf2002/stansbury.pdf (accessed 16 August 2002).

2. Dana Bartlett, *The Better City: A Sociological Study of a Modern City* (Los Angeles: Neuner Co. Press, 1907), 15.

3. *Los Angeles Times*, 17 June 1904, cited in Richard Connelly Miller, "Otis and His Times: The Career of Harrison Gray Otis of Los Angeles" (Ph.D. diss., University of California, Berkeley, 1961), 228.

4. These Progressive Era reforms were designed to provide opportunities for a more direct democracy and to undercut the force of powerful economic interests such as the Southern Pacific Railroad. However, by the turn of the century, each of these reforms—the recall (of an elected official), the initiative (to allow a policy to be adopted by direct vote), and the referendum (also to be used to overturn a policy by direct vote)—had become subject to the influence of money. The most notable example involved the 2003 recall of then governor Gray Davis.

5. Michael Paul Rogin and John L. Shover, *Political Change in California: Critical Elections and Social Movements, 1890–1966* (Westport, Conn.: Greenwood Publishing, 1970).

6. Steven J. Ross, *Working-Class Hollywood: Silent Film and the Shaping of Class in America* (Princeton, N.J.: Princeton University Press, 1998), 89–98.

226 / Notes to Pages 15-20

7. Robert Gottlieb and Irene Wolt, *Thinking Big: The Story of the* Los Angeles Times, *Its Publishers, and Their Influence on Southern California* (New York: G. P. Putnam, 1977), 82–105; Knox Mellon, "Job Harriman: The Early and Middle Years" (Ph.D. diss., Claremont Graduate University, 1973); Paul Greenstein, Nigey Lennon, and Lionel Rolfe, *Bread and Hyacinths: The Rise and Fall of Utopian Los Angeles* (Los Angeles: California Classics Books, 1992).

8. Tom Sitton, *John Randolph Haynes: California Progressive* (Stanford, Calif.: Stanford University Press, 1992), 99.

9. John C. Bollens, "A History of Charter Reform Efforts," in *A Study of the Los Angeles City Charter,* ed. John C. Bollens (Los Angeles: Town Hall, December 1963), 39–79.

10. Carey McWilliams, "The City That Wanted the Truth," *Pacific Spectator* (Spring 1949): 177–88.

11. Gottlieb and Wolt, *Thinking Big,* 185–201.

12. Job Harriman, cited in Dolores Hayden, *Seven American Utopias: The Architecture of Communitarian Socialism* (Cambridge, Mass.: MIT Press, 1976), 289–90.

13. Kevin Starr, *Material Dreams: Southern California through the 1920's* (New York: Oxford University Press, 1990).

14. On the Better American Federation, see Gottlieb and Wolt, *Thinking Big,* 190–91; on the KKK in Los Angeles, see Mike Davis, *City of Quartz: Excavating the Future in Los Angeles* (London: Verso, 1990), 162.

15. Greg Hise, "Industry and Imaginative Geographies," in *Metropolis in the Making: Los Angeles in the 1920s,* ed. Tom Sitton and William Deverell (Berkeley and Los Angeles: University of California Press, 2001), 13–44.

16. Vincent Ostrom, *Water and Politics: A Study of Water Policies and Administration in the Development of Los Angeles* (Los Angeles: Haynes Foundation, 1953), 61–71, 84.

17. John D. Weaver, *El Pueblo Grande: A Non-Fiction Book about Los Angeles* (Los Angeles: Ward Ritchie Press, 1973), 83.

18. Bessie Averne McClenahan, *The Changing Urban Neighborhood: A Sociological Study,* Social Science Series, no. 1 (Los Angeles: Semicentennial Publications of USC, 1929), 90.

19. Carey McWilliams, "Los Angeles," *Overland Monthly and Out West Magazine* 85 (May 1927): 135.

20. Sherry Katz, "Socialist Women and Progressive Reform," in *California Progressivism Revisited,* ed. William Deverell and Tom Sitton (Berkeley and Los Angeles: University of California Press, 1994), 117–43.

21. Philip Sonnichsen, " 'El Lavaplatos' (the Dishwasher)," *Texas-Mexican Border Music, Vols. 2 and 3: Corridos, Parts 1 and 2* (Arhoolie Records, 1975), cited in George J. Sanchez, *Becoming Mexican-American: Ethnicity, Culture, and Identity in Chicano Los Angeles, 1900–1945* (New York: Oxford University Press, 1993), 178; Merle E. Simmons, "The Ancestry of Mexican Corridos," *Journal of American Folklore* 76 (1963): 3.

22. Sarah Elkind, "The Public Good: Resource Policy and Southern Califor-

nia, 1910–1950" (paper presented to the American Society of Environmental History Annual Meeting, Denver, 21 March 2002); Greg Hise and William Deverell, *Eden by Design* (Berkeley and Los Angeles: University of California Press, 2000).

23. Greg Mitchell, *The Campaign of the Century: Upton Sinclair's Race for Governor of California and the Birth of Media Politics* (New York: Random House, 1992).

24. Frank J. Donner, *Protectors of Privilege: Red Squads and Police Repression in Urban America* (Berkeley and Los Angeles: University of California Press, 1990), 59–64, 245–89.

25. The view that Southern California had become a hotbed of radical ideas was widespread during the mid-1930s. George Creel, a northern Californian who was Upton Sinclair's opponent in the Democratic primary in 1934, made this widely cited comment about L.A.-based radicalism: "Northern Californians offered no problem," Creel commented, "for the hard-headed, hard-working native sons and daughters were in a majority, but when I crossed the Tehachapis into southern California, it was like plunging into darkest Africa without gun bearers." Cited in Robert E. Burke, *Olson's New Deal for California* (Berkeley and Los Angeles: University of California Press, 1953), 3.

26. Rose Pesotta, *Bread upon the Waters* (New York: Dodd, Mead, 1944), 19–63; Ronald W. Lopez, "The El Monte Berry Strike of 1933," *Aztlan* 1 (1970): 109–10.

27. Sanchez, *Becoming Mexican-American*, 239.

28. The gang episode is described in Mario T. Garcia, *Memories of Chicano History: The Life and Narrative of Bert Corona* (Berkeley and Los Angeles: University of California Press, 1994), 104–5.

29. It's important to note that some of the New Deal advances were limited in scope, such as the groundbreaking Wagner Act, which nevertheless still excluded rural laborers and thus significantly impacted Latino and African American workers. See George Lipsitz, *The Possessive Investment in Whiteness* (Philadelphia: Temple University Press, 1998), 5. For information on the Townsend Plan, see *Social Security Administration Agency History: The Townsend Plan Movement* (Washington, D.C.: Social Security Administration, n.d.), www.ssa.gov/history/towns5.html.

30. Herbert Klein and Carey McWilliams, "Cold Terror in California," *Nation* 141, no. 3655 (24 July 1935): 97–98.

31. The *Times* attack on Bowron is cited in Gottlieb and Wolt, *Thinking Big*, 224; see also John Anson Ford, *Thirty Explosive Years in Los Angeles County* (San Marino, Calif.: Huntington Library, 1961).

32. Clement E. Vose, *Caucasians Only: The Supreme Court, the NAACP, and Restrictive Covenant Cases* (Berkeley and Los Angeles: University of California Press, 1959); Charles Abrams, *Forbidden Neighborhoods* (Port Washington, N.Y.: Kemitat Press, 1971), 217–22; Lonnie G. Bunch, "A Past Not Necessarily Prologue: The Afro American in Los Angeles," in *20th Century Los*

Angeles: Power, Promotion, and Social Conflict, ed. Norman M. Klein and Martin J. Schiesl (Claremont, Calif.: Regina Books, 1990), 101–30.

33. For example, by the end of the decade the national Communist Party began to argue that the United States was on the verge of becoming a fascist state. Under the threat of legislation like the Smith Act, national Party leaders argued that local as well as national Party leaders needed to prepare to go underground, a position that had the potential to undermine the Los Angeles Party's ability to forge coalitions with non-Communist groups and individuals. Dorothy Healey and Maurice Isserman, *Dorothy Healey Remembers: A Life in the American Communist Party* (New York: Oxford University Press, 1990); John C. Culver and John Hyde, *American Dreamer: The Life and Times of Henry A. Wallace* (New York: W. W. Norton, 2000).

34. Mauricio Mazon, *The Zoot-Suit Riots: The Psychology of Symbolic Annihilation* (Austin: University of Texas Press, 1984), 15–30.

35. Deb Riechmann, "Government Releases Un-American Activities Files from the Forties," *Detroit News,* 25 August 2001; Larry Ceplair and Steven Englund, *The Inquisition in Hollywood: Politics in the Film Community, 1930–1960* (Garden City, N.Y.: Anchor Press/Doubleday, 1980), 258–60.

36. Gerald Horne, *Class Struggle in Hollywood, 1930–1950: Moguls, Mobsters, Stars, Reds, and Trade Unionists* (Austin: University of Texas Press, 2001); Brett L. Abrams, "The First Hollywood Blacklist: The Major Studios Deal with the Conference of Studio Unions," *Southern California Quarterly* 7, no. 3 (1997): 215–53; Janet Stevenson, *The Undiminished Man: A Political Biography of Robert Walker Kenny* (Novato, Calif.: Chandler and Sharp, 1980).

37. "Regents Demand Loyalty to U.S.," *Los Angeles Times,* 15 December 1945. The Regents had also been urged to investigate charges that "certain professors and instructors of UCLA are endeavoring to inculcate the students with communistic and extreme leftist doctrines rather than teaching them 'down the middle of the road.'. . ." "Howser Clashes with Inquiry Group," *Los Angeles Times,* 30 November 1945.

38. Thomas S. Hines, "Housing, Baseball, and Creeping Socialism: The Battle of Chavez Ravine, 1949–1959," *Journal of Urban History* 8, no. 2 (February 1982): 123–43.

39. Will Roscoe, ed., *Radically Gay: Gay Liberation in the Words of Its Founder, Harry Hay* (Boston: Beacon Press, 1996).

40. Charlotta Bass, *Forty Years: Memoirs from the Pages of a Newspaper* (Los Angeles: Charlotta Bass, 1960); Jeffrey C. Stewart, ed., *Paul Robeson: Artist and Citizen* (New Brunswick, N.J.: Rutgers University Press and the Paul Robeson Cultural Center, 1998).

41. Carey McWilliams, *The Education of Carey McWilliams* (New York: Simon and Schuster, 1978).

42. Myrna Oliver, "Phil Kerby: Times Editorial Writer Won Pulitzer Prize," *Los Angeles Times,* 30 April 1993, sec. A, 24.

43. Metropolitan Water District of Southern California, Los Angeles, "Statement of Policy" (the Laguna Declaration) (16 December 1952); Robert Gottlieb

and Margaret FitzSimmons, *Thirst for Growth: Water Agencies as Hidden Government in California* (Tucson: University of Arizona Press, 1991).

44. Cited in Kevin Lynch, *The Image of the City* (Cambridge, Mass.: MIT Press, 1971), 40.

45. Letter from Norman Chandler to Norris Poulson, 26 December 1952; *Elect Congressman Norris Poulson Mayor*, campaign brochure, n.d. (both the letter and brochure in possession of the authors); Robert Gottlieb, "Memories of Asa Call, L.A.'s Back-Room Mr. Big," *Los Angeles*, August 1978, 100–104.

46. Clora Bryant, Buddy Collette, William Green, Steven Isoardi, Jack Kelson, Horace Tapscott, Gerald Wilson, and Marl Young, *Central Avenue Sounds: Jazz in Los Angeles* (Berkeley and Los Angeles: University of California Press, 1998), 96, 154–59.

47. Michael Wilson, with commentary by Deborah Silverton Rosenfelt, *Salt of the Earth* (New York: Feminist Press, 1978).

48. Robin J. Dunitz, *Street Gallery: Guide to 1000 Los Angeles Murals* (Los Angeles: RJD Enterprises, 1993).

49. Edmund G. "Pat" Brown, inaugural address, 5 January 1959, www.governor.ca.gov/govsite/govsgallery/h/documents/inaugural_32.html.

50. Kenneth C. Burt, "Latino Empowerment in Los Angeles: Postwar Dreams and Cold War Fears, 1948–1952," *Labor's Heritage* 8, no. 1 (Summer 1996): 6–24; Don Normack, *Chavez Ravine, 1949: A Los Angeles Story* (San Francisco: Chronicle Books, 1999), 53, 135.

51. On the Civil Rights Congress, see Gerald Horne, *Communist Front?: The Civil Rights Congress, 1946–1956* (London: Associated University Press, 1988); Josh Sides, " 'You Understand My Condition': The Civil Rights Congress in the Los Angeles African American Community 1946–1952," *Pacific Historical Review* 67, no. 2 (May 1998): 233.

52. Dorothy Ray Healey and Maurice Isserman, *California Red: A Life in the American Communist Party* (Urbana: University of Illinois Press, 1993); Communist Party, Southern California District, Los Angeles, *A Municipal Program for Los Angeles* (April 1959).

53. Background and quotes by Ruben Salazar are from Albert Herrera, "The National Chicano Moratorium and the Death of Ruben Salazar," in *The Chicanos*, ed. Ed Ludwig and Tamis Santibanez (Baltimore: Penguin Books, 1971), 235–41; William Drummond, "The Death of the Man in the Middle," *Esquire*, April 1972; Gottlieb and Wolt, "The Odyssey of Ruben Salazar," in *Thinking Big*, 421–28.

54. Postcard in the possession of the authors.

55. Reyner Banham, *Los Angeles: The Architecture of Four Ecologies* (New York: Harper and Row, 1971), 195.

56. H. Marshall Goodwin, Jr., "The Arroyo Seco: From Dry Gulch to Freeway," *The Historical Society of Southern California* (June 1965): 73–95; HAER (Historical American Engineering Record), *The Arroyo Seco Parkway*, no. CA-265 (Berkeley: University of California, 1999).

57. Anthony M. Platt, ed., *The Politics of Riot Commissions, 1917–1970: A*

Collection of Official Reports and Critical Essays (New York: Collier Books, 1971). The McCone Commission also discussed the Proposition 14 repeal of the Rumford Fair Housing Act, arguing that "many Negroes *were encouraged to feel* that they had been affronted by the passage of Proposition 14" (4; our italics).

58. Rodolfo Acuna, *Occupied America: The Chicano's Struggle towards Liberation* (San Francisco: Canfield Press, 1972), 334–56. MEChA was founded following a 1969 conference at the University of California, Santa Barbara. MEChA de UCLA, "Las Fundaciones de MEChA" (Fall 2000), at Santa Rosa Junior College MEChA, www.srjcmecha.org/mecha101.html (accessed 5 January 2002 and 19 August 2002).

59. Ward Churchill and Jim Vander Wall, *Agents of Repression: The FBI's Secret Wars against the Black Panther Party and the American Indian Movement* (Boston: South End Press, 1990), 37–99.

60. One of the authors (Robert Gottlieb) took part in both these events.

61. The records of Southern California Women Strike for Peace are held at the Swarthmore College Peace Collection, inventoried at www.swarthmore.edu/Library/peace/DG100-150/DG115/seriesb.htm.

62. Kirkpatrick Sale, *SDS* (New York: Random House, 1973); Todd Gitlin, *The Sixties: Years of Hope and Days of Rage* (Toronto: Bantam Books, 1987); the personal experience of one of the authors (Robert Gottlieb) was that "voting in the streets" was a phrase commonly used at the time.

63. "Leaning on the Consumer," *Time*, 25 August 1975; personal communication with Tim Brick (2 July 2002); Campaign against Utility Service Exploitation, "Lifeline at Last," in *Public Power: A Report on Energy and Pasadena* (Pasadena, Calif., November 1979); Campaign against Utility Service Exploitation, "Action Update" (Pasadena, Calif., 7 October 1975).

64. The Coastal Commission was established by Proposition 20 in 1972. California Coastal Commission, *Who We Are* (Sacramento, 19 August 2002). The Political Reform Act of 1974 (Proposition 9) created a Political Reform Division within the California Department of State and a new Fair Political Practices Commission. Office of the California Secretary of State, *History of the Political Reform Division* (Sacramento, 3 April 1998), www.ss.ca.gov/prd/about_the_division/history.htm (accessed 19 August 2002).

65. David S. Broder, "The Canniness of the Long-Distance Runner," *Atlantic*, January 1978; Bob Gottlieb, "Jerry Brown," *Los Angeles*, October 1978.

66. Tom Hayden, *Reunion: A Memoir* (New York: Random House, 1988), 467–72.

67. Peter Dreier, "Rent Deregulation in Massachusetts and California: Politics, Policy, and Impacts," pt. 2 (paper for the Housing '97 conference, sponsored by New York University School of Law, Center for Real Estate and Urban Policy, and the NYC Rent Guidelines Board, New York University, 14 May 1997), www.tenant.net/Alerts/Guide/papers/dreier/dreier2.html (accessed 19 August 2002).

68. Terry Wolverton, *Insurgent Muse: Life and Art at the Woman's Building* (San Francisco: City Lights Books, 2002), xvi–xvii, 32–54; Lynell George, "Return to the Source," *Los Angeles Times*, 18 September 2002; Records of

Women against Violence against Women, 1972–85, Archives and Special Collections Department, Northeastern University Libraries, www.lib.neu.edu/archives/collect/findaids/m25find.htm (accessed 19 August 2002).

69. Liberty Hill Foundation, "Liberty Hill Statement of Purpose" (Los Angeles: Liberty Hill Foundation, 1976); *News from the Hill* 1, no. 1 (November 1976).

70. American Civil Liberties Union Freedom Network, "Joyce S. Fiske, First Woman President of ACLU of Southern California, Dies" (New York, 8 August 1998), www.aclu.org/news/n080898a.html (accessed 19 August 2002).

71. Personal communication from Torie Osborn (September 1998).

72. Georges Sabagh and Mehdi Bozorgmehr, "Population Change: Immigration and Ethnic Transformation," in *Ethnic Los Angeles,* ed. Roger Waldinger and Mehdi Bozorgmehr (New York: Russell Sage Foundation, 1996), 79–107.

73. On the March 1982 immigration demonstrations, see Garcia, *Memories of Chicano History.*

74. Lowell Turner, Harry Katz, and Richard Hurt, eds., *Rekindling the Movement: Labor's Quest for Relevance in the 21st Century* (Ithaca, N.Y.: Cornell University Press, 2001); Ruth Milkman, ed., *Organizing Immigrants: The Challenge for Unions in Contemporary California* (Ithaca, N.Y.: Cornell University Press, 2000).

75. Louis Blumberg and Robert Gottlieb, *War on Waste: Can America Win Its Battle with Garbage?* (Washington, D.C.: Island Press, 1989), 155–88.

76. Heal the Bay, "Who Is Heal the Bay?" www.aclu.org/news/n080898a.html (accessed 19 August 2002).

77. One of the authors of this book (Robert Gottlieb) was on the Liberty Hill Foundation's Community Funding Board (which reviewed and funded the work of many of the named groups) during this period.

78. Weed and Seed Program press release from U.S. Health and Human Services Department, 14 October 1992, www.hhs.gov/news/press/pre1995pres/921014.txt.

79. Industrial Areas Foundation, "A Win for the Working Poor: The Moral Minimum Wage Campaign" (Los Angeles, n.d.).

80. Robert Pollin and Stephanie Luce, *The Living Wage: Building a Fair Economy* (New York: New Press, 1998); Isaac Martin, "Dawn of the Living Wage: The Diffusion of a Redistributive Municipal Policy," *Urban Affairs Review* 36, no. 4 (March 2001): 470–96; David B. Reynolds, *Taking the High Road: Communities Organize for Economic Change* (Armonk, N.Y.: M. E. Sharpe, 2002).

CHAPTER 2. CHARLOTTA BASS

1. Kevin Starr, *Embattled Dreams: California in War and Peace, 1940–1950* (Oxford: Oxford University Press, 2002).

2. Biographical sources on Bass include Charlotta Bass, *Forty Years: Memoirs from the Pages of a Newspaper* (Los Angeles: Charlotta Bass, 1960); Char-

lotta A. Bass Papers and Manuscript Collection, Southern California Library for Social Studies and Research, Los Angeles; Jacqueline Leavitt, "Charlotta Bass, the California Eagle, and Black Settlement in Los Angeles," in *Urban Planning and the African American Community: In the Shadows*, ed. June Manning Thomas and Marsha Ritzdorf (Thousand Oaks, Calif.: Sage Publications, 1996), 167–86; Gerda Lerner, ed., *Black Women in White America: A Documentary History* (New York: Vintage Books, 1972); Rodger Streitmatter, *Raising Her Voice: African-American Women Journalists Who Changed History* (Lexington: University Press of Kentucky, 1994); Gerald Gill, "From Progressive Republican to Independent Progressive: The Political Career of Charlotta A. Bass," in *African American Women and the Vote, 1837–1965*, ed. Ann D. Gordon et al. (Amherst: University of Massachusetts Press, 1997), 156–71; and James Phillip Jeter, "Rough Flying: The California Eagle (1879–1965)" (paper presented to the Twelfth Annual Conference of the American Journalism Historians Association, Salt Lake City, Utah, 7 October 1993).

3. Bass, *Forty Years*, 27–33.

4. *California Eagle*, 8 March 1929, 1.

5. Gill, "From Progressive Republican," 160.

6. *Los Angeles Times*, 1 April 1945, sec. 2, 2.

7. Bass Collection, box 1, folder entitled "Bass—City Council Campaign 1945," platform of Charlotta A. Bass.

8. Ibid., folder entitled "Bass Congressional Campaign 1950."

9. Leavitt, "Charlotta Bass."

10. Bass Collection, box 1, folder entitled "Bass 1952 Vice Presidential Campaign."

11. Jeter, "Rough Flying," 13.

12. Emory J. Tolbert, *The UNIA and Black Los Angeles: Ideology and Community in the American Garvey Movement* (Los Angeles: Center for Afro-American Studies, University of California, 1980), 27.

13. Ibid., 63.

14. Ibid., 66.

15. Gill, "From Progressive Republican," 159; Tolbert, *UNIA and Black Los Angeles*, 67.

16. Gill, "From Progressive Republican," 165.

17. Bass, *Forty Years*, 134; Streitmatter, *Raising Her Voice*, 104.

18. Marion H. Jackson, letter to Bass, 14 August 1956, Bass Collection, box 2, folder 14.

19. Bass Collection, box 1, folder entitled "Bass—Articles and Speeches Undated," "NAACP."

20. Ibid., box 2, folder 13.

21. Ibid., box 1, folder entitled "Letters to C.A. Bass 1940's," "Notice of Libelous Statements Published and Demand for Retraction," dated 31 August 1948.

22. Streitmatter, *Raising Her Voice*, 102.

23. *California Eagle*, 26 April 1951.

24. According to Jeter, the *Eagle*'s circulation dropped from 17,600 in 1940 to 10,000 in 1950: Jeter, "Rough Flying," 11–12.

25. *California Eagle,* 29 January 1942, 8A.

26. Ibid., 15 November 1945.

27. Ibid., 5 August 1943, 8B.

28. Ibid., 16 July 1942, 8A.

29. For more information on how World War II impacted Bass and other African American leaders and their perspective on interracial cooperation in particular, see Kevin Allen Leonard, "'In the Interest of All Races': African-Americans and Interracial Cooperation in Los Angeles during and after World War II," in *Seeking El Dorado: African-Americans in California,* ed. Lawrence B. de Graaf, Kevin Mulroy, and Quintard Taylor (Los Angeles: Autry Museum of Western Heritage, 2001), 309–40.

30. Gerald Horne argues that the Civil Rights Congress (CRC) was not a "front organization" for the Communist Party, but rather had a number of members—including leaders—who were also members of the CP. There were in fact some leaders within the organization who criticized the civil rights group for not doing more to support CP members facing government persecution, even as the CRC was being labeled a CP front. Horne, *Communist Front?,* 23.

31. Bass, *Forty Years,* 179; Streitmatter, *Raising Her Voice,* 105–6.

32. U.S. Census Bureau, Executive Order 8802 (Washington, D.C., 25 June 1941), www.eeoc.gov/35th/thelaw/eo-8802.html.

33. Gill, "From Progressive Republican," 162.

34. Bass, *Forty Years,* 70.

35. Ibid.

36. Gill, "From Progressive Republican," 157.

37. The Sojourners for Truth and Justice organization was a small internationalist collective established in "the tradition of Harriet Tubman and Sojourner Truth," intended to "give inspiration and courage to women the world over, the colored women of African and Asia who expect us to make this challenge." Quoted in Gerald Horne, *Race Woman: The Lives of Shirley Graham Du Bois* (New York: New York University Press, 2000), 144.

38. Charlotta Bass, "On the Sidewalk: About Us Women," *California Eagle,* 27 August 1942, 1A.

39. Ibid., 14 February 1946, 1.

40. See Bass, *Forty Years,* chap. 25, "Labor on the Move."

41. See Rudy Acuna, *Occupied America* (San Francisco: Canfield Press, 1972), 202.

42. Leonard, "'In the Interest of All Races,'" 315–27.

43. Bass, *Forty Years,* 124.

44. Ibid.

45. Excerpted from text of a speech delivered in 1943: Bass Collection, box 1, folder entitled "Grand Jury 1943."

46. See Civil Rights Congress Collection at the Southern California Library for Social Studies and Research, Los Angeles.

47. "Father of Vets to Be Deported," *California Eagle*, 23 February 1950, 2A.

48. The Double V campaign was initiated on February 7, 1942, in the pages of the *Pittsburgh Courier*—one of the most widely read Black newspapers in the 1940s. The campaign involved articles, editorials, letters to the editor, and an official logo. Black newspapers across the country, including the *California Eagle*, picked up the cause, demanding that African Americans called to fight in the war receive full citizenship rights at home. See Patrick S. Washburn, "The Pittsburgh Courier's Double V Campaign in 1942," *American Journalism* 3, no. 2 (1986): 73–86.

49. Though it is unclear just how active she was as "honorary cochairman," the presence of her name on letterhead of both organizations and her reelection to this office several times on the Protection Committee are at the very least suggestive of her commitment to their cause. See American Committee for the Protection of the Foreign Born Collection, Southern California Library for Social Studies and Research, box 1, folder 25.

50. Ibid., 12 February 1958.

51. Speech delivered at Pilgrim Baptist Church, n.d., Bass Collection, box 1, folder entitled "Bass—Progressive Party 1952 Speeches."

52. Mario T. Garcia, *Memories of Chicano History: The Life and Narrative of Bert Corona* (Berkeley and Los Angeles: University of California Press, 1994), 119.

53. *California Eagle*, 5 August 1943, 8A; emphasis in original.

54. Bass, *Forty Years*, 95.

55. The Home Protective Association was formed specifically to rally support for the Laws family. The group later offered help in other, similar cases. See Bass, *Forty Years*, 197.

56. Ibid., 110.

57. Ibid., 95.

58. "IPP Calls," *California Eagle*, 18 August 1950, 3.

59. Bass, *Forty Years*, 99.

60. *California Eagle*, 15 March 1929, 1.

61. "Be in City Council Chambers Tuesday A.M.," *California Eagle*, 11 November 1943, 1A.

62. "How City Council Feels about Democracy," *California Eagle*, 18 November 1943, 1A.

63. "IPP Calls," *California Eagle*, 18 August 1950, 3.

64. "A Call for Control Not De-Control," *California Eagle*, 16 March 1950, 6.

65. "Rent Controls Voted Off Hotels by City Council Majority," *California Eagle*, 23 March 1950, 3.

CHAPTER 3. THE CONTINUING DIVIDE

1. Governor's Commission on the Los Angeles Riots (McCone Commission), "Violence in the City: An End or a Beginning?" (Sacramento, December

1965), in Robert M. Fogelson, *The Los Angeles Riots* (Salem, N.H.: Ayer Company, 1988), 3.

2. U.S. Commission on Civil Rights, cited in "Watts: An Analysis," *Campus CORE-lator* (University of California, Berkeley) 1, no. 4 (Fall 1965).

3. See www.usc.edu/isd/archives/cityinstress/analysis/main.html.

4. Lou Cannon, *Official Negligence* (Boulder, Colo.: Westview Press, 1999), 350; Hiroshi Fukarai, Richard Krooth, and Edgar W. Butler, "The Rodney King Beating Verdicts," in *The Los Angeles Riots: Lessons for the Urban Future*, ed. Mark Baldassare (Boulder, Colo.: Westview Press, 1994), 73–102; Peter A. Morrison and Ira S. Lowry, "A Riot of Color: The Demographic Setting of Civil Disturbance in Los Angeles," in *The Los Angeles Riots*, ed. Mark Baldassare, 19–46; James H. Johnson, Jr., et al., "The Los Angeles Rebellion: A Retrospective View," *Economic Development Quarterly* 6, no. 4 (November 1992): 356–72.

5. Pauline Kael, *New Yorker*, 2 December 1974; Morrow Mayo, *Los Angeles* (New York: Alfred A. Knopf, 1933); Clive James, "Postcard from Los Angeles 1," *London Observer*, 16 June 1979; Ann Magnuson, *Interview* 18, no. 8 (August 1988): 34; Bob McEnery, commentary on L.A. CBS-TV, 18 January 1994.

6. U.S. Census Bureau, *Profile of General Demographic Characteristics*, Summary File 1 (SF 1), 100 percent data, Los Angeles (Washington, D.C., 2001).

7. Official web site of the City of Los Angeles, 2001, www.ci.la.ca.us (accessed 12 August 2002).

8. "About Los Angeles County," L.A. County web site, www.co.la.ca.us/overview.htm (accessed 12 August 2002).

9. The remaining million or so residents live in unincorporated sections of the county, with county government providing all local services and in effect serving as their home town. The county also contracts its services out to a number of the newer, smaller cities, with county sheriffs providing law enforcement coverage, waste management removing trash, and the county otherwise fleshing out the skeletal government infrastructure of newly incorporated locales. In California, counties bear chief responsibility for the provision of health and many social welfare services, so L.A. County operates an extensive network of hospitals and clinics and administers multibillion-dollar public assistance programs.

10. Robert Gottlieb and Margaret FitzSimmons, *Thirst for Growth: Water Agencies as Hidden Government in California* (Tucson: University of Arizona Press, 1991).

11. Margaret FitzSimmons and Robert Gottlieb, "Bounding and Binding Metropolitan Space: The Ambiguous Politics of Nature in Los Angeles," in *The City*, ed. Edward Soja and Allen Scott (Berkeley and Los Angeles: University of California Press, 1996), 186–224.

12. U.S. Census Bureau, *Population of Counties by Decennial Census: 1900 to 1990, California* (Washington, D.C., n.d.).

13. U.S. Census Bureau, data from 1940 and 2000 decennial censuses; Southern California Area Association of Governments, "Census 2000 Questions and

Answers," www.scag.ca.gov/census (accessed 12 August 2002); Los Angeles Almanac, "Historical Demographics," 2002 (accessed 12 August 2002).

14. Southern California Studies Center, University of Southern California, *Sprawl Hits the Wall: Confronting the Realities of Metropolitan Los Angeles* (March 2001), 13.

15. Twenty-three percent fewer babies were born in 2000 than in 1990, a phenomenon extending to all the region's ethnic groups. United Way of Greater Los Angeles, *From Cradle to K: Ensuring Success by Six for All Los Angeles Children* (November 2001), 4.

16. Southern California Association of Governments, *The State of the Region, 2000: The Region at the Dawn of the 21st Century* (Los Angeles, May 2000), 15.

17. At its most basic, *sprawl* means the physical, geographical expansion of urban and suburban areas, usually through a growth pattern in which the outer fringes of a metropolitan area grow faster than its historic core. Planning Commissioners Journal, Planners Web, "How Do You Define Sprawl?" 2001, www.plannersweb.com/sprawl/define.html (accessed 12 August 2002).

18. SCAG, *State of the Region, 2000*, 15; U.S. Census Bureau, data from 1940 and 2000 decennial censuses.

19. Fourteen of the twenty fastest-growing cities in California between 1990 and 2000 were located in Riverside and San Bernardino Counties; Scott Gold, "The Costs of Growth: Paying Price of Growth in Inland Empire," *Los Angeles Times*, 25 November 2001.

20. Los Angeles County, the core of the region, accounted for a larger percentage of the region's population growth over the past twenty years (46 percent) than from 1960 to 1980 (38 percent): U.S. Census Bureau, data from 1960, 1980, and 2000 decennial censuses.

21. Regarding Latinos, considering L.A. once again as concentric circles, with the City of L.A. as the innermost ring, surrounded by Los Angeles County and then by the multicounty region, there is an ethnic gradient running from core to periphery. With the exception of outlying, majority-Latino Imperial County, the Latino share of the region's population is highest in the city and lowest outside of L.A. County (U.S. Census Bureau, *Profile of General Demographic Characteristics*, Summary File 1 [SF 1], 100 percent data, Imperial County, Los Angeles City, Los Angeles County, Orange County, Riverside County, San Bernardino County, and Ventura County, Calif. [Washington, D.C., 2001]). Regarding Whites and Asians, in 1965, changes to federal immigration laws that had previously granted preferential access to Western Europeans spurred Asian immigration into the region. The area's Asian population jumped more than tenfold after 1960, and the Asian *share* of the regional population increased more than fivefold, to 10.2 percent in 2000 (U.S. Census Bureau, data from 1960 and 2000 decennial censuses). However, not all Angelenos are members of one of the four largest ethnic groups. Nearly all the cities in Los Angeles County were built on the sites of Tongva villages. The Gabrieleno-Tongva, the Native American group living in the greater Los Angeles area at the time of European

contact and Spanish conquest, had inhabited the region for two thousand years. Today more Native Americans live in Los Angeles than in any other metropolitan area in the United States, except New York City (just under 1 percent of City of Los Angeles residents), but most of them are members of tribes from other parts of the country, led by Cherokee. The Los Angeles area is also home to communities of native Hawaiians, Samoans, and other Pacific Islanders, who constitute 0.2 percent of the population of the city. The 2000 census for the first time gave respondents the option of describing themselves as multiracial. More than 5 percent of residents of the City of L.A. placed themselves in the multiracial category: U.S. Census Bureau, including *The American Indian and Alaska Native Population, 2000* (Washington, D.C., 2002), 8; Gabrieleno-Tongva Tribal Council, "Welcome to the Land of the Tongva" (San Gabriel, Calif.: Gabrieleno-Tongva Tribal Council, 1998).

22. U.S. Census Bureau, Summary File 4 (SF 4), Los Angeles County, Calif. (Washington, D.C., 2002).

23. James P. Allen and Eugene Turner, *The Ethnic Quilt: Population Diversity in Southern California* (Northridge, Calif.: Center for Geographical Studies, California State Northridge, 1997); U.S. Census Bureau, Summary File 4 (SF 4), City of Los Angeles, Los Angeles County, Calif. (Washington, D.C., 2002).

24. U.S. Census Bureau, *Profile of General Demographic Characteristics*, Summary File 1 (SF 1), 100 percent data, Santa Ana, Calif. (Washington, D.C., 2001).

25. Lisa Richardson, "Language Statistics Overlook Nuances," *Los Angeles Times*, 25 November 2001.

26. U.S. Census Bureau, *Profile of General Demographic Characteristics*, Summary File 1 (SF 1), 100 percent data, Monterey Park, Calif. (Washington, D.C., 2001).

27. Wei Li, "Ethnoburbs versus Chinatown: Two Types of Urban Ethnic Communities in Los Angeles" (10 December 1998), www.cybergeo.presse.fr/culture/weili/weili.htm (accessed 12 August 2002).

28. U.S. Census Bureau, data from 1990 and 2000 decennial censuses, Compton and Inglewood, Calif.

29. Ibid.

30. Hector Tobar, "Cityhood Fever—It's Catching," *Los Angeles Times*, 16 July 1990; SCAG, *Sprawl Hits the Wall*, 39.

31. Korean Immigrant Workers Advocates fact sheet (13 May 2002), www.kiwa.org/e/homefr.htm (accessed 12 August 2002).

32. Jennifer Sinco Kelleher, "Advocates for Immigrant Worker Rights," *Los Angeles Times*, 26 July 2002.

33. Priscilla Murulo and A. B. Chitty, *From the Folks Who Brought You the Weekend* (New York: New Press, 2001), 70–71, 123–24, 130.

34. AFL-CIO, Executive Council Action, "Immigration" (16 February 2000), www.aflcio.org/publ/estatements/feb2000/immigr.htm (accessed 12 August 2002).

35. Los Angeles Almanac, "Los Angeles' Auto Manufacturing Past," www

.losangelesalmanac.com/topics/Transport/tro4.htm; and "Auto Plants in Los Angeles County," www.losangelesalmanac.com/topics/Transport/tro5.htm.

36. Eric Mann, *Taking on General Motors: A Case Study of the UAW Campaign to Keep GM Van Nuys Open* (Los Angeles: Center for Labor Research and Education, University of California, 1987).

37. James Rainey and Marc Lacey, "Riordan's First Year at the Helm," *Los Angeles Times*, 3 July 1994.

38. California Employment Development Department, "Monthly/Annual Average Unemployment Data" (Los Angeles County, 7 August 2002), www .calmis.ca.gov/htmlfile/subject/lftable.htm.

39. Neeta Fogg and Paul Harrington, "Growth and Change in the California and Long Beach/Los Angeles Labor Markets" (Center for Labor Market Study, Northeastern University, 3 May 2001).

40. California Employment Development Department, "Unemployment Data" (Los Angeles County, 2002).

41. Fogg and Harrington, "Growth and Change."

42. Paul More et al., *The Other Los Angeles: The Working Poor in the City of the 21st Century, 2001* (Los Angeles Alliance for a New Economy, August 2001), 30–31; Fogg and Harrington, "Growth and Change," 13.

43. The Los Angeles Economic Development Corporation, a business entity, ranks Los Angeles' fourteen leading economic sectors, in order of the number of workers employed, as business and professional management services, health services and bio-med, tourism, international trade, wholesale trade, technology, motion picture and TV production, financial services, apparel, agriculture and food products, furniture manufacturing and wholesaling, auto-parts manufacturing and wholesaling, petroleum production and refining, and toy manufacturing and wholesaling: Los Angeles Economic Development Corporation, "The Economic Base of the Los Angeles Five-County Region (2000)" (Los Angeles, 2001), www.laedc.org/about_L.A._county/14industry.shtml (accessed 12 January 2002). Source for wages needed to support families: California Budget Project, *Making Ends Meet: How Much Does It Cost to Raise a Family in California?* (Sacramento, September 2001).

44. Roger Waldinger et al., "Helots No More: A Case Study of the Justice for Janitors Campaign in Los Angeles," working paper no. 15, Lewis Center for Regional Policy Studies, Los Angeles, April 1996, 4; Robert Gottlieb, *Environmentalism Unbound: Exploring New Pathways for Change* (Cambridge, Mass.: MIT Press, 2001), 145–80.

45. Waldinger et al., "Helots No More," 8.

46. John Howley, "Justice for Janitors: The Challenge of Organizing in Contract Services," *Labor Research Review* 15 (1990): 64; Richard W. Hurd and William Rouse, "Progressive Union Organizing: The SEIU Justice for Janitors Campaign," *Review of Radical Political Economics* 21, no. 3 (Fall 1989): 70–75.

47. Lydia A. Savage, "Geographies of Organizing: Justice for Janitors in Los Angeles," in *Organizing the Landscape: Geographical Perspectives on Labor*

Unionism, ed. Andrew Herod (Minneapolis: University of Minnesota Press, 1998), 225–52.

48. Christopher L. Erickson et al., "Justice for Janitors in Los Angeles: Lessons from Three Rounds of Negotiations" (Institute for Work and Employment, MIT, November 2001), mitsloan.mit.edu/iwer/justiceforjanitors.pdf (accessed 12 August 2002).

49. Harold Meyerson, "The Red Sea: How the Janitors Won Their Strike," *L.A. Weekly,* 28 April 2000.

50. Forbes.com, "The Forbes 400," 27 September 2001, www.forbes.com/2001/09/27/400.html (accessed 12 August 2002). Los Angeles' richest provide an evolutionary tableau of the ways that fortunes have been accumulated in the region: a reasonably instructive facsimile of the economic transformation of L.A. Money from real estate (number 5) and oil (3) anchor the list firmly in the twentieth century's land-based deal making. Donald Bren, for example, America's forty-second wealthiest person, is majority owner of the Irvine Company and, through it, the largest landowner in Orange County. Bren, who also has extensive commercial real estate holdings in Los Angeles and Silicon Valley, got his start in residential real estate in the late 1950s. The "Getty" in Anne Catherine Getty Earhart's (336) name gives her away. Granddaughter of oilman and art collector J. Paul, she inherited $400 million when Getty Oil was sold to Texaco in 1986. To many, Los Angeles wealth and glamour are synonymous with Hollywood. Twelve L.A.-area media or entertainment industry billionaires and multi-multimillionaires prove that airtime, while more ethereal than land, holds lucrative possibilities. In the 1980s Haim Saban developed the *Mighty Morphin' Power Rangers,* a kids' TV show marrying frenetic action and cheesy special effects. Saban sold the Power Rangers franchise (later called Saban's Power Rangers) to Rupert Murdoch for half of the Fox Family Network. When Disney bought the Fox Family Network for $5 billion in 2001, Saban's fortune grew again, and he is now the 172nd wealthiest person in this country. Moving along, five high-tech pioneers and eight investment, insurance, and finance mavens are evidence that L.A. was not bypassed by the new economy. But what comes up can go down. Nicolas Henry III and Henry Samueli, tied for ninety-seventh on the 2001 list of richest Americans, were tied for eighteenth place in 2000. Broadcom, the computer-chip company they cofounded, lost much of its value when the late-1990s Internet stock market bubble burst. While waiting out the return of an upswing in the cyclical world of finance, they can take heart in the rebound of Angeleno Michael Milken, who flew high in the 1980s as a junk bond king, was imprisoned for securities fraud, and now is known for medical philanthropy while cruising comfortably at number 340 on the Forbes list. Rounding out the L.A. thirty-nine are a supermarket maven, a soft-drink distributor, a self-storage facility owner, and three leasing/transport moguls: representatives of the retail and business-services sectors that are the greatest employers of Angelenos today. Though she lives near San Diego rather than in greater L.A., Joan Beverly Kroc (85), the widow of McDonald's founder Ray

Kroc, could be considered an honorable fortieth member, since the very first McDonald's restaurant, and through it the entire fast-food industry, was founded in San Bernardino in 1948.

51. Ann W. O'Neill, "Kerkorian Answers Ex-Wife's Charges," *Los Angeles Times*, 25 January 2002, Business section, 1; U.S. Department of Labor, Bureau of Labor Statistics, Consumer Expenditure Survey, *Region of Residence: Average Annual Expenditures and Characteristics, Consumer Expenditure Survey, 2000* (Washington, D.C., 7 August 2002), http://ftp.bls.gov/pub/special.requests/ce/standard/2000/region.txt.

52. Sources: U.S. Census Bureau, data from 1990 and 2000 decennial censuses; Howard Fine, "Ranks of Pentamillionaires Swell throughout L.A., U.S.," *Los Angeles Business Journal*, 27 May 2002; Los Angeles Alliance for a New Economy, *The Other Los Angeles: Working Poverty in the City of the 21st Century* (Los Angeles, 2000); United Way of Greater Los Angeles, *From Cradle to K*, 41–42.

53. Fogg and Harrington, "Growth and Change," 41–42.

54. An estimate based on national household net worth statistics. Michael E. Davern and Patricia J. Fisher, *Household Net Worth and Asset Ownership, 1995*, prepared by U.S. Census Bureau (Washington, D.C., February 2001).

55. Essayist Richard Raynor portrays this area, west of La Cienega Boulevard and north of the Santa Monica Freeway, as constituting a "magical divide." "By entering this area," Raynor quotes a friend, "I would be safe, secure, and white. Latinos would be the people who didn't speak English; they would clean the house and clip the lawn, then get on the RTD and disappear back to the netherworlds of East and South Los Angeles. And Blacks wouldn't exist at all, unless they wore Armani and worked at CAA." Richard Raynor, "Los Angeles," in *Another City: Writing from Los Angeles*, ed. David L. Ulim (San Francisco: City Lights Books, 2001).

56. The wealthiest three City Council districts are home to sixteen, sixteen, and fourteen commissioners; the poorest three districts to four, two, and three members: Matea Gold, "Most Hahn Appointees Are from Wealthy Areas," *Los Angeles Times*, 24 January 2002.

57. Nancy Cleeland, "Lives Get a Little Better on a Living Wage," *Los Angeles Times*, 7 February 1999.

58. Santa Monica Coalition to Protect the Living Wage; John Wood, "Living Wage Supporters Call for Investigation," *Santa Monica Mirror*, 28 June 2003.

CHAPTER 4. STRESSES IN EDEN

1. The Ramos family's name and that of the Edwards family, discussed in the next paragraph, have been changed to protect their privacy.

2. Reyner Banham, *Los Angeles: The Architecture of Four Ecologies* (Berkeley and Los Angeles: University of California Press, 2001), 195–204.

3. Don Normack, *Chavez Ravine, 1949: A Los Angeles Story* (San Francisco: Chronicle Books, 1999); Thomas S. Hines, "Housing, Baseball, and Creep-

ing Socialism: The Battle of Chavez Ravine 1949–1959," *Journal of Urban History* 8, no. 2 (February 1982).

4. Payton Phillips Garcia, *Notice of Displacement: The Real Cost of the Staples Center and Downtown Revitalization* (Los Angeles: Urban and Environmental Policy Institute, 2002).

5. Los Angeles Housing Crisis Task Force, *In Short Supply* (Los Angeles, May 2000). Affordable rental housing is defined by the federal government as costing no more than 30 percent of income.

6. Federal housing subsidies have declined by 75 percent since 1978, with Los Angeles receiving just $57.5 million in federal funding for housing.

7. Southern California Area Association of Governments, *Housing in Southern California: A Decade in Review* (Los Angeles, January 2001), 12–13.

8. Southern California Studies Center, University of Southern California, *Sprawl Hits the Wall: Confronting the Realities of Metropolitan Los Angeles* (Los Angeles, March 2001), 23.

9. The City of L.A.'s housing wage (the wage required to afford an average-priced house) is thirty-one dollars per hour, or sixty-six thousand dollars annually: Housing L.A., *Out of Reach* (Los Angeles, April 2001). As a result, while the national homeownership rate is 67 percent, in Los Angeles it is just 39 percent: Los Angeles Housing Crisis Task Force, *In Short Supply: Recommendations of the Los Angeles Housing Crisis Task Force* (Los Angeles, 2002), 8.

10. The City of L.A.'s rental wage (the wage required to afford an average-priced two-bedroom apartment) is $15.35 per hour, or $31,000 annually: Southern California Association of Non-Profit Housing (SCANPH), *The Southern California Housing Crisis* (Los Angeles, May 2002).

11. In 1999, poor households in L.A. County paid 52 to 73 percent of their income for housing, two to three times the 26 to 27 percent spent on housing by average L.A. residents: U.S. Census Bureau, *American Housing Survey for the Los Angeles–Long Beach Metropolitan Area* (Washington, D.C., 1999).

12. Southern California Association of Nonprofit Housing, "Affordable Housing Crisis in Los Angeles" (Los Angeles: SCANPH, 2002).

13. Jenny Hontz, "Digs of Doom: The Story of Life and Death inside the Echo Park Apartment House," *L.A. Weekly*, 2–8 March 2001.

14. Weingart Center Institute for the Study of Homelessness and Poverty, *Who Is Homeless in Los Angeles?* (Los Angeles, June 2000); United Way of Greater Los Angeles, *A Tale of Two Cities* (Los Angeles, 2003), 13.

15. Peter Dreier and Kelly Candaele, "Housing: An LA Story," *Nation*, 15 April 2002, 22.

16. Jan Breidenbach, director of SCANPH, quoted in ibid., 22–24.

17. Ibid.

18. Martin Webster, "Transportation: A Civic Problem," *Engineering and Science* (December 1949): 11–15; *The Arroyo Seco Parkway Dedication Ceremonies Program* (Pasadena, Calif.: n.p., 1940).

19. Historical American Engineering Record (HAER), *Arroyo Seco Parkway*, no. CA-265 (Berkeley: University of California, 1999).

20. The motorist's statement is quoted in Cecilia Rasmussen, "Harrowing Drive on State's Oldest Freeway," *Los Angeles Times*, 6 November 2001; Anastasia Loukatiou-Sideris and Robert Gottlieb, *Putting Back the Pleasure in the Drive: Reclaiming Urban Parkways for the 21st Century* (Los Angeles: Urban and Environmental Policy Institute, Occidental College, 2003), can be accessed at http://departments.oxy.edu/uepi/arroyo/ParkwaysAccess.htm.

21. Even as late as 2000, automotive ways of getting around—cars, trucks, and motorcycles—accounted for 49 percent of the region's smog and 89 percent of the cancer risk from air pollution: Gary Polakovic, "There's Hope in the Air: L.A. Is Winning the Smog War, Though Battles Remain," *Los Angeles Times*, 14 January 2001; Southern California Air Quality Management District, *Multiple Air Toxics Exposure Study (MATES-II)* (Diamond Bar, Calif., March 2000).

22. Los Angeles County Metropolitan Transit Authority, *Data and Statistics* (Los Angeles: estimate for 1998).

23. Southern California Studies Center, *Sprawl Hits the Wall*, 17.

24. The rate of growth slowed in the 1990s; it was just 9 percent in L.A. County, 12 percent in Orange County, and 20 percent or more in outer counties: ibid.

25. L.A. County MTA, *Long Range Transportation Plan* (Los Angeles, 2000).

26. Scott Gold, "Paying Price of Growth in Inland Empire," *Los Angeles Times*, 25 November 2001.

27. Ibid.

28. Seventy-six percent of users of the MTA's bus system, for example, did not have access to a car: Bus Riders Union: James Corliss, *Beyond Gridlock: Meeting California's Transportation Needs in the Twenty-First Century*, Surface Transportation Policy Project (San Francisco, May 2000).

29. Bus Riders Union, *Labor Community Strategy Center vs. Los Angeles County MTA: Summary of the Evidence* (Los Angeles, 1995).

30. See www.arroyofest.org.

31. Brownfields are abandoned or underused plots of land, often former industrial sites, where redevelopment is complicated by environmental contamination.

32. Jesus Sanchez, "L.A.'s Cornfield Row," *Los Angeles Times*, 17 April 2001. The developer's pledge to abandon the warehouse project was cemented when the state provided $44 million in park funding in its 2001–2 budget to acquire the land: Julie Tamaki, "Davis Signs $103 Billion State Budget," *Los Angeles Times*, 27 July 2001.

33. The City of L.A. covers almost four hundred square miles; L.A. County, over four thousand; the SCAG six-county region, nearly forty thousand. San Bernardino County is the largest county in the continental United States; Manhattan, San Francisco, and Milwaukee could all fit inside the City of L.A., with no overlap and plenty of room to spare; Carey McWilliams, *Southern California: An Island on the Land* (Santa Barbara, Calif.: Peregrine Smith, 1973).

34. South Coast Air Quality Management District (SCAQMD), *Historic*

Ozone Air Quality Trends (Diamond Bar, Calif., 5 March 2002), www.aqmd.gov/smog/o3trend.html (accessed 13 August 2002).

35. American Lung Association, *State of the Air Report* (Los Angeles, 2002); Gary Polakovic, "Southland Smog Reaches Highest Level in Six Years," *Los Angeles Times*, 24 September 2003.

36. Environmental Defense Fund, *Scorecard* (San Francisco, 2002), www.scorecard.org (accessed 17 September 2002), based on EPA 1996 National-Scale Air Toxics Assessment modeling.

37. According to the American Lung Association, in 2002, San Bernardino County had the worst ozone of any county in the United States. Riverside County was fourth, L.A. County eighth, and Ventura County twenty-first (it had been seventh worst in 2000): American Lung Association, *State of the Air*.

38. Scott Gold, "Paying Price of Growth in Inland Empire," *Los Angeles Times*, 25 November 2001.

39. Four hundred thousand to five hundred thousand acre-feet were brought in by aqueduct; one hundred thousand each came from local wells and from imported water purchases from the Metropolitan Water District; recycled water accounted for just 0.3 percent of total supply and use: Los Angeles City Planning Department, *1996–1998 Annual Report on Growth and Infrastructure* (Los Angeles, 2000), 74–75.

40. Environmental Defense Fund, *Scorecard*.

41. Rachel T. Noble et al., "Storm Effects on Regional Beach Water Quality along the Southern California Shoreline," *Journal of Water and Health* 1 (2003).

42. Environmental Defense Fund, *Scorecard*.

43. Ibid.

44. Ibid.

45. Los Angeles County Department of Health Services, Maternal, Child and Adolescent Health, Childhood Lead Poisoning Prevention Program web site, "Surveillance/Data," 2003, www.inpublichealth.org/lead/reports/leaddata.htm.

46. Greg Hise and William Deverell, *Eden by Design: The 1930 Olmsted-Bartholomew Plan for the Los Angeles Region* (Berkeley and Los Angeles: University of California Press, 2000).

47. Plans for the park would create one of the largest urban green areas established in a century, with a million residents living within a three-mile radius: Community Conservancy International, "The Baldwin Hills Park Project," 2003, www.ccint.org/; Joe Mozingo, "State Helps Buy Land for Park in Baldwin Hills," *Los Angeles Times*, 22 December 2000; Steve Hymon, "On the Trend of Better Health in South L.A.," *Los Angeles Times*, 16 November 2003.

48. Los Angeles has just over an acre of neighborhood park land per thousand residents, far less than the ten acres per person recommended by the National Recreation and Parks Association; Verde Coalition, *Los Angeles Needs Neighborhood Green Space* (Los Angeles, 2000).

49. University of Southern California, Sustainable Cities Program, *Parks*

and Park Funding in Los Angeles: An Equity Mapping Analysis (Los Angeles, May 2002).

50. See Manuel Pastor, Jr., Jim Sadd, and John Hipp, "Which Came First? Toxic Facilities, Minority-Move-In, and Environmental Justice," *Journal of Urban Affairs* 23, no. 1 (2001): 1–21. Comparisons of demographics and pollution loads in L.A County show small disparities by race or income in terms of Superfund sites, toxic releases, or cancer risks, but neighborhoods with lower-income residents and people of color have a significantly (60 percent) higher concentration of facilities emitting air pollution: Environmental Defense Fund, *Scorecard.*

51. SCAQMD, *Multiple Air Toxic Exposure Study.*

52. Natural Resources Defense Council and Coalition for Clean Air, *No Breathing in the Aisles: Diesel Exhaust inside School Buses* (Los Angeles, February 2002).

53. SCAQMD, rule no. 1195. On air pollution from shipping, see Gary Polakovic, "Finally Tackling L.A.'s Worst Air Polluter," *Los Angeles Times*, 10 February 2002.

54. Rebuild L.A., *Rebuilding L.A.'s Urban Communities* (Los Angeles, 1997).

55. Linda Ashman et al., *Seeds of Change: Strategies for Food Security for the Inner City* (Los Angeles: California Interfaith Hunger Coalition, 1993).

56. Amanda Shaffer, Center for Food and Justice, Urban and Environmental Policy Institute, *The Persistence of L.A.'s Grocery Gap* (Los Angeles: Center for Food and Justice, 2002), 16.

57. Ashman et al., *Seeds of Change.*

58. Ali H. Mokdad et al., "The Spread of the Obesity Epidemic in the United States, 1991–1998," *JAMA* 282, no. 16 (27 October 1999): 1539–46.

59. Amanda Shaffer and Robert Gottlieb, "Promises of Renewal Broken," *Los Angeles Times*, 10 March 2002.

60. Los Angeles Regional Food Bank, *Hunger in Los Angeles County, 2001* (Los Angeles, 2002).

61. Shaffer, *Persistence of L.A.'s Grocery Store Gap.*

62. Center for Food and Justice, Urban and Environmental Policy Institute, *A Taste of Justice: Conference Discussions and Opportunities for Future Action* (Los Angeles, 2002).

63. Wendy Slusser, M.D., M.S., Principal Investigator, School of Public Health, University of California, *Evaluation of the Effectiveness of the Salad Bar Program in the Los Angeles School District* (Los Angeles, 24 June 2001); Center for Food and Justice, Occidental College, *The Farmers' Market Salad Bar: Assessing the First Three Years of the Santa Monica–Malibu Unified School District Program* (Los Angeles, October 2000). The Alice Waters comment was made at Roosevelt Elementary School in Santa Monica, at a salad bar tour attended by one of the authors (Robert Gottlieb).

64. ACLU Foundation of Southern California, *Williams v. California, First*

Amended Complaint for Injunctive and Declaratory Relief (Los Angeles, 14 August 2000).

65. California Department of Education, Educational Demographics Unit, *Dataquest,* data1.cde.ca.gov/dataquest (Sacramento, 2002); and Los Angeles Unified School District (LAUSD), *Fingertip Facts, 2001–2002* (Los Angeles, 2002).

66. Ibid.

67. *Fingertip Facts, 2001–2002.*

68. *Dataquest* and *Fingertip Facts, 2001–2002.*

69. Ibid.

70. LAUSD, *Strategic Execution Plan: Building a Learning Environment* (Los Angeles, December 2001).

71. California Department of Education, *Dataquest;* LAUSD, *Fingertip Facts, 2001–2002.*

72. LAUSD, "School Accountability Report Cards," 2002, search.lausd.k12 .ca.us/cgi-bin/fccgi.exe?w3exec=sarco.

73. Ibid.

74. Community Coalition, *Fremont 911! Students Declare Emergency at South L.A. High School* (Los Angeles, 2001).

75. The district estimated its construction would displace 896 renting families, 227 home-owning families, and 250 businesses, nonprofits, churches, and so forth: LAUSD, Office of Inspector General, *Report of Audit: Relocation Program* (Los Angeles, 5 March 2002).

76. Los Angeles County Department of Health Services, Public Health, *L.A. Health at a Glance* (Los Angeles, October 2000).

77. Los Angeles County Department of Health Services, *Recent Health Trends in Los Angeles County* (Los Angeles, June 2002).

78. Los Angeles County Department of Health Services, *Health-Related Quality of Life in Los Angeles County* (Los Angeles, March 2001).

79. Los Angeles County Department of Health Services and UCLA Center for Health Policy Research, *The Burden of Disease in Los Angeles County: A Study of the Patterns of Morbidity and Mortality in the County Population* (Los Angeles, January 2000).

80. Los Angeles County Department of Health Services, HIV Epidemiology Program, *Adult and Adolescent Spectrum of HIV Disease (ASD) Semi-Annual Summary Report 1989–2000* (Los Angeles, January 2002).

81. United Way of Greater Los Angeles, *From Cradle to K: Ensuring Success by 6 for All Los Angeles Children* (Los Angeles, 2001).

82. Richard Brown, Roberta Wyn, and Stephanie Teleki, UCLA Center for Health Policy Research, *Disparities in Health Insurance and Access to Care for Residents across U.S. Cities* (Los Angeles, August 2000).

83. California Department of Health Services, Medical Care Statistics Section, *Medi-Cal Program: Persons Certified Eligible by County, Sex, and Age* (Sacramento, October 2000).

84. California Department of Health Services, Office of Statewide Health Planning and Development, Healthcare Information Resource Center (Sacramento, 2002).

85. Charles Ornstein and Lisa Richardson, "County OKs Hospital Cuts," *Los Angeles Times*, 30 October 2002; Sue Fox, "Court to Rule on Health-Care Cuts," *Los Angeles Times*, 2 December 2003.

86. Esperanza Community Housing Corporation, "Focus Areas: Health," www.esperanzachc.org/focus/health/html (accessed 17 September 2002).

87. Erwin Chemerinsky, *An Independent Analysis of the Los Angeles Police Department's Board of Inquiry Report on the Rampart Scandal* (Los Angeles, September 2000); *Report of the Rampart Independent Review Panel* (Los Angeles, November 2002).

88. *Report of the Independent Commission on the Los Angeles Police Department* (Christopher Commission Report) (Los Angeles, July 1991).

89. Los Angeles Police Department, *10 Year Violent Crime Statistic Charts* (Los Angeles, March 2002).

90. California Department of Corrections, *Historical Trends 1980–2000* (Sacramento, August 2001), 3a.

91. Ryan S. King and Marc Mauer, Sentencing Project, *Aging behind Bars: "Three Strikes" Seven Years Later* (Washington, D.C., 2001).

92. In March 2003, a sharply divided Supreme Court upheld California's three-strikes law in a pair of cases based on the golf clubs and videotape circumstances: *Lockyer v. Andrade*, no. 01-1127, and *Ewing v. California*, no. 01-6978.

93. California Department of Corrections, Data Analysis Unit, *Second Strikers in the Institution Population by Gender, County of Commitment, and Racial/Ethnic Group, as of December 31, 2001* (Sacramento, January 2002).

94. California Department of Corrections, *Historical Trends 1980–2000*, 1.

95. Ibid., 10a.

96. *USA Today*, 6 August 1992.

97. ACLU of Southern California, press release, "Civil Rights Groups Announce Formation of Coalition for Police Accountability," 16 December 1999.

CHAPTER 5. SHIFTING COALITIONS

1. Michael Finnegan and James Gerstenzang, "Bush Cites Hope That Emerged from Violence 10 Years Ago," *Los Angeles Times*, 30 April 2002; Elisabeth Bumiller, "Bush in Los Angeles on Riot Anniversary," *New York Times*, 30 April 2002.

2. Gary J. Miller, *Cities by Contract: The Politics of Municipal Incorporation* (Cambridge, Mass.: MIT Press, 1981).

3. Robert Gottlieb and Irene Wolt, *Thinking Big: The Story of the* Los Angeles Times, *Its Publishers, and Their Influence on Southern California* (New York: G. P. Putnam, 1977); Frank Clifford, "Gates Affair Stirs Nostalgia for Elites," *Los Angeles Times*, 2 June 1991; Bill Boyarsky, "March toward an Uncer-

tain Future," *Los Angeles Times*, 2 August 1996; Joel Kotkin, "The Powers That Will Be," *Los Angeles Times*, 14 December 1997. A biography of McCone is available on the web at www.cia-on-campus.org/usc.edu/mccone.html.

4. Edward Banfield, *Big City Politics* (New York: Random House, 1965), 80.

5. Michael J. White, "Racial and Ethnic Succession in Four Cities," *Urban Affairs Quarterly* 20 (December 1984): 165–83; the discussion of the ethnic and racial composition of the L.A. City Council is informed by Raphael J. Sonenshein, *Politics in Black and White: Race and Power in Los Angeles* (Princeton, N.J.: Princeton University Press, 1993); Raphael J. Sonenshein, "The Los Angeles Jewish Community: An Examination of Its History of Activism for Human Rights" (Sacramento, March 2000), www.csus.edu/calst/Government_Affairs/Reports/ffp34s.pdf (accessed 8 August 2002); Fernando J. Guerra and Dwaine Marvick, "Ethnic Officeholders and Party Activists in Los Angeles County," working paper 11, in *Minorities in the Post-Industrial City*, vol. 2, Institute for Social Science Research (ISSR), UCLA (Los Angeles, 1986); and authors' communication with Raphael Sonenshein via email.

6. This Black-Jewish alliance is discussed in detail in Sonenshein, *Politics in Black and White.*

7. Greg Mitchell, *The Campaign of the Century: Upton Sinclair's Race for Governor of California and the Birth of Media Politics* (New York: Random House, 1992), 577–80.

8. Brief histories of the California Democratic Clubs and an L.A. area affiliate can be found online: "History of the California Democratic Party," 2001, www.ca-dem.org/cdphistory.html/ (accessed 8 August 2002); "The Jerry Voorhis Claremont Democratic Club," www.claremontdems.org/who.htm (accessed 8 August 2002).

9. Sonenshein, *Politics in Black and White*, 56–66.

10. No major American city had elected an African American mayor until 1967, when Gary, Indiana, elected Richard Hatcher and Cleveland, Ohio, elected Carl Stokes.

11. See Sonenshein, *Politics in Black and White*, on the 1969 and 1973 elections.

12. Brian Jackson and Michael Preston, "Race and Ethnicity in Los Angeles Politics," in *Big-City Politics: Governance and Fiscal Constraints*, ed. George E. Peterson (Washington, D.C.: Urban Institute Press, 1994), 85–104; and Sonenshein, *Politics in Black and White*, 139–55; James A. Regalado, "Los Angeles Labor and Los Angeles City Politics: An Assessment of the Bradley Years, 1973–1989," *Urban Affairs Quarterly* 27, no. 1 (September 1991): 87–108.

13. John Mollenkopf, *The Contested City* (Princeton, N.J.: Princeton University Press, 1983).

14. Robert Ajemian, "Person of the Year, 1984: Peter Ueberroth," *Time*, 7 January 1985, www.time.com/time/poy2000/archive/1984.html.

15. "Malign Neglect" and "Malign Neglect II," *L.A. Weekly*, 30 December 1988–5 January 1989, 28 August–3 September 1992, cited in Susan Anderson, "A City Called Heaven: Black Enchantment and Despair in Los Angeles," in *The*

City: Los Angeles and Urban Theory at the End of the Twentieth Century, ed. Allen Scott and Edward W. Soja (Berkeley and Los Angeles: University of California Press, 1996), 350.

16. Hahn Quach and Dena Bunis, "All Bow to Redistrict Architect: Secretive, Single Minded Berman Holds All the Cards," *Orange County Register*, 26 August 2001.

17. Fernando J. Guerra and Dwaine Marvick, "Ethnic Officeholders and Party Activists in Los Angeles County," Institute for Social Science Research, vol. 2, 1986–87, *Minorities in the Post-Industrial City* (University of California, Los Angeles, 1986), paper 11, 4–5.

18. Sonenshein, *Politics in Black and White*, 122.

19. The account of Waters's career draws on Michael Barone and Richard E. Cohen, *The Almanac of American Politics, 2002* (Washington, D.C.: National Journal Group, 2001), 250–52; Sonenshein, *Politics in Black and White*, 125–30, 216–17, 223–24; and various web sites.

20. Los Angeles City Council, "Los Angeles City Council Biography," www .lacity.org/council/cd8/cd8b01.htm (accessed 25 September 2002).

21. Albert Herrera, "The National Chicano Moratorium and the Death of Ruben Salazar," in *The Chicanos*, ed. Ed Ludwig and Tamis Santibanez (Baltimore: Penguin Books, 1971), 235–41.

22. Tony Castro, "Eastside Story: Rivals Jockey for Position as Alatorre Plays Out Hand," *L.A. Weekly*, 13–19 March 1998.

23. Marc Haefele, "Alatorre Takes the Fifth—108 Times," *L.A. Weekly*, 23– 29 April 1999.

24. James A. Regalado, "Organized Labor and Los Angeles City Politics: An Assessment in the Bradley Years, 1973–1989," *Urban Affairs Quarterly* 27 (September 1991): 87–108.

25. Pamela Moreland, " 'The Only Thing She's Changed Is Her Hair Color': A Community Volunteer; Weintraub, Old and New: Conservative Image Blurs," *Los Angeles Times*, 5 April 1985.

26. Robert Kuttner, *Revolt of the Haves: Tax Rebellions and Hard Times* (New York: Simon and Schuster, 1980).

27. Ames Rainey, "Voters Rejecting Measures to Raise Taxes for Schools," *Los Angeles Times*, 6 November 1991; Amy Pyle, "L.A. School Bond Measure Appears Headed for Defeat," *Los Angeles Times*, 6 November 1996.

28. Mark Purcell, "The Decline of the Political Consensus for Urban Growth: Evidence from Los Angeles," *Journal of Urban Affairs* 22, no. 1 (2000): 85–100; and Mark Purcell, "Ruling Los Angeles: Neighborhood Movements, Urban Regimes, and the Production of Space in Southern California," *Urban Geography* 18, no. 8 (1997): 684–704.

29. William Fulton, *The Reluctant Metropolis* (Point Arena, Calif.: Solano Books, 1997), 51–66.

30. Tom Hogen-Esch, "Urban Secession and the Politics of Growth: The Case of Los Angeles," *Urban Affairs Review* 36, no. 6 (July 2001): 794.

31. Julie-Anne Boudreau and Roger Keil, "Seceding from Responsibility?

Secession Movements in Los Angeles," *Urban Studies* 38, no. 10 (2001): 1701–31; and Hogen-Esch, "Urban Secession and the Politics of Growth."

32. Lou Cannon, *Official Negligence* (Boulder, Colo.: Westview Press, 1999).

33. For a discussion of this conflict, as well as efforts to bridge the cultural divide, see Regina Freer, "Black-Korean Conflict," in *The Los Angeles Riots*, ed. Mark Baldassare (Boulder, Colo.: Westview Press, 1994), 175–204; and Raphael J. Sonenshein, "The Battle of Liquor Stores in South Central Los Angeles: The Management of Interminority Conflict," *Urban Affairs Review* 31, no. 6 (July 1996): 710–37.

34. Karen M. Kaufman, "Racial Conflict and Political Choice: A Study of Mayoral Voting Patterns in Los Angeles and New York," *Urban Affairs Review* 33, no. 5 (May 1998): 655–85.

35. Daniel B. Wood, "Now There's Even Less 'There' There," *Christian Science Monitor*, 20 April 2000. As an example of the indirect fallout of corporate relocation, the ARCO Foundation, which had provided a significant source of grants for L.A-area nonprofit organizations and charitable projects, was restructured along with the company, losing its Los Angeles focus in the process. Harold Meyerson, "Who Owns L.A.?" *L.A. Weekly* (itself New York–owned), 7 April 2000.

36. Ronald Brownstein, "On the Move with Richard Riordan: Quiet Clout, Big Money, and Questions of Obligations," *Los Angeles Times Magazine*, 21 August 1988; Riordan for Governor, "Biography" (Los Angeles, 2002), www .library.ucla.edu/libraries/mgi/campaign/2002/cal/primary/gov/riordan/ website/biography.htm (accessed 30 September 2002).

37. Barbara Bliss Osborn, "Election Neglected on L.A.'s Local TV: Exploring an Empty News Hole," *Extra!* July–August 1997, 14.

38. Los Angeles Philharmonic, "Lillian Disney and the History of an Inspiration," www.laphil.org/wdch/vision (accessed 25 September 2002); Associated Press, "Houston Gets Expansion Franchise," 7 October 1999; Jim Newton and Mark Z. Barabak, "DNC Selects Los Angeles for 2000 National Convention," *Los Angeles Times*, 12 March 1999.

39. Doug Smith, "Mayor Raises $1.4 Million to Back School Board Slate," *Los Angeles Times*, 6 March 1999.

40. Field Poll, California Opinion Index, "A Summary Analysis of Voting in the 1994 General Election" (San Francisco, January 1995).

41. Patrick J. McDonnell and Robert J. Lopez, "Some See New Activism in Huge March," *Los Angeles Times*, 18 October 1994.

42. Simon Romero, "Citizenship Classes Swell at L.A. Unified Adult Schools," *Los Angeles Times*, 11 December 1994.

43. Ted Rohrlich and Dan Morain, "The Man Driving the Latino Machine," *Los Angeles Times*, 14 October 1999; California State Legislature, Latino Caucus, "Latino Legislative Caucus History and Purpose," www.democrats.assembly .ca.gov/latinoCaucus/history.htm (accessed 26 September 2002).

44. Hugo Martin, "Katz Rejects Alarcon's Apology over Flier," *Los Angeles Times*, 30 June 1998.

45. Michael Barone, *The Almanac of American Politics, 1998* (New York: Crown Publishing Group, 1997).

46. Harold Meyerson, "California's Progressive Mosaic," *American Prospect* (18 June 2001): 17–23; Barone and Cohen, *Almanac of American Politics, 2000.*

47. California Secretary of State, "1998 General Election Returns" (Sacramento, 1998), http://vote98.ss.ca.gov/Misc/Summary.htm (accessed 30 September 2002); Mark Z. Barabak, "Big Democratic Turnout Aids Candidates, Causes," *Los Angeles Times,* 3 June 1998.

48. Harold Meyerson, "Primary Concerns," *L.A. Weekly,* 14–20 January 2000.

49. California State Assembly, "California State Assembly Biography" (Sacramento), http://democrats.assembly.ca.gov/members/a45/a45bio.htm (accessed 26 September 2002).

50. Greg Krikorian, "Council Overrides Veto, OKs Wage Law," *Los Angeles Times,* 2 April 1997.

51. Steve Proffitt, "Bringing Hollywood—the Place—Back into the Limelight," *L.A. Times,* 1 June 1997.

52. Julian Gross, Good Jobs First and the Los Angeles Alliance for a New Economy, *Community Benefits Agreements: Making Development Projects Accountable* (Los Angeles, 2002).

53. Los Angeles City Council, "Biography," www.lacity.org/council/cd13b01.htm; Mason Stockstill, "Council Approves Plan for $100 Million Housing Trust Fund," *City News Service,* 1 March 2002.

54. "Candidate Profile, Antonio Villaraigosa," http://student-voices.org/candidates/index.php3?CandidateID = 2 (accessed 25 September 2002).

55. Harold Meyerson, "L.A. Story," *American Prospect* 12, no. 12 (2–16 July 2001): 14–16.

56. Raphael J. Sonenshein and Susan H. Pinkus, "The Dynamics of Latino Political Incorporation: The 2001 Los Angeles Mayoral Election as Seen in Los Angeles Times Exit Polls," *PS* (March 2002): 67–74. The exit polls reported in this article did not include Asian voters.

57. Patt Morrison, "Hahn Pulls Ahead of Villaraigosa in the Polls, but by What Method?" *Los Angeles Times,* 30 May 2001.

58. This dilemma was partly a consequence of California's nonpartisan system of municipal government. In a party system, Villaraigosa's victory over Hahn in April's primary would have put the former Speaker into a runoff against Republican Steve Soboroff rather than against Hahn, and Villaraigosa would then have picked up the great majority of the Black vote in June. Without that vote, however, Villaraigosa needed to best Hahn among the centrist and center-right Democrats of the San Fernando Valley and Los Angeles' Westside—a formidable challenge at best, and an impossible one after Hahn's ads went on the air.

59. Sonenshein and Pinkus, "Dynamics of Latino Political Incorporation," 67–74.

CHAPTER 6. SETTING AN AGENDA

1. Al Martinez, "Committee of 25—L.A.'s Super Government?" *Los Angeles Times*, 3 December 1972. Soon after the *Times* article appeared, the committee changed its name to the Community Committee, although its orientation and membership remained the same. Burt Hubbard, "The 'Community Committee': L.A.'s Secret Government," *Los Angeles*, September 1977; also, New American Movement, "Who Rules Los Angeles" and "How Los Angeles Is Ruled" (Los Angeles, April 1975).

2. Bob Gottlieb, "Is This the Tom Bradley We Elected to Office?" *Los Angeles*, 1977.

3. Ron Curran, "Future Imperfect," *L.A. Weekly*, 2–8 December 1988.

4. L.A. 2000 Partnership, *L.A. 2000: A City for the Future*, final report of L.A. 2000 (Los Angeles, 1988).

5. William Trombley, "2 New Agencies Proposed to Set Regional Policy," *Los Angeles Times*, 16 November 1988; Catherine C. Templeton, "Los Angeles from Above: The Oneness of Our Plight," *Los Angeles Times*, 27 November 1988.

6. Richard W. Stevenson, "Patching Up L.A.: A Corporate Blueprint," *New York Times*, 9 August 1992; also, Kenneth Reich, "The Days of Glory," *Los Angeles Times*, 28 July 1994.

7. Stevenson, "Patching Up L.A."; Robert Scheer, "Peter Ueberroth: A Man of Privilege Aims to Get Down and Dirty to Rebuild L.A.," *Los Angeles Times*, 17 May 1992.

8. Don Lee, "Bagging a Career," *Los Angeles Times*, 12 February 1995.

9. Ronald W. Cotterill and Andrew W. Franklin, *The Urban Grocery Store Gap*, Food Marketing Policy Issue Paper, no. 8 (Bridgeport: Food Marketing Policy Center, University of Connecticut, April 1995); Nancy Cleeland and Abigail Goldman, "The WAL-MART Effect: Grocery Unions Battle to Stop Invasion of the Giant Stores," *Los Angeles Times*, 25 November 2003; Melinda Fulmer, "Wal-Mart Food Fight Leaves Big Rivals Standing," *Los Angeles Times*, 27 November 1999; Denise Gellene, "Warehouse Clubs, Grocers Feed the Frenzy for Value," *Los Angeles Times*, 27 September 1993.

10. Henry Weinstein and George White, "Vons to Open 12 Stores in Inner-City Locations," *Los Angeles Times*, 24 July 1992.

11. Cited in ibid. The press conference proceedings are available in Center for the Study of Los Angeles Research Collection, "History: Rebuild L.A. Collection," http://lib/lmu.edu/special/csla/rla/rla_hist.htm (18 June 2001).

12. Henry Weinstein, "Rebuild L.A. Struggles to Establish Its Role," *Los Angeles Times*, 4 November 1992.

13. Paul Feldman and George White, "Vons Opening in Compton Stirs Economic Hopes," *Los Angeles Times*, 12 January 1994; Kevin Herglotz, "Vons Closure Was a Business Decision," *Los Angeles Times*, 21 May 2000; Melinda Fulmer, "Some Supermarkets Thrive in Inner City," *Los Angeles Times*, 13 May

2000; Amanda Shaffer and Robert Gottlieb, "Promises of Renewal Broken," *Los Angeles Times*, 10 March 2002.

14. Rebuild L.A., *RLA Grocery Store Market Potential Study* (Los Angeles, October 1995); Amanda Shaffer, Center for Food and Justice, Urban and Environmental Policy Institute, *The Persistence of L.A.'s Grocery Gap* (Los Angeles: Center for Food and Justice, 2002).

15. Mary Hendrickson et al., *Consolidation in Food Retailing and Dairy: Implications for Farmers and Consumers in a Global Food System* (Columbia: University of Missouri and the National Farmers' Union, January 2001).

16. Kami Pothukuchi, *Attracting Grocery Retail Investment in Inner-City Neighborhoods: Planning Outside the Box* (Detroit: Department of Urban Planning, Wayne State University, October 2001); Linda Ashman et al., *Seeds of Change: Strategies for Food Security for the Inner City* (Los Angeles: California Interfaith Hunger Coalition, 1993); "Pathmark and New Communities Corporation—Joint Venture Helps Revitalize Newark," *FMI Issues Bulletin* (Food Marketing Institute, Washington, D.C., January 1993).

17. Henry Weinstein, "Janitors Lash Out at Rebuild L.A. in Rally," *Los Angeles Times*, 18 December 1992.

18. Michael Lipsky and David J. Olson, *Commission Politics: The Processing of Racial Crisis in America* (New Brunswick, N.J.: Transaction Books, 1977), 6; Anthony M. Platt, ed., *The Politics of Riot Commissions, 1917–1970: A Collection of Official Reports and Critical Essays* (New York: Collier Books, 1971).

19. Liberty Hill Foundation, "Our History" (Los Angeles, 2001), www.libertyhill.org/donor/d_about_content4.html (accessed 12 August 2002).

20. Regina Freer, "From Conflict to Convergence: Interracial Relations in the Liquor Store Crisis in South Central Los Angeles" (Ph.D. diss., University of Michigan, 1999).

CHAPTER 7. A VISION FOR THE CITY

1. Gary Polakovic, "Finally Tackling L.A.'s Worst Air Polluter," *Los Angeles Times*, 10 February 2002.

2. The water table is sufficiently high in three different areas of the L.A. River that any attempt to lay concrete in these areas would be problematic. These "soft bottom" areas, including the site for the studios in North Hollywood, became the initial focus for some of the earliest "greening the river" advocacy. See Blake Gumprecht, *The Los Angeles River: Its Life, Death, and Possible Rebirth* (Baltimore: Johns Hopkins University Press, 1999).

3. Wender's comments are cited in Urban and Environmental Policy Institute, *Re-Envisioning the Los Angeles River: A Program of Community and Ecological Revitalization*, final report to the California Council of the Humanities (Los Angeles: Urban and Environmental Policy Institute, Occidental College, 2001).

4. James Preston Allen, "L.A. Secession and Empire," *Random Lengths News*, 19 April–2 May 2002.

5. Sue Fox, "San Pedro Tells the Mayor It's Nothing Personal," *Los Angeles Times*, 9 May 2002; James Preston Allen, "Pound of Flesh, Pound of Sand," *Random Lengths News*, 8–21 March 2002.

6. Sharon Bernstein, "City Would Emerge Fully Formed from Valley," *Los Angeles Times*, 26 May 2002.

7. Kristina Sauerwein, "An X-Rated Issue: Will Secession Be Good for Valley Porn Industry?" *Los Angeles Times*, 1 November 2002.

8. Of Valley voters, 50.7 percent supported secession; 66.9 percent opposed it citywide. Patrick McGreevy, "Valley Secession Group Facing Its Own Breakup," *Los Angeles Times*, 27 November 2002.

9. Elizabeth Hardwick, "After Watts," *New York Review of Books*, 31 March 1966, 3–4.

APPENDIX. A POLICY AGENDA FOR THE NEXT L.A.

1. The Field Act and its regulations require schools to be constructed using designs and materials that resist earthquakes.

Acknowledgments

This book was inspired by the work of progressive activists and thinkers who have worked hard to make Los Angeles a more just, democratic, and livable city during the past century. Its immediate origin was the conference held at Occidental College in 1998 to celebrate the history of Progressive L.A. and help the current generation of activists to learn from the past in order to shape the future. The five-hundred-plus people who attended this event were inspired by the reminiscences of activists who had participated in the key struggles from the 1930s through the 1960s, and continued to believe in the ideals of social justice.

Harold Meyerson, then editor of the *L.A. Weekly* and currently editor of *American Prospect*, deserves special thanks not only for his detailed knowledge of L.A. history and politics (and his coauthorship of chapter 5 of this book), but also for the *L.A. Weekly*'s support of the Progressive L.A. conference.

The 1998 conference eventually led to the formation of the Progressive Los Angeles Network (PLAN), a broad group of organizers, practitioners, and academics who worked for almost two years to develop a comprehensive progressive policy agenda for Los Angeles. This process and the agenda document that was created helped in turn to shape public debate in the 2001 municipal elections for mayor and City Council. Several hundred people participated in PLAN's task forces on a variety of issues, bringing together people who shared underlying ideas about social justice but whose busy political lives made it difficult to work together on a common project. The key players in this process included the cochairs of the PLAN task forces and the PLAN advisory board members: Karen Bass (California State Assembly member), Jan Breidenbach (SCANPH), E. Richard Brown (Center for Health Policy), Marianne Brown (UCLA LOSH), Kelly Candaele (L.A. Community

256 / *Acknowledgments*

College Board), Tim Carmichael (Coalition for Clean Air), Sharon Delugach (L.A. City Council member Martin Ludlow), Sister Diane Donoghue (Esperanza), Alice Walker Duff (Crystal Stairs), Maria Elena Durazo (HERE Local 11), Randy Jurado Ertll (CARECEN), Denise Fairchild (Community Development Technologies Center), Larry Frank (National Lawyers Guild), Robert Garcia (Center for Law in the Public Interest), Antonio Gonzalez (Southwest Voters Registration Education Project), John Grant (UFCW 770), Roy Hong (Korean Immigrant Workers Advocates), Sue Horton *(L.A. Times)*, Madeline Janis-Aparicio (Los Angeles Alliance for a New Economy), Roger Lowenstein (ACLU Foundation), Michelle Mascarenhas (Center for Food and Justice), Jerilyn Mendoza (Environmental Defense), Harold Meyerson *(American Prospect)*, Sam Mistrano (Human Services Network), Gloria Ohland (Surface Transportation Policy Project), Torie Osborn (Liberty Hill Foundation), Manuel Pastor (UC Santa Cruz), Rev. Altagracia Perez (St. Philip's Episcopal Church/Coalition L.A.), Gary Phillips (Southern California Library for Social Studies and Research), Sarah Pillsbury (Sanford/Pillsbury Productions), Carlos Porras (Communities for a Better Environment), Neal Richman (UCLA Department of Urban Planning), Vivian Rothstein (HERE International Union), Teresa Sanchez (SEIU 347), Paul Schrade (United Auto Workers), Amy Schur (ACORN), Matt Sharp (California Food Policy Advocates), Gary Stewart (Rhino Entertainment), Frank Tamborello (Los Angeles Coalition to End Hunger and Homelessness), Anthony Thigpenn (AGENDA), Robin Toma (L.A. Human Rights Commission), Goetz Wolff (L.A. County Federation of Labor/UCLA Department of Urban Planning), and Kent Wong (UCLA Labor Center). Their hard work is reflected in the vision and policy agenda described in chapter 6. An abridged version of the PLAN policy agenda is provided in the appendix.

We owe thanks to many people who provided us with information about L.A.'s history and its current conditions. These include Tim Brick, Sarah Cooper and the staff of the Southern California Library for Social Research, William Deverell, Larry Frank, John Grant, Marge Nichols of the United Way of Greater Los Angeles, Barbara Osborn, Torie Osborn, Manuel Pastor, Raphael Sonenshein, Jennifer Wolch, and Goetz Wolff.

A number of other people worked hard to make PLAN an effective vehicle for injecting progressive ideas into L.A.'s political world. These include Ankine Aghassian, Catherine Carter, Michael Christensen, Nicole Drake, Eric Garcetti, Mahnaz Ghaznavi, Ana Guerrero, Josh Kamensky, Sandra Martinez, Alessandro Morosin, Angelica Salas, Kelly Swegan, and Amy Wakeland.

Khara Ali'l, Michelle Ashley, Andrea Azuma, Katie Brewer-Ball, Megan Buchanan, Nikolay Filchev, Brooke Gaw, Chris Green, Jordan Hawkes, Kyle Kitson, Walter Moran, Tucker Neal, Sarah Pope, Jonathon Tracy, and Heather Weaver provided valuable volunteer assistance. Thanks to Robert Borosage and Roger Hickey of the Campaign for America's Future in Washington, D.C., which cosponsored a conference with PLAN at the California Science Center in October 2001. Thanks to Patricia Bauman of the Bauman Foundation, Ken Gregorio of the California Community Foundation, Gary Stewart of Rhino Records, the Roth Family Fund, Lanny Gertler, John Guerra of the Gas Company, the Liberty Hill Foundation, Ruth Holton of the California Wellness Foundation, the California Council for the Humanities, the ACLU, and the Gertler Family Fund for supporting PLAN's work.

Sylvia Chico, the administrator at the Urban and Environmental Policy Institute at Occidental College, has played a major role at every stage of this project. We thank her for her hard work, her support, and her ability to help us to maintain our equilibrium in the midst of chaos. Thanks to Occidental College President Ted Mitchell and Professor David Axeen, as well as our colleagues and students, for helping to make Occidental a wonderful place to teach, research, write, and participate in community service.

Several Occidental College students and Urban and Environmental Policy Institute staff—including Andrea Azuma, Brooke Gaw, Tegan Horan, Kelci Lucier, Marcus Renner, Amanda Shaffer, Natalie Tagge, and Jonathan Taylor—provided valuable research assistance.

At the University of California Press, Sheila Levine and Charlene Woodcock have been extremely supportive of this project.

Index

Page numbers in italics indicate figures.

43; City Beautiful vision of, 12–13; collapse of, 101; communal experiment in, 16–17; crisis of, 99–101; federal subsidies for, 241n6; jobs separated from, 34, 100–1, 105; L.A. 2000 on, 176, 177–78; landlords' responsibilities for, 164; lead-contaminated, 110, 204; legislation on, 34–35, 229–30n57; organizing on, 39, 43–44, 101–2, 166; racial discrimination in, 61–63; recommendations on, 197–200, 204–6; rent levels for, 101, 241n5; secessionist movement and, 193; shortage of, 24, 194–95. *See also* public housing; restrictive housing covenants

Housing Court, 199
Housing L.A., 101–2, 170
Housing Trust Fund: funds for, 170; plans for, 101–2; recommendations on, 197–98; sponsor of, 165
housing wage, 241n9
Huerta, Dolores, 37
Hughes Aircraft, 155
hunger: persistence of, 113–14; plan of action for, 210, 212
Hynes, William "Red," 21, 23

IAF (Industrial Areas Foundation), 31, 44, 119
immigrants and immigration: amnesty for undocumented, 82–83, 219–20; borders closed against, 23; citizenship classes for, 159; hostility toward, 81–82, 166–67; income inequality and, 92; increase in, 76–80, 150; as janitors, 88–90; LAPD's treatment of, 25–26, 57–58, 123–24; legislation on, 32, 60, 228n33, 236–37n21; as not yet voting, 152, 154–55; organizing of, 41–42, 47, 163, 185; organizing on behalf of, 59–60, 234n49; recommendations on, 219–20; rights of, 59–60, 80–83; secession movements and, 191; tuition issues and, 83, 119; wage

concerns of, 160. *See also specific groups*
Immigration and Nationality Law (McCarran Act, 1952), 60
Immigration and Naturalization Service (INS), 47
incinerators, waste, 42–43
Inclusionary Zoning Policy (proposed), 198–99, 208–9
income distribution. *See* economic divisions; poverty; wealth, extent of
Independent (London), 87
Industrial Areas Foundation (IAF), 31, 44, 119
industrial growth, advocates of, 29. *See also* manufacturing
Industrial Workers of the World (IWW, or Wobblies), 17
infant mortality, 121
initiative (political), 13, 225n4
International Ladies Garment Workers' Union (ILGWU), 21–22
International Longshoremen's and Warehousemen's Union, Local 26, 41
Internet, 215–16
interurban system, 104, 137
investment, governmental, 222–23
Iota Phi Lambda (sorority), 53
Iranians, immigration of, 76–77
Irvine Company, 239–40n50

Jackson, Jesse, 147
Jacobs, Steven, 89
James, Clive, 71
Janis-Aparicio, Madeline, 45, 171
janitors: strikes by, 87–90, 170, 183; wages of, 87, 94
Japanese Americans: internment of, 57; racist fear campaigns against, 25
Jarrico, Paul, 30
Jarvis, Howard, 151–52, 167
Jefferson High School, 116
Jet Propulsion Laboratory, 74
Jews: Black political alliances with, 139–43; elites' fears of, 137; immigration of, 76–77

urban centers: federal policies as detri-
mental to, 134; food issues in, 112–
15; fostering innovations in, 67–68;
population remaining in, 76; possibilities in, 182–83; Rebuild L.A.
on, 179–81; undermining of, 136–
37. See also neighborhoods and
communities
urban environment: crisis of, 107–12;
obesity and, 113, 120; recommendations on, 200–6
urban greening approach, 20
urban growth: advocates of, 13, 18, 29;
conflicts over, 12–13; as decentering
process, 136–37; L.A. 2000 on, 176–
77; resistance to, 152–53; suburbanization and decline in, 33–34. See
also real estate development
Urban League, 69
urban policy: cyclical interest in, 133–
34; fostering innovations in, 67–68;
on growth, 74; newspaper on, 16
urban renewal, L.A.'s version of, 31, 99
urban sprawl: air pollution linked to,
109; definition of, 236n17; fostering
of, 75–76, 104; jobs and housing
separated in, 34, 100–1, 105; smart
growth vs., 208–9
U.S. Commission on Civil Rights, 70
U.S. Congress, 26, 54, 147, 162
U.S. Department of Defense. See
defense industries
U.S. District Court of Appeals, 25–26
U.S. Employment Service, 27, 56
U.S. Immigration and Naturalization
Service (INS), 47
U.S. Supreme Court: lawsuit against
MTA refused by, 106; on restrictive
housing covenants, 24; on Smith
Act, 32; on three-strikes law, 246n92
utilities, 12. See also public utilities
utopianism, 13, 16–17

Valley Industry and Commerce
Association, 153
Ventura County, 73, 243n37
veterans, 62

Vietnam War: opposition to, 35–36,
140, 143, 148; radicalization in, 33
Villaraigosa, Antonio: campaign of,
165–71, 190, 250n58; as influence,
135; on secession movements, 194
Vons (food retailer), 113, 180–81
Voorhis, Jerry, 21, 137
voting: immigrants as not yet, 152,
154–55; recommendations on, 214–
16

wages: call to investigate, 19; decline
of, 85; housing costs and, 241nn9–
10; of janitors, 87–90, 94; moral
minimum, 44; raising of minimum,
160, 161; statistics on, 19, 86;
Ueberroth on, 183; of waiters,
97. See also living wage
Wagner Act, 227n29
walking, 103, 107, 206–7
Wallace, George, 141
Wallace, Henry, 25, 27
Wal-Mart, 180, 182
Wardlaw, William, 156
Washington, Kenneth, 146
Waters, Alice, 115
Waters, Maxine: career of, 134, 146–
47, 148; Hahn's relationship with,
169, 190
water supplies: conflicts over, 73;
development of, 18; imported,
14, 110, 243n39; L.A. 2000 on,
176–77; pollution of, 43, 110;
recommendations on, 203–4
Watts, 138
Watts Labor Community Action
Committee, 36
Watts riots: aftermath of, 64, 139;
context of, 34–35; implications of,
134, 175
WAVAW (Women against Violence
against Women), 39
Waxman, Henry, 134, 143–44, 145,
162
wealth, extent of, 90–91, 163, 239–
40n50
Weiner, Maury, 140–41

Text:	10/13 Aldus
Display:	Aldus
Compositor:	BookMatters, Berkeley
Printer and Binder:	Edwards Brothers, Inc.